A Peace of Africa

A Peace of Africa

Reflections on Life
in the Great Lakes Region

*Enjoy and I hope you
get some new insights.*

David Zarembka

David Zarembka

Madera Press
Washington, DC

Published by Madera Press, Washington, DC

Printed in the United States of America

ISBN — 0-9791003-1-3
ISBN — 978-0-9791003-1-4

Contents

When I was a child, we had goats at home. While we were at school, we tied them to a tree so they could not destroy the fields. Upon getting back from the school, we usually untied them so that they could find grasses wherever they might. However, most of the time, the goats would remain standing at the same place although they were no longer tied to the tree. Sometimes I think that something similar happens in people's minds.

Adrien Niyongabo

It was easy to love God in all that was beautiful.
The lessons of deeper knowledge, though,
    instructed me to embrace God in all things.

St. Francis of Assisi

Introduction

Why I Write

Since 1964 when I first lived in the Great Lakes region of Africa, my heart and concern have been for the area. I have been married on separate occasions to two women from Kenya, have lived there for a total of ten years plus uncountable trips, and am actively involved in peacebuilding activities both in the United States and Africa. With such an unusual background, I have, over the years, developed my own perspective which is frequently at odds with the American "conventional wisdom" on Africa. My opinions are based on my observations and experience. The purpose of this book is to convey to others my understanding of the culture, politics, development, interaction with the Western world, shortcomings, and potential for the people in East and Central Africa. I explain cultural aspects of these societies that are difficult for the average American to understand because they have had little exposure to the region. I focus on healing, reconciliation, and peacebuilding. This is not a work of certitude, but of exploration as I feel that life is really about trying to understand the world we all live in together.

In essence, I started writing this book when I first went to Africa to teach Rwandan refugees in Tanzania in 1964 and wanted to share my experiences. I took a year off after my junior year at Harvard College. When I returned to the United States after fourteen months aboard, I was amazed at some of the naïve, uninformed questions I was asked about Africa. I was also discouraged by the continued perpetuation of negative stereotypes of Africans.

One extreme example I still vividly remember occurred when I was first preparing to go to Tanzania. A doctor on the staff of Harvard Medical School gave our group of volunteers a presentation on the health issues in Africa. She advised us never to shake hands with an African because we might get worms since Africans were so dirty. She went on to describe the various kind of worms we might contract. Even as a young student, I realized that this was nonsense. Since that bizarre lecture, I have shaken the hands of tens of thousands of Africans and I have not yet gotten worms.

The people I have met and the lives we have shared tell a wholly different story. The Africa I had experienced was far from the images of a distant place filled with exotic animals, chaotic wars, natural beauty, and utter poverty painted in the American media. Now, decades later, I am pleased to have completed the task of writing this book. I am glad I waited because my life experiences in Africa and with Africans have continually added to my understanding of human nature and how various societies can organize themselves, for better or for worse.

The early 1960's were the time of hopeful optimism in Africa as country after country gained independence from colonialism. People were enthusiastic as they joined together to build schools, health clinics and hospitals, cultivated crops such as tea and coffee that had been forbidden by the colonialists, and began the adventure of charting their own destiny in world affairs. Alas, this euphoria soon evaporated as neo-colonialism by the former colonialists, corruption, struggle for power, civil wars, and military coups instigated frequently by Cold War concerns left the part of Africa that I knew with disillusionment and lack of economic progress.

I am still the heir to that youthful optimism for Africa. I have had to try to understand why things went wrong and what is needed to rectify the situation so that people in Africa can have adequate shelter, food, health care, education, employment, and good governance. This is what I share in this book. I come from the perspective of the grassroots, the common people I have been in contact with throughout these many years. These include the large families of my first wife, Rodah Wayua Zarembka, from eastern Kenya and that of my second wife, Gladys Kamonya, from western Kenya. It also includes those I taught in a refugee camp in 1964-65, those I interacted with while I was in the Peace Corps in 1966 to 1968, as founding principal of a high school in Kenya in 1968, and those I have been working with since 1998 as Coordinator of the African Great Lakes Initiative of the Friends Peace Teams.

My hope is that, as the reader, you learn to empathize with Africans and then question some of the unexamined assumptions of American society. I will explain, as best as I am able, the reality of Africa as I have seen and lived it, with both its warts and beauty — the problems that have held it back during these decades as well as the wonderful resilience of the people that could make the future so positive, promising, and productive.

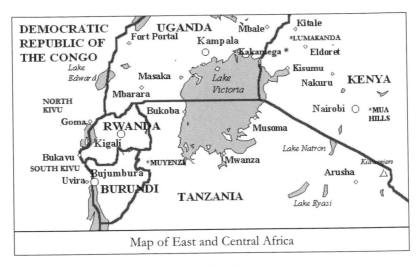

Map of East and Central Africa

The Positive Future

The Great Lakes region of Africa — Tanzania, Kenya, Uganda, Rwanda, Burundi, eastern Democratic Republic of the Congo, and the southern Sudan — is a geographical area. The Great Lakes includes Lake Victoria, Lake Tanganyika, Lake Turkana, Lake Kivu, and many, other smaller lakes. This region is defined by the use of Swahili as a common language. Unfortunately, this region does not have a succinct name for the people who live here. Therefore, in this book when I use the word "African," I am referring to people from this region. Things could be different elsewhere in Africa. I have placed a glossary at the end of the book to help with Swahili words, places, and people mentioned in this book.

There is no reason why this Great Lakes region cannot be vibrant, healthy, prosperous, and peaceful. Geologically, it is a spectacular place. While the tourist attractions are well known, there are so many other wonders. I once sat on the veranda at the Bethany Retreat Center in Kibuye, Rwanda, on the shores of Lake Kivu, watching the volcano, Nyiragongo, fifty or more miles away in North Kivu giving off sparks and smoke against the evening sky.

It would be nice if the people of the region were affluent enough to visit their own wonderful attractions. When my father-in-law came to the United States shortly after Gladys and I were married, we had to take him to a zoo in Washington, DC. Although elephants lived in the wild only a hundred miles from his home in Kenya, he had never seen one.

Most of the area where people are densely settled has fertile, volcanic soil with excellent, if at times inadequate, rainfall. Since most of the area transfixes the equator at three to six or more thousand feet above sea level, the climate is mild in most places. At our home in Lumakanda, Kenya, which is about six thousand feet above sea level, the temperature on my thermometer ranges from fifty-six degrees to eighty degrees Fahrenheit. Here there is no hot summer or cold winter. Rather the distinctions on climate are made by whether it is the rainy season or the dry season. Since we are only about fifty miles north of the equator, there are two of these seasons each year.

Economically, in most countries the region has been doing much better during this last decade. Burundi began to revive at the end of the twelve-year civil war in 2005, Kenya with regime change in 2003, Rwanda with the stabilization after the 1994 genocide, and even in North and South Kivu in mid 2000s where fighting has not finished. In recent years, the gross domestic product of some of these countries has been increasing by up to eleven percent per year. Of course, this is from a low level, so a country needs five to ten percent growth year after year for decades before it can become prosperous enough to fulfill the necessary food, shelter, health, and education needed for all its inhabitants. Even during the world financial crisis that began in 2008, most of these countries have experienced growth of at least five percent, except Kenya in 2008 because of the post election violence.

This growth is obvious to me on the ground. I live right off the main highway, called Uganda Road, that runs from the port at the coast of Kenya, through Nairobi, and then on to Uganda, Rwanda, Burundi, and eastern Congo. It is a two lane paved highway with small turn-offs for buses and minibuses to load and unload their passengers. The number of large trucks with "transit" marked on them — meaning that they are going to other countries — has been increasing at such a rate that it is noticeable. The truck are beginning to clog up the road and unfortunately destroying it because it was not built for such heavy traffic. A contract has been awarded to rebuild the road from Eldoret to the border with Uganda as other sections from the coast have already been rebuilt.

Has this increased wealth trickled down to the average person? While I am certain that the elites have done well, I have my *mabati* test. *Mabati* are corrugated iron sheets that are expensive to buy since they are about $10 per two feet by ten feet sheet. Only someone who has extra cash is able to roof a house with them. When they are first attached, they gleam brightly in the sun so one can observe how much building is going on at the local level by the amount of shiny *mabati*. This building may be anywhere from a latrine roof to the roof of a large church. In the last few years, the amount of *mabati* has increased substantially. This is particularly true in Kenya, but going down the hill to the lakeside town of Gisenyi in Rwanda, one is blinded by the glare of all the new *mabati* roofs. Unfortunately, many of these new houses are not yet finished since they do not yet have doors and windows, but eventually most of them will be completed. Burundi after twelve years of civil war was almost totally destroyed so that the per capital income was one of the lowest in the world at about thirty cents per day per person. The rebuilding since the war ended are obvious with even shiny *mabati* roofs near Bujumbura and the major towns, although not yet in some of the rural areas.

In short, the region is on the move, probably at the most sustainable rate since independence fifty years ago. This progress will only continue if the fighting, wars, and corruption end.

Where I'm Coming From

My father, Richard Zarembka, was born in Russian-controlled Poland in 1913. My grandfather left as a migrant laborer to the US in 1914 just before the beginning of World War I (WWI). At this time in history, less than 100 years ago, there were no immigration restrictions. WWI changed this and it was only with the passage of a family reunification act that allowed my grandmother and my father to immigrate to the United States. My grandfather was of peasant background as his family had a small plot of land to cultivate, similar to the peasant farmers in Kenya. My grandmother, on the other hand, was of middle, artisan class because her father was a bricklayer. She loved classical music and made sure my father had violin lessons even when finances were tight. After my father finished high school during the Depression, he decided to become a violin teacher, but soon realized that he could not make a living as a violin teacher and decided to become a photographer, an occupation that he followed the rest of his working life, specializing particularly in children's portraits.

My mother, Helen Jane Colvin Zarembka, had a typical American background. Her great grandfather came to Ohio from Scotland in 1826. One of her great grandmothers was of German-Jewish background and came to New Orleans in 1810. Other relatives came before the American Revolution so my mother could have become a member of the Daughters of the American Revolution, but never considered it, as I will describe below. She graduated from the University of Missouri at Columbia in 1936, with a major in math and a minor in astronomy.

My mother also played the violin and my parents met at the St. Louis Philharmonic Orchestra, an amateur orchestra. My father was first violinist and my mother was third violinist. The conductor noticed some sparks there and asked the second violinist if he would change positions with my mother so that they would then be sharing the same music stand with my father. He agreed and my parents married in 1940.

For many years, my mother's father had been the music critic for the *St. Louis Star* newspaper and then the *St. Louis Post Dispatch*. In 1939, the Daughters of the American Revolution (DAR) refused to allow Marian Anderson, a renowned African-American opera contralto, to sing to an integrated audience in its Constitution Hall in Washington, DC. As a result, she sang outdoors at the Lincoln Memorial to a crowd of seventy-five thousand plus millions on the radio. Decades later, when my mother related this story to me, she was still irate about this slight to one of most celebrated singers of the twentieth century. My mother said that she had no intention of joining the DAR because she did not think that a stuck-up ancestry was important and disapproved of her relative who did join the DAR as a person with no confidence in her own intrinsic worth.

Clayton, Missouri, the suburb of St. Louis where my parents bought a house when I was three years old, was at the time an isolated world all to itself. Clayton was a professional, middle class community where people were comfortably employed, but not members of the wealthy class. As I grew up, except for visiting my grandparents, I really had little exposure outside of Clayton.

In the 1950's, the United States was still recovering, rebuilding from the Depression and the diversion of resources during World War II. One of the fads was "do-it-yourself" as people tried to improve their housing and condition. There was little focus on the rest of the world. In Clayton students were not required, nor even expected, to do any kind of community service. There were no soup kitchens, homeless shelters, or other volunteer activities. At least I never heard of any. These all became common beginning in the mid-1960s when America began to wake up to the inequalities, poverty, and injustices not only at home but also abroad. Yet, I, like many of my generation who grew up without the scars of the Depression and World War II, realized that the world was more than a smug, comfortable place.

As a child, one learns by observing. Usually there is no instruction to synthesize all those random observations so the individual has to figure out how society works by him or herself. Race is something many people have to unravel and attempt to understand. When I was six or seven years old, I remember my mother commented that, on the corner where we were driving past, the boy there was half black and half white. In my young mind, I expected that this meant that half of the boy's body would be black on one side and the white on the other. Since the dividing line did not seem to come from the forehead through the nose and on down, I concluded that the top half must be one color and the bottom half the other color. Later I did well remember when the Clayton Public Schools were integrated. I was also aware when the Shaw Park swimming pool was restricted to only residents of Clayton, after too many African-Americans from St. Louis city were coming to swim.

I was a frequent visitor to the Polish ghetto in St. Louis where my paternal grandparents lived. I remembered my grandfather telling me about the terrible working conditions in Danzig, now called Gdansk and a part of Poland, but then controlled by Germany, where he worked under the cruel whip of the Germans. He also told me about the Depression when he worked pulling ice for St. Louis Coal and Ice only a few days per week, but twelve hours per day and paid only for eight hours. When I asked him why he did not complain, he replied that there was a long line of men waiting to take his place. My father, of course, had his own Depression stories and his climb to respectable middle-class status in Clayton was the motivating factor in his life. My mother would give the clothes we had out-grown to the African-American maid who came in each week to help her clean the house. A few times, we gave those clothes to my grandmother to send to her relatives in Poland. I also was aware the number of times one of my uncles was unemployed and his family had difficulty making ends meet.

Perhaps due to my dad's pursuit of "the American Dream" from humble origins in Poland, I realized even when in high school that if I did not spend money, I would not have to make it. Therefore, if I limited by expenditures, I would be free of the constraints of the consumer society and the rat race to make more and more money. As a result, I never smoked, drank, or gambled even during high school when these were the major activities of some of my classmates.

My mother was a victim of her time — perhaps we all are. Women's role was to stay home and raise the children. My mother, though, had a liberal, even radical outlook, at least for those myopic conservative times. Each week she would sit down and have lunch with the African-American maid. While this might seem trivial today, in those days the vast majority of white Americans would not eat with African-Americans. First lady Eleanor Roosevelt created a scandal in 1939 when she invited Marian Anderson to eat at the White House after her famous concert mentioned above. Later in life, after we children had grown up and the zeitgeist of America had changed, my mother volunteered every week at Malcolm Bliss Hospital and supported such groups as the American Friends Service Committee (after I had become a Quaker) and Dorothy Day's Catholic Worker Movement.

Consequently, by the time I reached Harvard I was curious about social justice issues. I wanted to explore, interact, learn about, and understand that wider world. I knew that out there was a "How beauteous mankind is! O brave new world! That have such people in it!" as my mother would quote from Shakespeare's *The Tempest*. I did not want to be stuck in the ivory tower, a fate that befell many of my classmates. I immediately signed up to volunteer with the student run Phillips Brooks House, the social service arm of Harvard students. I was placed as a volunteer at the Cambridge Neighborhood House that was close enough for me to ride by bike. I went there once a week for an afternoon and mostly tutored high school students. This settlement house was in the African-American section of Cambridge, but I really did not have much culture shock, as it was similar to the Polish community where my grandparents lived.

At the beginning of my junior year, I also volunteered for a program that gave away books to disadvantaged students at an elementary school in Roxbury. Two other volunteers were Alison Liebhafsky (Des Forges) (see page 24) and Karen Weisskopf (Worth). They had just returned from the summer on a Phillips Brooks House's sponsored summer project, called Project Tanganyika, teaching Rwandan refugees in the northwestern part of then Tanganyika. When Tanganyika became Tanzania, the name of the project was changed to "Volunteer Teachers for Africa." I heard their wonderful tales of their experiences. Alison, in particularly, encouraged me to apply to the project as both Alison and Karen were on the selection committee for the following year. Volunteer Teachers for Africa had decided that the cost of the airfare did not justify just a short summer tour and changed to a year-long program.

I considered this a great opportunity to see another part of the world. I wanted to see how people in a remote part of the world lived — that is, remote from the worlds of Clayton and Cambridge. Of course, for the students I would teach, it was the US that was "remote." How were they the same? How were they different?

Yet there were deeper questions I wanted to consider. What values did I have that were important, core ones that I could not give up without giving up myself? What values were just superficial characteristics I had picked up while growing up and were not essential to my personality? I have to admit that after my so safe cultural upbringing, there was a sense of adventure, a sense of wanting to see the unknown, to discover those places difficult for me to imagine.

Peacemaking Background

My interest in and dedication to peacemaking began in May 1961 when I turned eighteen and I was required to register for the draft. As I walked across the park from my high school to the draft board on that warm, sunny day, I said to myself, "I can not kill anybody." It did not occur to me at that time that I also might be killed. When I signed up, I ticked the box to register as a conscientious objector as one unwilling to fight in wars. This was well before the Vietnam War and at that time, in order to be approved by the draft board, I had to prove that I was a "sincere" conscientious objector. There was a long form with difficult questions to fill out. I remember that at the young age of eighteen, one needed to give evidence of past non-violent actions. There were hypothetical questions on how one would react in life and death situations such as if a robber is about to kill your grandmother. At this time, in reality only members of the recognized pacifist churches — Quakers, Mennonites including the Amish, and Church of the Brethren — were given this classification.

When I got home from my initial trip to the draft board and told my mother that I had signed up as a conscientious objector, she was as supportive as she could be. She was a great storyteller. One of the stories she told me many times when I was a child was about her second cousin, Dan Suits. They had grown up together in St. Louis, although Dan was somewhat younger than my mother. During World War II, when few people became conscientious objectors, he became a conscientious objector and joined the Quakers — I do not know which was first. My mother would comment that she did not approve of his becoming a conscientious objector because it was so necessary to defeat Hitler. When I walked across the park and decided that I could not kill another person, I did not remember this story. I have continued throughout my life to be 100% against war, preparation for war, use of war as a tool of diplomacy, and payment of taxes in support of war and war making.

My parents had sent my siblings and me to the Episcopal church, perhaps as a compromise between the Methodist/Presbyterian religion of my mother and the Catholic background of my Polish dad. The Church of the Holy Communion we attended was definitely not a pacifist church as I remember the minister frequently preaching on the ungodliness of the evil Communists. The church was right wing and I do not understand why my mother, who was quite liberal, sent us there.

Although I had a deferment as a college student, I nonetheless had to fill out that long application form about conscientious objection. I knew little about this issue and I realized that I had to study up. The first book I read was Leo Tolstoy's *The Kingdom of God Is Within You*. Most of the first chapter was about the pacifism of the British Quakers. Tolstoy's description of the pacifism of the British Quakers made me interested in Quakerism, which is officially called "the Society of Friends."

As soon as I went to college, I attended Friends Meeting at Cambridge and was most comfortable with all aspects from the first meeting for worship I attended. This Quaker meeting, as most in the eastern United States, was a silent meeting with no preacher. If a person felt so moved, he or she could stand up during the silence and give a message. During a good meeting, a message would be followed by silence until another person built upon the words spoken by the previous speaker, and so on. I liked the thoughtful silence and the lack of preaching. I was already in sympathy with what the Quakers call "the Peace Testimony." Likewise, I already agreed with their concerns for simplicity, community, integrity, equality, and internationalism. I also agreed with their approach to human beings as conveyed in their belief that "there is that of God in every person," to look positively at a person and find the goodness in them. Moreover, this is not a passive activity, but a requirement for the active involvement in the affairs of humanity. George Fox, one of the founders of the Quaker faith conveys this nicely in his 1656 quote:

> Be patterns, be examples in all countries, places, islands, nations, wherever you come, that your carriage and life may preach among all sorts of people, and to them: then you may walk cheerfully over the earth, answering that of God in everyone.

Another aspect I appreciated about the Quaker religion was the focus on "continuing revelation." This is the concept that not only does one have to assess one's values and ideas in the current context and condition, but that all the truths in the world have not yet been necessarily discovered. Therefore, rather than looking back to a predetermined past, life includes seeking new meaning allowing a person and his or her community to grow and change. I have appreciated their use of terminology such as "divine wisdom," "eternal truth," and "speaking truth to power."

From that first meeting, I have never looked elsewhere as I had found my spiritual home. I have been intimately involved in Quaker worship and Quaker affairs. I have served on numerous committees, sometimes as clerk (chair) or treasurer for my Quaker meeting (church), yearly meeting (equivalent to a diocese in other religions), Quaker organizations, and a Quaker school.

Although most people make firm statements and sound certain, I think that many aspects of life evolve and the certainty is something more often solidified in hindsight. So it is with my interest in Africa. In my social studies class in my freshman year of high school, there was a one or two week section on Africa. The test at the end of the lessons was to take a map of Africa and to place the names of all the countries in the correct spot. I was the only one in the class who got this test 100% correct. Did this academic success lead to an interest in Africa, or did I ace the test because, somehow or other, I already had an interest in Africa? I do not know. Did I become a conscientious objector because of the stories of my relative or did I arrive at that conclusion on my own? I do not know.

This type of uncertainty, the possibility of multiple interpretations of the same thing without knowing which is correct, the ambiguity of life, and the complexity of it all are themes that will run though this book.

Background in Africa

After I finished two years (1966 to 1968) in the Peace Corps in Tanzania and Kenya, I was asked by one of my former Swahili teachers if I would like to start a self-help secondary school in his home area of the Mua Hills, just east of Nairobi. I agreed and was the founding principal of the Mua Hills Harambee Secondary School. At that time, it was a co-ed day and boarding school.

I lived in the Mua Hills for a little over two years, married Rodah Wayua Zarembka, a local Kenyan from the Kamba ethnic group. Let me tell a story about how I became engaged to Rodah. I had already met her father, Wilson Malinda, because he was on the school board for the Mua Hills Harambee Secondary School. One Sunday in April 1969, I needed to visit her parents in order to obtain "blessings" for our marriage. Normally someone does this from the groom's family, but since I had no family in Kenya, I had to do it myself. Our marriage was going to be no surprise to them and Rodah had arranged for my formal visit.

After I reached their house and gave the usual greetings, I was escorted inside and was given the obligatory cups of tea. Although they knew me well, they did not know much about my family so Wilson and Priscilla, my future in-laws, asked me about my family.

Who are you father and mother? Richard and Helen Jane Zarembka. *Good as there was only one wife which showed that I came from a good Christian family.*

How many brothers and sisters did I have? One brother and two sisters. *A small family since Wilson and Priscilla had nine children.*

What does your father do? He is a portrait photography. *This was quite understandable because most African houses had pictures of family members tacked to the wall of the living room.*

Some of the founders of the Mua Hills Harambee Secondary School. From the left, Chief Philip Nzioka, myself, Motheke Ndeti, and a neighbor of the school.

How much land does your father have? One-quarter acre. *I could see Wilson's shoulders slump. Only the poorest people have one quarter of an acre. Wilson himself had fifteen acres! With a quarter acre, one cannot feed even one person, let alone a family. I had clearly been raised in poverty.*

In order to salvage this disappointment, Wilson asked me what we grew on that small plot. *One apple and one peach tree,* was my feeble answer. This was a strange disconnect between the cultures, but fortunately they blessed our wedding and Rodah and I were married on May 10, 1969.

After we moved to the United States in December 1970, we had two children, Joy Mutanu and Thomas (Tommy) Mutinda. We lived in Pittsburgh, Pennsylvania, for fourteen years. I earned a master's degree from the University of Pittsburgh in International and Development Education. Later I studied for a PhD in Educational Administration again at the University of Pittsburgh, but never completed my thesis. During this time, I became involved with the Peace Center of Pittsburgh Friends Meeting in promoting the anti-apartheid movement against South Africa. The Meeting passed a resolution against Pittsburgh National Bank, which had bailed out the South African government after the death of Steve Biko in 1976. I visited Kenya in 1974 and 1979 and we usually had African students living with us, particularly Kenyans, who kept me well informed of developments there. Rodah and I separated in 1985 when I moved to the New York City area for a job.

My Involvement with the African Great Lakes Initiative

My continued interest in peacemaking, particularly among Quakers, led me to be appointed in 1996 to be the Baltimore Yearly Meeting's representative to a Quaker organization called Friends Peace Teams. There are about thirty-six yearly meeting — the equivalent of a diocese in other Christian religions — in the United States. In 1993, sixteen of these yearly meetings had come together to form the Friends Peace Teams in order promote more active peacemaking in the world by Quakers.

In March 1998, I was at a Friends Peace Teams' meeting and there was a discussion about the Balkans and if the Friends Peace Teams should send a team there to try to nonviolently promote peace. During the meeting, I asked, "Why are we always talking about the Balkans? There are many Quakers in East and Central Africa involved in conflict, wars, and genocide with little outside support. Why are not we talking about them?" One of the other members, Mary Lord, then responded, "What do you have in mind?" I asked for the evening to think it over and the following day, I proposed that Friends Peace Teams send a delegation to visit the Quakers in Rwanda, Burundi, eastern Congo, Uganda, and Kenya. The purpose was to find out three things:

• How were the conflicts in the region impinging upon the African Quakers themselves?

• What peacemaking activities were the Quakers doing?

• Were there possibilities of American Quakers partnering with the African Quakers in peacebuilding activities?

This was agreed and what came to be called the African Great Lakes Initiative (AGLI) began. I first wrote to all the yearly meetings in East and Central Africa, asking them if they would welcome a visit from us. I quickly received positive responses, particularly from Burundi, Rwanda, and eastern Congo. In January 1999, seven people — a Canadian Quaker couple, a German Quaker, an Ameri-

Members of the initial AGLI delegation to the Great Lakes region. Back from left, me, Bill McMechan, Rosemarie McMechan, Ute Caspers, and Derrick Kayongo. Front from left, Carl Stauffer and Jill Sternberg

can Mennonite working in South Africa, a Ugandan living in the United States, and two American Quakers including myself visited Burundi, Rwanda, Uganda, and Kenya. I was on the team of three that visited Burundi and Rwanda.

The visit was successful. We learned numerous things. For instance, Burundi in 1999 was in the sixth year of what would be a twelve-year civil war. Although Quakers first went to Burundi in 1934 and there were perhaps eight thousand Quakers at that time, the AGLI delegation had been only the second American Quaker group to visit. There is a Burundian saying, "A real friend comes in a time of need." Clearly, the Quakers were not acting like "real friends" to the eyes of the Burundians. The peacemaking work by the Burundi Quaker church had been supported by the Mennonites, another one of the pacifist churches.

Our delegation visited Musama Friends Church. It was up-country perhaps five miles off the main road on a rugged, gutted dirt road. We went to visit this church because the youth of the church — meaning those under 35 years of age — had identified ninety-seven vulnerable families in the community, the elderly, the blind, women without husbands. They rebuilt their houses when they were destroyed in the fighting. We stopped at the house of a blind man whose home had been rebuilt four times by the group. This was all done without outside support belying the common belief in America that things only happen in Africa when funds are pumped in from the wealthy countries. They showed me their church and the clinic which was no more than a few poles and some plastic sheeting and spoke of their hopes for a better future.

For me, the important point was that they were so pleased that someone from the outside had come to visit. They felt that someone recognized and remembered them. This gave them hope. I myself never did so little — all I did was look around, ask a few questions, shake hands with lots of people, and show interest in their existence and well-being. The lesson here is that when there are conflicts in the world, we must visit those who are afflicted by war.

The result of the delegation was that, yes, the Quakers in this region were much affected by the violence; yes, they were doing peacemaking work; and yes, they would like to partner with American Quakers in future peacemaking activities. Since that time, I have been the Coordinator of the African Great Lakes Initiative. We have survived mostly on small donations from individuals, and the support of Quaker meetings and churches of various denominations. The most we raised in any one-year (2008) was $480,000. As far as non-governmental organizations go, AGLI is small. Yet in the last twelve years, AGLI has, I believe, done good work. The African Great Lakes Initiative's activities include the following:

1. **Alternatives to Violence Project (AVP):** This program, developed in Green Haven Prison near New York City in 1975, teaches respect for self and others, communications skills, cooperation, and non-violent conflict resolution to those with a history of violence. AGLI introduced this program to Rwanda (2001), Burundi (2002), Kenya (2003), and South Kivu in the Democratic Republic of the Congo (2005). These are three-day experiential workshops. In the Great Lakes region, we bring equal numbers from both sides into the same workshop.

2. **Healing and Rebuilding Our Communities (HROC):** During the first delegation, African Quakers indicated that they needed trauma healing. Beginning in 2003, the African Quakers developed a personal and community trauma healing program, based on the methodology of AVP. The basic workshop covers psycho-social trauma, grieving, negative and constructive uses of

My daughter, Joy, in middle, with two Burundian work campers at the first AGLI work camp in Kamenge, Burundi in 1999.

anger, and the rebuilding of trust between individuals and the opposing communities. Chapter 9 covers this program in detail. The program is currently in Burundi, Rwanda, Kenya, and North Kivu province of the Democratic Republic of the Congo.

3. **Mediation**: The facilitators from the above two programs are frequently asked to resolve disputes. As a result, AGLI helped to introduce transformative mediation, a version that fits in well with the experiential nature of the two programs, into the region.

4. **The Friends Women's Association's (FWA) Kamenge Clinic**: This is a small clinic in Kamenge, a slum of Bujumbura, that focuses on HIV+ women and other health and peace issues in an area mostly destroyed during the Burundi civil war.

5. **Bududa Vocational Institute (BVI):** This is a post elementary technical institute in Bududa, Uganda, an out-of-the way place surrounded by Mt Elgon.

6. **Orphans and scholarship programs**: In Bududa, Uganda, two hundred orphans and destitute children are supported in the Children of Peace Program. In Rwanda, up to twenty orphaned and/or poor students are sponsored for their middle and high school education. In Burundi, eighteen Hutu and Tutsi high school

students in and around Kamenge are given scholarships and meet together in an association.

7. **Speaking tours**: Since most westerners have little understanding of the conditions in Africa, AGLI brings two or three "missionaries" from our programs in the Great Lakes region to inform Americans, Canadians, and Brits about the work that AGLI is doing in the region. Our biggest problem here is getting a visa for the young speakers to enter the US, Canada, or the UK.

8. **Work camps/Extended Service Volunteers**: To give foreigners a chance to experience living conditions in the region, AGLI sponsor three or four work camps each year, usually one each in Rwanda, Burundi, Uganda, and Kenya, including both non-African and African work campers. We also place volunteers in our African programs for three months to three years.

If you would like to know more about any of these programs, visit the AGLI website found at www.aglifpt.org. Friends Peace Teams also has similar programs in Central America and Colombia and in Indonesia. More information can be found at www.friendspeaceteams.org.

My Present Life

My second wife, Gladys Kamonya, is a Luhya, from the main ethnic group in Western Province of Kenya. She was born in Vihiga District, which even in the 1920's was overpopulated. Lumakanda, where we live now, is in Lugari District about seventy miles to the north. This had been part of the White Highlands during the colonial period when British settlers owned large farms. When Kenya independence came in 1963, a program financed by the British government bought out the British and the large plots were divided up into smallholdings of around twenty acres each. Since Vihiga District was so overcrowded, many people from Vihiga District obtained plots in the Lugari District and moved there.

As the oldest of seven daughters, Gladys spent years overseas working for a Kenyan diplomat so that she could support her family including her two children, Douglas and Beverly. She lived two years in Zambia, three years in Pakistan and then came to the United States. Not once in the three years Gladys was in Pakistan did any Pakistani, male or female, sit next to her on the bus. With

Above is a picture of Gladys and me with a little lamb born just before Christmas 2010. We were married in November 1999 in the United States so none of Gladys' relatives from Kenya were able to attend the wedding, although her father visited us for three months shortly thereafter. In November 2009, we decided to have a 10th Anniversary celebration in Kenya so that her Kenyan relatives could participate. As it often happens here in Kenya, our plans for a simple anniversary were overwhelmed by high expectations. In the end, our small gathering turned into over seven hundred and fifty relatives, friends, and church members attending! One of the traditions is for people to line up and hand gifts to the bride and groom. For us, this lasted forty-five minutes. Three sheep were among the presents and one of these sheep gave us the gift of this little lamb just before Christmas

her usual good humor, Gladys says, "That was fine with me as I always had a seat to myself."

Gladys's grandmother had become a Quaker in Kenya sometime around 1920 as one of the first few thousand converts there. Gladys came to the United States in May 1995 to take care of the children of an Indian couple, though the wife had grown up in Kenya. One of the girls was going to Sidwell Friends School where Bethesda Friends Meeting is. We met at the meeting. We were married in November 1999. After my father died, we moved to St. Louis, Missouri, to help take care of my mother, who had a slowly progressing case of Alzheimer. Two years after my mother died in April 2005, we moved to Kenya to be near to Gladys' father who, now in his mid-eighties, was healthy but clearly declining.

Lumakanda Rock with small shops on the road. From the right, a motorcycle taxi repair shop, a welding shop, and a store selling electrical supplies.

Lumakanda is headquarters for Lugari District. The town houses the district government, a hospital, schools, district and local police station, churches, and shops. Most of the government workers' homes are elsewhere so there are many one-room hostels that employees rent. It is only a few blocks in size. There are somewhere between five hundred and a thousand people living here.

For those who pine for that old self-sufficient village life that Wendell Berry and other back-to-landers promote, a move to Lumakanda is the answer. We buy much of what we need from the town shops and farmers nearby. A relative of Gladys brings us milk every morning and evening. The children of local farmers bring various greens that Gladys and others like so much. The charcoal man brings large bags of charcoal on his bicycle to see if we need some more. At the many, too similar shops in town, we can buy all essential items including airtime for our cell phones, Internet con-

Main street in Lumakanda. The building on the right is the nicest one in town and is owned by the teachers' credit union.

nection and the daily newspaper. There are three butchery shops that slaughter local cows, goats and sheep plus another one that slaughters pigs. Since there are Muslims in the area, the pig butchery is separate from the others. If we do not have enough chicken of our own, we can buy others from neighbors.

When we built our house, the metal doors and windows were made at the metal working shop, the interior wooden doors and rafters were made from locally cut trees, planed and built in one of the number of carpentry shops, sand came from the local river, and the bricks were made from clay and burnt close by. The masons, plumbers, electrician, and other workers who built our house were people who lived in the neighborhood.

Unlike the Quakers in the eastern United States who meet in silent worship, Quakers in Kenya have a programmed service including songs, prayers, a sermon by a pastor, and a collection after the sermon. In Lumakanda, we attend Lumakanda Friends Church each Sunday when we are in town. It is only a block from our house. We attend the early 8:00 o'clock service which lasts about an hour and a half. This is the village meeting. Lumakanda Monthly

Meeting (meaning it meets once per month to conduct business) is composed of three village meetings like the one we attend. On a typical Sunday, there are about eighty adults at the service we attend and thirty-five children in Sunday school. Within in a mile there is another Friends church where Gladys' sister and her family attend.

Differences

Throughout my life of traveling back and forth from the United States to Eastern and Central Africa, I have been struck by the stark differences.

- While there are many unmet basic needs for food, shelter, clothing, health service, and education in the African Great Lakes region, in the United States for most, but certainly not all, those basic needs are provided.
- While the first has a scarcity of goods, the later is overwhelmed by materialism.
- While the first is based on community sharing and support, the latter is based on the isolation of individualism.
- While the first has extreme diversity, the latter has a deadening conformity promoted by the mass media
- While one lives close to the earth, the other lives more and more in cyberspace.
- While the former is economically fugal, the latter is sucking up the resources of the world at an unsustainable rate.
- While East and Central Africa has had many conflicts since independence in the early 1960's, the United States has been perpetually in high tech, expensive wars or preparing for such wars which are fought outside the United States itself.

Conclusion

When my son, Tommy, was at the University of Rochester and majoring in religion, he asked me to write up my philosophy of life — what made me tick, what were my religious convictions, what was internally important. It was a hard task to actually think and write about. In the end it was one of those things that was put off numerous times until it was never completed. In a sense, this book, which took me a year and a half to write, is finally a response to his request.

I have outlined my Quaker faith in humankind and social justice that I had developed as a young person, my early interest in Africa, and my conviction that a person needs to go out into the world and work to alleviate injustice. I believe that my firm roots in Quakerism, in finding that of God in everyone, in the importance in mending the ills of the world is the basis for my long term commitment to the challenging, but rewarding work that I do.

In 1964, one of the Harvard group members, Sally Pettus, died from a ruptured diaphragm in Dar es Salaam. I decided to travel to Dar to meet with the rest of the members of the group. It was seven hundred miles and took me two days on a bus over nondescript dusty roads. For some reason, during the ride at the end of the first day as the sun was setting, I noticed a boy herding about fifteen cows passing by a baobab tree. It was a perfect picture. I love looking at baobab trees. They are so big, so interesting in shape with a massive trunk but not much in the way of branches. Some of the larger ones are reputed to be many thousands of years old. When I was born, my mother's best friend gave my mother the book, *The Little Prince*. In his tour of the asteroids, the Little Prince came upon one which was being overgrown by three baobab trees because the owner was too lazy to take proper care of his asteroid. I think it was my emotional state that made this incident so memorable — the ancient age of the tree, the pastoral scene, the death of my friend, the thought about what life was really all about. In the end, I was no more exempt from the rhythms of life than anyone else was.

Section 1

Understanding the Context

Children in the internally displaced persons' camp in Igunga, North Kivu, Congo. Note the plastic trap huts in the background where the children sleep and the volcanic rock they are standing on. Luckily they have all been supplied with plastic shoes since it would be extremely difficult to walk on the sharp rocks.

Even though these children are living in terrible conditions, none of them are malnourished and they have decent clothes, probably used clothes from the US. This is in contrast to the usual media pictures of children in such conditions where often a sick, emaciating looking child is pictured in order to bring pity to those seeing him or her. This picture would not be useful for fundraising purposes for a relief organization.

Chapter 1
From Genocide to Relief

The Rationale for Genocide

> There was one little child, probably three years old, just big enough to walk. The others had gone ahead, and this little child was behind following after them. The little fellow was perfectly naked. I saw one man at a distance of about seventy-five yards, draw up his gun and fire — he missed the child. Another man came up and said, "Let me try — I can hit him." He kneeled down and fired at the little child, but he missed him. A third man came up and made a similar remark, and fired, and the little fellow dropped.

Such is the reality of genocide. One can pray for the soul of this little boy who never had a chance in life. The totally innocent are slaughtered as if they are no longer human beings. In talking with many survivors of the Rwandan genocide that I know personally, the wedge between life and death was no more than some chance happening. Note that we only hear the stories of those who survived, as dead people tell no tales.

A young Rwandan who was thirteen years old at the time of the genocide told me this story. At one point, he had on an oversized coat. An *interahamwe* ("those who work together," youth militia who were responsible for much of the killing during the genocide) seized him by the back of the coat in order to kill him. He quickly shed the coat and ran through the forest with the *interahamwe* in fast pursuit. As he ran, another man who had been hiding in the forest became scared and ran. The *interahamwe* then ran after the other man and probably killed him. The boy was saved because someone else took his place.

Solange Maniraguha, one of the lead HROC facilitators in Rwanda, was also saved. On the first day of the genocide, the *interahamwe* attacked her house. They broke through the roof, entered, and killed her parents. Then the one who killed her parents turned to Solange and her sisters and said, "Run, run." They ran. So the man who killed parents helped save her life.

Surveys have found that most of the people who participated in the genocide felt that they had no other choice. In 2002, Scott

2

Strauss, in *The Order of Genocide: Race, Power, and War in Rwanda,* interviewed 209 genocide perpetrators who were in prison. Before the genocide most of the perpetrators had had good relations with their Tutsi neighbors (positive 87%, "no problem" 11%, negative 2%). Almost all (99%) would have allowed their child to marry a Tutsi. This is not too surprising when one realizes that 69% had Tutsi family members. The 5% who were married to Tutsi wives or were hiding Tutsi were most reluctant, but felt forced to commit atrocities. Only a small percentage, perhaps 5%, were "true believers" and killed willingly. The largest percentage (64%) said that they were coerced by other Hutu to participate. If someone actively opposed the genocide, he was frequently killed himself. Most of the killings were done in large groups — 76% were in groups of over ten people. In other words, it was mostly mob killings.

What does one do when one's government is the motivator and instigator in a plan to kill one's neighbors, including perhaps one's relatives? How many people have the moral strength to resist when there is a great possibility of being killed? Like everyone, I fantasize that I would have resisted, but that is in the comfort of my quiet study. Can anyone really predict how he or she would have responded in such an impossible situation?

It is remarkable that after one hundred days of daily "hunts" by a large percentage of the adult male population, about twenty-five percent of the Tutsi survived. Almost all of those Tutsi who survived had to be helped Hutu.

What was the rationale behind all this senseless killing? The architect of the genocide, Theoneste Bagasora, with his extremist group called "Hutu Power," had this underlying goal: If they could get all the Rwandan Hutus to participate in the genocide and exterminate all the Tutsi, then there would be a conspiracy of silence. This would develop into Hutu solidarity and their reign over Rwanda would be secure. Since everyone participated, everyone would be guilty. This is why they worked so hard to force people to participate. With this unity in crime, there would be total impunity for everyone. I think that this justification is one of the greatest horrors of the Rwandan genocide. Nazi Germany killed their millions of victims in concentration camps out of sight and sound from most Germans because Hitler, Himmler, and Goebbels did not want to upset the German population with direct knowledge of the magnitude of the Holocaust. Most Germans could claim that they did not really know what was going on — although I think that they had to be blinding themselves to the people missing around them. Others, of course, were willing participants.

At this point, I need to add a few words that I left out of the quote at the beginning of this section:

> There was one little child, probably three years old, just big enough to walk through the sand. The Indians had gone ahead, and this little child was behind following after them. The little fellow was perfectly naked, traveling on the sand. I saw one man get off his horse, at a distance of about seventy-five yards, draw up his rifle and fire – he missed the child. Another man came up and said, "Let me try the son of a bitch; I can hit him." He got off his horse, kneeled down and fired at the little child, but he missed him. A third man came up and made a similar remark, and fired, and the little fellow dropped.

This is from the testimony of Major Scott J. Anthony, First Colorado Cavalry before the United States Congress, House of Representatives, "Massacre of Cheyenne Indians," in the Report on the Conduct of the War (38th Congress, 2nd session, 1865), page 27.

The extermination of the Native Americans in the United States and the marginalization of the few remaining Native Americans, is the same rationale as that of the Hutu Power group in Rwanda. Although it took about three hundred years rather than one hundred days, there is today a conspiracy of silence in the United States about this genocide.

Willing Participants

"How could so many people have participated in the Rwandan genocide?" This is one of the most difficult questions to understand. Even Rwandans ask, "How could we have killed each other like this?"

Deborah Wood, a teacher at Westtown Friends School near Philadelphia, was an AGLI work camper in Rwanda in the summer of 2008 and wrote the following article, "Just Say No? Reflections on Peace Work in Rwanda," for the school's newsletter, "Professional Development at Westtown" (Volume 8, Issue 1, December 2008). She began the article by quoting one of the Rwandan facilitators she worked with there:

"We Rwandans like to follow orders. That is how we so easily killed each other in the genocide. We just follow orders. We do not think about them."

These were the words of one of the facilitators of the Alternatives to Violence Project (AVP) workshop I was a part of in Gisenyi, Rwanda. I was there under the auspices of a Quaker organization to help the local Friends church build a peace center in their community that had been in the home territory of many of the leaders of the Hutu Power movement that orchestrated the 1994 genocide. The words, an undenied truth, were spoken as we debriefed a workshop activity. There were signs of agreement from all the Rwandans in the room. For the activity, the facilitators had lined the nineteen other participants and myself up face to face and instructed the line on the left to push our partner out the door, then to switch roles.

When given this task we had already been working together for over a day talking about the roots of violence in our communities, hearing about the twelve steps to transforming power, and playing silly games with each other to keep us awake and get us laughing. We had grown comfortable with each other and our facilitators. No one had asked for the purpose of this activity, we just did it. In the first round, my partner had not made me move an inch or even put me off balance. When we switched roles, I pushed my partner halfway to the door. She had flexed her knees and staggered her stance, just egging me on; she had read my competitive athletic nature accurately. Another participant, a mother and deacon in the Friends church who taught other church members to embroider so they might be able to earn money, pushed her partner, a young man, a third of the way to the door. When asked why we had pushed our partners off balance and toward the door, most of us answered that we were following the instructions and I added that my partner had prepared to push back and so I pushed hard and moved her backwards to the door.

Then came the point to the lesson, the facilitator asked, "But why would you push your partner out a door?" One or two of us chuckled to break the sudden shame-filled tension. The mother and church deacon, feeling a bit defensive, replied again, "You told us to, so I just followed instructions." Then the facilitator said the words above about how easily Rwandans follow orders, how much more comfortable they are when they are doing what they have been told to do.

In the following days, I saw that characteristic mirrored in other people and activities. Perhaps I saw that willing obedience because I wanted an answer for how it was that the people I lived, worked, played, and worshipped with for five weeks could have killed their families, neighbors, and colleagues. Yet at the same time, I did not want to see how it was that a few years of propaganda, free beer for the militia, economic hardship, a supply of French ammunition and Chinese machetes, and a tendency to follow orders was all it took to trigger the most intensive killing of the twentieth century. Close to 1 million people of the country's 8 million died at the hands of fellow citizens in just 100 days during the spring and summer of 1994. In no other conflict has the rate of killing been as quick as it was at the start of the Rwandan genocide. The AVP workshop, one of the ways communities in Rwanda are hoping to prevent genocide from happening there again, gave me insight into the social framework of Rwandan society that eased individual Rwandans into the role of *genocidaires*.

Roots of Genocide

For years, I have been thinking about the psycho-social root of genocide and other acts of extreme violence. These are not particularly common but do happen frequently enough to show a pattern. Why do some places have a genocide and others places do not? I am not talking about the specific socio-political causes or the role of those at the top who are most responsible. Rather I am thinking about the issue, what is the real root?

My thesis is that the Hutu's untreated trauma from being at the bottom of society during colonial times gave them justification to later use extreme violence against the Tutsi. As we have learned from the testimonies of many participants in the HROC workshops, unacknowledged trauma leads to withdrawal from others, a feeling of isolation, lack of communication, anger, hostility, revenge, family violence, substance abuse, and a sense that the person is no longer human. When many people in a society have these feelings, this becomes the zeitgeist of the society. Societal violence is a probable outcome. Latent, unresolved trauma, which can be passed down for generations, is the root cause of the extreme violence.

Let us look more closely at Rwanda. In the early 1930's, the Belgians who considered the almost white "Hamitic Tutsi" to be superior to the black "Bantu Hutu," divided everyone in Rwanda into Tutsi and Hutu, making the Tutsi the ruling class and the Hutu the subservient class. The Tutsi were then instructed to treat the Hutu severely. They required the local Tutsi leaders in each community to recruit forced labor Hutu gangs. Rwanda is a hilly country and these forced labor gangs, controlled by whips used by the Tutsi, built spectacular roads by hand throughout Rwanda. If a Tutsi did not fulfill his quota of Hutu laborers or did not drive them hard enough, he was relieved of his duties, punished, and another Tutsi was put in place.

Could there be a more vicious system designed to create hostility between groups of people? Experiments have shown that if you divide individuals into two groups and make one superior to the other, within forty-five minutes you can create great antagonism.

The Alternatives to Violence Project has an exercise in the advanced workshop called "Masks" on exactly this topic. It is commonly used in the workshops in Africa. Its purpose is "to help explore the feelings that surround social discrimination of all sorts and to inform a discussion about the roots of violence/conflict that live in that discrimination." The twenty participants are divided into two groups. One group, the inferior one, is given masks. The unmasked are the rulers and they take off their shoes and put them in a pile in the center. The members of the unmasked group can speak at any time, address everyone as they wish, and even change the rules of the game. The masked can only speak with permission and must address the unmasked by their formal name —— Mr., Ms., or Mrs. and the last name. An issue is introduced that needs to be solved. After twenty minutes or so of discussion, the masked must find the shoes of the unmasked and put them on their feet.

The instructions for this exercise states "Do not push too hard. This exercise explores some of our most emotionally charged areas. Allow the participants their defenses!"

The Mask Game

In Africa there is an additional element added to this exercise. Those who were masked become the unmasked and the unmasked become masked. In other words, the ruler and ruled are reversed. This mirrors what happened in Rwanda when with the connivance of the Belgians, the ruling hierarchy, reversed their established pattern at the time of independence; making the majority Hutu now the ruling class and the Tutsi subordinate. When this is done in the exercise, the result is that the new unmasked who were formerly the abused become much more abusive to their former abusers than the original abusers were to them.

Sometimes this exercise gets so out of hand that it has to be stopped. After the exercise is finished, a long discussion ensues. How did you feel as a ruler? How did you feel when you were discriminated against? What feelings/emotions did you have? Relate these feelings and observations to situations in your own setting and culture? The discussion is always illuminating and profound.

During the colonial period the Tutsi were given all the positions of authority, education, and wealth while the Hutu were whipped and taxed into submission. No one can doubt the anger, bitterness, and sense of injustice that the Hutu felt. A few years before independence in 1961, the Belgians decided to switch sides and support the Hutu over the Tutsi. The first attacks against the Tutsi began in 1959 and the Belgians did nothing to stop them. Now the Hutu victims were on the top and, as predicted by the AVP exercise described above, they wreaked revenge against their former Tutsi masters. Let us apply this to the other examples.

Germany lost World War I. Large numbers of young Germans were killed in the war, much of the country was destroyed, and reconstruction was curtailed by the demands of the victors for restitution. Germans felt that they were victims. It makes no difference if their feelings were "right" or "wrong," real or imagined. The trauma of WWI and its aftermath pervaded the population and therefore the society as a whole. Hitler read this wounded psychology correctly and was able to channel it first into his rise to power and then into finding convenient scapegoats in Jews, gypsies, communists, the mentally retarded, Jehovah Witnesses, and gays — those who were seen as deviant from the ideal norm.

It has been frequently stated that the saturation bombing of Cambodia by the United States during the Vietnam War totally disrupted normal Cambodian society. This disruption led to the rise of the Pol Pot regime of severely traumatized people. In this case, they took their revenge on their own countrymen — those who were educated, those who had previously been on the top, or those who just happened to be in the way.

I have never seen any plausible explanation of why the Afrikaners, when they won control of the South African government in 1948, decided to impose apartheid. Why were they so adamant about apartheid and so cruel and relentless about enforcing it? The Afrikaners considered themselves victims also. The turn of the century Boer War with the British was probably genocide. The Boer men became fighters, leaving their women and children at home. The British rounded up these women and children and placed them in concentration camps without adequate food, health care, or shelter. Then they hunted down the Boer soldiers and killed as many as possible. Those who were captured were treated severely. The result was not only the displacement of a large percentage of the Boer/Afrikaner population, but an extremely high death rate. It took the Boers/Afrikaners over forty years to gain control of the South African government, but when they did, their wounded, traumatized psyches made apartheid seem justified. Then it became time for the black South Africans to resist. I am convinced that the high homicide rate and other violence in the South African population after independence from apartheid in 1994 are due to the traumatization of the black population during apartheid.

This is similar to the segregation in the southern states of the US. The US Civil War was brutal to the southern states. Nineteen percent of the adult white male population were killed. General Sherman's March to the Sea was just one of the many northern campaigns to loot, destroy, and kill in the South. By the end of the war, the South was devastated, traumatizing the entire population. It ended in 1865 and northern control through reconstruction ended in 1877. While it seems "natural" to us today that the South would re-construct slavery through segregation, in fact this was not the only option. There could have been a "live and let live" attitude. Again, the whites traumatized by the war needed a scapegoat to vent their anger, fears, and feelings of revenge. The former slaves were an easy, available, marginalized group to attack.

When a group has been traumatized by war, it is necessary and imperative to deal with the resulting trauma. If not, in the years or decades ahead, that trauma which can be passed down through the generations, may lead to another, perhaps worse, war or genocide, frequently against disposed, marginalized people close at hand.

After September 11, 2001, the Bush Administration quickly used the anger, fear, and feelings of revenge from the attack on the World Trade Center and the Pentagon to psychologically enable traumatized Americans to attack Afghanistan and Iraq. In both places, the American actions may be planting the seed of another genocide or acts of extreme violence in the years or decades ahead.

These are not happy thoughts, but we need to explore those roots of extreme violence and genocide if we are going to prevent them in the future.

Soldiers versus Civilians

I had a great uncle, Donald Colvin, who was building railroads in Mexico during the time of the Mexican Revolution in 1912. I have his letters written home to his mother and sister. In one of these letters, the Mexican army and the Zapata rebels were fighting in a town close by. Even though he was a gringo working for the American imperialists, he showed absolutely no alarm about the nearby fighting. In those honorable days, soldiers fought each other and did not bother the civilians. When the Zapata rebels won, he continued to live in Mexico, building railroads for the new government until, unfortunately, he drowned in a flash flood.

Alas, this is not the case in the African Great Lakes region. Soldiers rarely fight each other, but attack and terrorize citizens to get them to flee. There is not going to be any lasting resolution to the fighting and wars until the international community understands this aspect of the conflict.

This is how it works. An armed group, which can include government troops, decides that they are going to attack and conquer a village and its surrounding area. They announce their intention by such means as wounding a townsman, and telling him to return home and tell the villagers that the group is going to attack. He returns to his community, raises the alarm, and people take what they can carry and flee. One frequently sees pictures of these people with large loads on their heads or pushing a loaded wheelbarrow fleeing along crowded escape routes. If a few soldiers or other armed actors are in the town, they also flee knowing they will be overwhelmed. The conquering group then enters an almost deserted town, loots it, takes over the best residences and businesses, and controls the territory. Either the original inhabitants then return under the control of the conquering group or they flee to internally displaced camps.

This works best when the invading group has a fearsome reputation. They get this reputation by killing civilians, raping women and men, looting, setting fires, and feasting on livestock. The more terror the armed group spreads the easier it is to conquer territory.

In the meantime, the fleeing people are subject to all kinds of hazards: lack of food and medicine, exposure at night when they sleep outdoor in the forests, the possibility of being raped or killed, and the breakdown of cohesion, which is what keeps a community functioning. This explains why so many people in the region have died — not by being killed by armed actors, except during the Rwandan genocide, but due to exposure, hunger, and disease.

The armed group now controls the area with few people in it. If people decide to return, then they must do so under the terms of the new rulers of their area. This can mean "taxation," conscription into forced economic activities, and whatever the new military rulers of the area demand. The armed groups wish to control various territories for different reasons. There may be a lucrative illegal mine in the area or it might be on the route to export minerals that can be taxed as they move through. In addition, they may have used up the resources of a prior conquered area and need to move on to more "fertile" territory. Frequently when a group conquers a village, they accuse those who remain of supporting the "enemy." In retaliation, they revenge by killings those people they have accused.

Soldiers in this scenario are dispensable. When there are reports that so many soldiers from an armed group have been killed, this has little meaning in a strategic sense. New soldiers can be recruited immediately because there are many unemployed, uneducated youth with nothing to do and little prospects for a bright future. I was once told that youth could join Nkunda's rebel army for a bonus of $100 which was a lot considering that the daily wage was $1. Since there is little training, these new recruits are soon ready for action and usually put on the front lines, as they are the ones who are killed in any combat. This is to say, regardless of the numerous campaigns to wipe out this group or another — they have been trying to wipe out the Lord's Resistance Army in northern Uganda for the last quarter century — this never happens.

The international community continues to support military solutions like the 2009 Congolese and Rwandan armies' attempts to kill and capture the former Hutu *genocidaires* in North Kivu. Since the Congolese army is one of these armed actors — controlling mines for the benefit of the soldiers only, sometimes looting, raping, and killing — the expansion of area controlled by the present Congolese army is not a solution to the problem.

Nonetheless, this is the solution supported by the international community including the UN forces in North and South Kivu. The fact that this "solution" has failed for years, even decades, does not seem to deter the international community, students of the region, and the involved governments from trying it over and over again. A more creative, workable solution to the wars in the region needs to be developed. The first step is to understand that these are wars of armed actors against unarmed civilians.

My friend, Alison Des Forges, from Human Rights Watch summarized it like this:

> We need to be ready for the future. These kinds of wars directed against civilians are increasing. The kind of war that happened in the middle of the twentieth century, where you had professional armies confronting each other, has given way now to another kind of war, which is being wages

against civilians. The laws of war that we drew up were mean to protect civilians. Now the context has changed and the civilians are becoming the object. Are those laws of war still valid? Can we enforce them? And what will we do the next time a civilian population becomes the objective for extermination?

Where Will the Women Sleep Tonight?

While a certain amount of attention has been devoted to the use of rape as a weapon of war, particularly in North and South Kivu, I have not seen many explanations of why this happens.

One of the most effective methods of terrorizing a population is "rape" — particularly gang rape. It is more effective than killing someone because the raped person is traumatized and he or she then affects his or her family, neighbors, and community. A killed person's body would just lie there and, if no one saw it, it would not "terrorize" anyone. Reports of the mutilation of bodies have this same affect — the mutilation terrorizes people who then flee.

Note that above I did not use only the female gender. Peter Yeomans, a doctoral student in psychology at Drexel University, conducted a survey of seventy-nine HROC participants in Burundi and of the nine people who reported being raped; two were men. As everywhere in the world, rape is underreported and I expect the rape of males is even more underreported.

Here is the testimony of an anonymous female HROC workshop participant in North Kivu who was raped during the First Congo World War in 1996.

I was raped and contracted HIV/AIDS. So is my daughter of twelve years. We all lost hope — no one to comfort the other. We just saw death as the next thing happening to us anytime. But God has been gracious. People have stood by us and those [HROC] teachings have really helped me to live positively. I am always bitter about the rapists but that had not changed me. Instead it worsens the situation because whenever I think about it everything comes back fresh in my mind. I have understood the meaning of forgiveness. Many times we wait for offenders to ask for forgiveness. In my case where will I meet them? And I would not like to meet them anyway. I have decided to forgive them. I am going to share with my daughter what we learnt. I believe it will help her so that we may begin this journey together.

In North and South Kivu provinces of the Congo, where rape is prevalent, it is difficult to understand all the consequences. Not only is the woman exposed to pregnancy, gynecological problems, and becoming HIV+, but she is stigmatized and ostracized by her husband, her family, and the larger society. Here is the testimony of Rebecca, a thirty-five year old rape survivor with three children. Her husband divorced her after he discovered she had been raped. She lived in the Mugunga Internally Displaced Persons camp outside of Goma until it was dispersed in September 2009.

In 1998, I was in the house with my younger siblings and my mom. We were all raped. Even my mother was raped, and she died as a result. It was all in the night. The men were all in the military, or at least they wore military uniforms. We do not really know who they were, but the *interahamwe* used to wander through that area at night. The *interahamwe* would mix with the locals and the locals would tell them where to loot and who to attack.

After it happened, we took my mom to her brother. He had no money for medical care either and so we took her home. That is where she died. My dad died a year later.

After that, we moved to another territory. I took all of my siblings with me. But it was insecure and we could not stay there, so we came to Goma. Everything was difficult. My sisters, in desperation, would go out to meet men [exchange money for sex]. Then they would get married [live with the man for a short while]. Things would not work and then they would come back to me. Things got bad. They would get jobs at factories picking through beans, working long hours, and making less than $1 per day. My brother in desperation joined the army; he was only 14 years old. Today, we do not know where he is. One of my sisters has gotten married in Muaso. The other two have given birth twice, but they live with me.

My sisters still have flashbacks. When one of my sisters gets a flashback, her eyes will get stuck in one direction. She fears something coming at her day and night. She can never stay alone or sleep near the door. I personally do not get flashbacks like I used to. That has come with time and the [HROC] teachings. It was at the workshop that I realized I was not alone. And through that I felt I was able to take the first step towards forgiveness.

In November 2008, Gladys and I visited the IDP camp mentioned above and talked with thirteen rape survivors. We met secretly in a small office because the women were afraid to be identified as rape survivors. Here is my report of the meeting:

While we were there thirteen women, many with children, one by one entered this office. We did a listening session with them. One woman had gone with ten others to get some small branches to support the four-foot plastic hovels of the IDP people in Goma. They were all raped by government soldiers. During the fighting the previous year, another woman watched as her husband and three of her children were killed. She, in turn, was first beaten so badly that she is now blind in her right eye and then raped. She is now sixty-five years old. A sixteen-year-old girl had also been raped and sat with her six-month-old little boy. The girl next to her, also with a baby, was only fifteen, meaning she was raped when she was fourteen. Most of the women were gang raped and many had incurred major gynecological problems including the removal of their uterus. As a group, the only support they get is medical care at one of the Goma hospitals. One woman was clearly psychologically deranged.

I was surprised by how graphic the women were in their descriptions of the rapes and their results since in their culture talking about anything sexual in front of a male is taboo. As usual in these situations, all the women were anxious to tell their stories, as if the telling itself was a healing act. The rest of the time, they had to go around hiding in shame, pretending that nothing had happened.

I asked if any of them had been tested for HIV/AIDS. They almost unanimously agreed that they had been tested by the doctors but the doctors had refused to tell them the results. This is criminal! Women have a low status in this region and women who have been raped really have no status at all. Therefore, they are no longer considered human, e.g. they are unworthy of being told their status.

One forty-two year old woman was in a Catch 22 situation. She was unwilling to tell her husband that she had been raped because if she did she would be thrown out of the household. Her husband wanted her to return home in the rebel controlled area, but she was afraid that she might be HIV+, although she did not know for sure, and she did not want to go back and perhaps infect her husband. So what could she do? I admired her because there are many people who do not wish to know their status so that they can be oblivious about whether they are passing AIDS on to their unsuspecting partners. I asked Zawadi, the HROC coordinator, how much it cost to be tested for AIDS and she immediately called someone she knows who works at a testing center. The cost of the necessary AIDS test is only $5!

This kind of rape is only the most obvious, what I would call "violent rape." When you see all those pictures of people fleeing with goods on their heads, where will the women sleep that night? Many will have to find a man, perhaps a soldier or policeman, to protect them for the night. The cost is "consensual rape" — the agreement to have sex with the protector. This "relationship" might last a night or two, or a week, or a month, but in the end, it is temporary and the woman is turned out and has to find another "protector." The result is unwanted pregnancies and HIV.

The Healing and Rebuilding Our Community (HROC) program in North Kivu has begun HROC workshops with these rape survivors using only female facilitators. In addition to dealing with the trauma, the intent is to bring the women together into support groups as I describe in Chapter 4. The hope is that they will no longer be alone in their sorrow and problems, but will have the benefit of a cohesive group.

The Best Side of Human Nature

On the Sunday after post election violence broke out in Kenya in 2008, a woman came to the front of Lumakanda Friends Church and gave the customary closing prayer. After church, Gladys told me that this woman was hiding a neighboring Kikuyu woman in her house. The trauma of the violence had induced labor and the Kikuyu woman gave birth that night. Of course, we could not tell anyone about this because the Quaker woman's house could have been burned down if the attackers knew she was hiding a Kikuyu.

When politically induced ethnic violence breaks out, the media covers the atrocities but rarely covers attempts by people to save others from the opposite side. They report on the worst aspects of human nature rather than the best of human nature.

On October 21, 1993, President Ndadaye, the Hutu democratically elected president of Burundi, was assassinated by the Tutsi military. This led to countrywide chaos as Hutu attacked Tutsi in their communities and then the Tutsi military retaliated by killing Hutu. One of the worse massacres occurred at the gas station on the road below Kibimba, the first and largest Quaker mission station in Burundi. Tutsi students from Kibimba Secondary School along with other Tutsi were herded into the gas station office which was then set on fire. Sixty people died and forty escaped. The next day the Tutsi military arrived, killed Hutu at the gas station, and looted the small community. I remember reading about this massacre in the US media at the time.

Three weeks later, my friend, Alison Des Forges, was at the site of the massacre doing an investigation for American and European human rights groups, including Human Rights Watch. She later returned to continue the investigation. Her report was published in French, but she never translated it into English because, in April 1994, she immediately began reporting on the Rwandan genocide.

I recently obtained a French copy of two sections of the report; one on the Kibimba massacre and the other on violence in Mutaho where AGLI has done HROC workshops. I then sent the French version to Sheila Havard, a former AGLI work camper from Canada, to make a rough translation. In her email she wrote, "There are a lot of references to people saving or trying to save others." In only eight pages of the report, there are fourteen incidents of people trying to save others. I quote them here:

1. There was even a Hutu teacher who tried to save some of the Tutsi and he was killed. He was a biology teacher. His nickname was Kavyimabuhiye.

2. According to other testimony, the principal [of Kibimba Secondary School] did all he could to save the hostages.

3. Mutoya Parish: many Hutu families hid and kept neighboring Tutsi families in their homes.

4. Mutaho Commune: A Hutu priest from the parish said that some parish workers had come to get him to save a Tutsi on Thursday 21st at 9 p.m. He said, "We went to tell the people who were all worked up not to shed any blood."

5. A Hutu nun recounted that she had hidden an UPRONA [Tutsi] supporter and his family on Friday morning. He already had a head wound. In the afternoon, a gang armed with spears came to get him but the nun managed to trick them.

6. The same nun said, an old woman came to seek refuge. Her husband and son had been captured. She only had a blanket left.

7. She continues, then, with the priest, we rescued a young man who was being arrested/stopped on the road. There was a shouting crowd on the road going to Mutaho. We've been told that people were dying on the road.

8. In the Mutaho trading center, on Friday morning, a group of Hutu armed with *pangas* [machetes] and clubs went round from house to house inviting everyone to come and demonstrate against the assassination of President Ndadaye. Those who refused were threatened with death. So an UPRONA supporter had to seek refuge in the house of a neighbor who was a Hutu shopkeeper, a member of FRODEBU [Hutu party] and a Muslim.

9. Somewhat later, this same shopkeeper intervened to prevent a rich Tutsi shopkeeper from being killed. He was hit with a stick and had to flee without being able to save the Tutsi.

10. The same Muslim shopkeeper, later on hid the principal of the commune college and an English teacher in his home, both Tutsi, as well as a Hutu supporter of UPRONA and the wife of the rich shopkeeper who had just been killed. He hid them for two days until the military came on Monday morning and took them to an IDP camp.

11. Again the same shopkeeper, The Hutu Muslim shopkeeper risked being killed at this time but the people he had saved pleaded for him and saved him in turn.

12. A 53-year-old Tutsi, a member of UPRONA living on Nyakero Hill explained how he had fled from the killers: "They wanted to exterminate only the UPRONA/Tutsi ethnic group. We fled into the bush. When the soldiers arrived, most were dead. Three of us escaped out of a group of eighteen. I fled when I saw that my brothers and neighbors were being killed. I was saved by a

Hutu from my hill, who hid me. Then I went to my Muslim boss, who hid me in his ceiling until the military arrived."

13. On Wednesday, after the 7 AM mass, the parishioners again went to clear the road near Mubarazi River. After the road had been cleared, the soldiers fired on the people who had helped them, killing about fifteen or twenty of them. A student was able to escape, as was a young teacher from Muyange, called Félix, who had a bayonet wound. We thought he was going to die. But the Tutsi nurses who had been hidden in the parish cared for this young Hutu. The priest recommended that they not say anything to the soldiers. Félix was transported to the Kibuye Hospital by the Red Cross.

14. Priests from the parish stated that they were aware of numerous cases of solidarity where Hutu had risked their lives to save, hide and feed neighbors.

I want to end this section with a testimony of a Tutsi survivor in Burundi which renews one's faith in humankind:

"During the crisis, Hutus took me from home and brought me down here to hang me on that big tree you are seeing outside. I thank so much those Hutus for when we got here, they told me to run away. And then they started to shout loudly as if I am shouting for being killed. They told their friends that they killed me already and that the screaming they heard was from me. I am thankful to them so much. They saved my life. One of them is here." Then they hugged each other.

This testimony has another lesson. It is a joint Hutu-Tutsi statement. In a country racked with such violent conflict as Burundi and Rwanda, each side tends to have its own history. The narrative of each side is to emphasize its victimization and downplay its deadly actions during the conflict. There can be no reconciliation without a shared history. This testimony is one of a shared history. In Israel, there is a synagogue that has the Garden of the Righteous that commemorates with a ceremony and tree those non-Jews who helped with saving Jews during the Holocaust. Its webpage states, "The teaching component is intended to show children and adults that the lesson of the Holocaust is not only one of sadness, but also a lesson in courage, honor, compassion, and heroism. It emphasizes that during the Holocaust there were righteous non-Jews who actually helped, rather than hurt, Jews." In Jerusalem, a similar official project has recorded the names of twenty-three thousand righteous gentiles.

Neither Rwanda nor Burundi has launched such a project. In Rwanda, every Hutu is still considered "suspect" as a *genocidaire*. The tens of thousands, even hundreds of thousands, of Hutu who helped save those Tutsi who survived the genocide after being hunted down for a hundred days need to be acknowledged and commemorated. This is a significant step in developing a shared history that will bring true reconciliation.

Dying for Peace

In January 2010, I received an email from an American asking for help and advice on getting a Kenyan out of Kenya because he was being threatened due to his possible testimony in the International Criminal Court about the 2008 post election violence. There is no doubt that Kenyans were being threatened. Two human rights workers had recently been assassinated. However, the request was from an American in the United States and I saw no indication that the Kenyan had asked to be rescued. Perhaps he wanted this, but I would have wanted to hear from him directly.

This illustrates one of the major differences between Western thinking and African thinking. American thinking puts individual survival as the highest priority. African thinking, under the concept of *ubuntu* [humanness], considers the individual only in the context of the larger community. Let me give you a number of examples to illustrate how this plays out.

The first occurred with a report I received from Adrien Niyongabo, the HROC Coordinator in Burundi, about a project we planned to do for the upcoming elections. HROC/AGLI planned to train citizen reporters who had attended our HROC workshops and to join them together in Democracy and Peace Groups to observe and try to make the elections fair and non-violent. Since the citizen reporters would be known by the population and government authorities, there was a certain amount of risk in doing this work. The response of one of the HROC committee members was, "You cannot do much for peace if you fear dying for peace."

I have observed this before. A number of years ago, I was at an AVP meeting in Kigali, Rwanda and Eddie Kalisa, a young Tutsi facilitator, brought up the request from Kaduha government officials for AVP workshops. In this remote hilly area, Hutu were still killing Tutsi. Among the eight or so people at the committee meeting, not one, including Eddie who would be an obvious target, expressed any comment or reservation about going to do three-day workshops in this clearly dangerous place. Their work was to bring reconciliation and that was what they were dedicated to do, without any qualms or hesitancy whatsoever over safety.

Alison Des Forges once told me that before the genocide, when she was doing investigations of the small massacres that were then taking place, whenever she asked a Rwandan informant if she could use his or her name, he or she always replied in the affirmative. A frequent comment was, "These people massacred here have died for no reason whatsoever and, if I die because of what I have told you, then I will have at least died for a reason."

Theoneste Bagasora, the "architect" of the genocide, and the other *genocidaires* understood this Westerners' individualistic thinking. They realized that, when they brutally killed and mutilated ten Belgian UN peacekeepers, all the Europeans and Americans would flee the country enabling them to do the "work" — as they called the killing of Tutsi — by themselves without outside knowledge or intervention. They were absolutely right. The American government was concerned about getting the two hundred fifty-four Americans out of Rwanda, but when this was accomplished, the plight of the estimated five hundred thousand Rwandans who were killed in the genocide was not its concern.

At the beginning of the genocide in Rwanda, all expatriates who so desired were evacuated while their Rwandan Tutsi colleagues were left behind for slaughter. However, one American, Carl Wilkens, a Seventh Day Adventist aid worker, evacuated his wife and four children but refused to leave his Rwandan colleagues and stayed behind. During the genocide, Carl was supplying Gicimba orphanage, housing about four hundred Tutsi orphans, with food and water. As the *interahamwe* were closing in to kill the Tutsi boys at that orphanage, Carl spent the night in the orphanage to protect them and then, by chance, the next day he ran into the Rwandan Prime Minister, Jean Kambanda. Carl asked him to call off the *interahamwe*. This the Prime Minister did and the boys were saved. Another time he saved a hundred children and then again twelve genocide survivors. In other words, this one American who stayed behind saved more Rwandans from genocide than did the entire United States government with its military might of awe-inspiring weaponry and hundreds of billions of dollars.

There is the little known fact about the Rwandan genocide. A number of Tutsi men living in Rwanda were married to Belgian, French, or French-Canadian women. When the genocide came, these women had the choice of leaving Rwanda and their husbands and children, who were considered "Tutsi" by the rules used in Rwanda, to almost certain death or staying with their families and risk being killed as well. As far as I can tell, most stayed with their families and most were also killed. However, in the weird way that the world thinks of "significant people," when these "white" women married Africans they gave up the privileges of being "significant." Their deaths, like that of so many Rwandans, were little noted and not remembered. The important point here is that it was because they were women, wives of Rwandan men, that they lost them that significant status. French, Belgium, or Canadian men, I believe, would have been evacuated with their Tutsi wives.

This may all sound academic, but is a crucialfor me. When the 2008 post election violence occurred in Kenya, Eden Grace, a Friends United Meeting's staff member living in Kisumu, offered to put me on the list of Americans to be evacuated, if necessary, by the US Embassy. This was not unlikely as the Americans in Kisumu — a city with a lot of violence at that time — were evacuated twice. She indicated that Gladys as my spouse, although not an American citizen, would be evacuated along with me.

I declined for two reasons. First, I might potentially save myself and Gladys, but what about her father, six sisters, son, daughter, two grandchildren and so many other members of her family? Could we flee leaving them to perhaps perish? While I might be in more danger by staying, there was also the possibility that Gladys and I, having more resources — contacts, money, knowledge of the way the world works — might be able to assist other family members to survive. Would we live with souls at ease if we were evacuated, but other family members were killed?

The second reason is that if I fled I would be an accomplice to the violence. The whole concept of protecting human rights is based on the fact that an observer — and as an American, whether I like it or not, I am one of those "significant people" — might be a deterrent. Moreover, since I had a cell phone and Internet access, might not my reporting from such an out-of-the-way place as Lumakanda be a testimony and witness to what was going on? Might this not alert the rest of the world — at least my contacts — about the unfolding events?

"Do Unto Others as They Do Unto You"

Shortly after Hurricane Katrina hit in 2005, I was passing through Kampala, Uganda. I read the following story in *The Monitor*, one of the major papers in Uganda.

There is a group of HIV+ women in Kampala who work together in an association. Their work is to pound rocks into gravel which is then sold for construction. I have seen these women along one of the roads next to a ridge full of large rocks. They sit on the ground and with a small sledgehammer pound away turning the rocks into a heap of gravel. The paper indicated that they earn about $1.00 per day for this backbreaking work. These women had heard about Hurricane Katrina and how it had destroyed so many homes and possessions of the people of New Orleans. They decided to donate over $900 for the relief of the victims of Hurricane Katrina. When one of the women was asked why they would do this, when their own condition was dire, she replied, "Our custom is to help people when they are in difficulties. We see that those people have lost everything so we want to help out."

It is sad to think how little $900 contributed to the relief of Hurricane Katrina victims. On the other hand, the response of these HIV+, rock-breaking women through their humanness, their connection to suffering all over the world, is overwhelming.

Chapter 2
My Heroes

Fearless Alison Des Forges

Alison Des Forges, senior researcher for Human Rights Watch for Rwanda, Burundi and the eastern Congo, died on Thursday, February 12, 2009 in an airplane crash near Buffalo, New York.

I met Alison Des Forges in college in 1963 when she had just returned from a summer of teaching Rwandan refugees through a Harvard/Radcliffe program, Project Tanganyika. When her boyfriend, Roger Des Forges, came to town, I would put him up in my dorm. She encouraged me to apply for the program and I ended up spending a year teaching Rwandan refugees in the West Lake region of Tanzania. Her boyfriend became her husband and we stayed in close contact through the years. In the late 1960's, when she finished her research in Rwanda, Alison and Roger came to visit me in Kenya.

She received her PhD in African history from Yale in 1972. Her thesis is unique and now impossible to replicate. She interviewed over a hundred elderly Rwandans who could remember when the Europeans first arrived in Rwanda in the 1890's. Some of these people were over a hundred years old. Her thesis, "Defeat is the Only Bad News: Rwanda under Musinga, 1896-1931," gives the history of the European conquest from the African point of view. In contrast, a few years ago, I read, *The Scramble for Africa: White Man's Conquest of the Dark Continent from 1876 – 1912* by Thomas Parkenham (1992) which had no reference that I can remember to any African's opinion regarding this conquest. Alison's thesis illustrated how various Rwandan political factions manipulated the German and then the Belgian colonialists to their own advantage. *Defeat Is the Only Bad News* has now been published in paperback.

As our children grew up, we would frequently visit each other. My family lived in Pittsburgh and they lived in Buffalo where Roger was a Professor of Chinese History at the University of Buffalo. When my son, Tommy, went to the University of Rochester from 1991 to 1995, I would stay with the Des Forges' whenever I visited him. Throughout the time preceding the genocide, Alison and I would discuss the looming catastrophe as neither of us had any

24

Alison Des Forges

doubt that terrible things were being planned.

She was fearless. Everyday she would go for a walk — a real power walk — because she was quite short and she would walk very fast. I almost had to run to keep up with her. When she crossed a street, she would just walk right in front of an oncoming car. When I asked her about this, she replied, "They will always stop." Was this bravery or foolhardiness? They always stopped.

Before the genocide in 1994, Alison had been investigating the many small massacres of Tutsi that were occurring in Rwanda, usually in out of the way places. The local authorities would always try to keep her from visiting these remote areas, saying the road was too bad, it was too dangerous, or that she needed permission, etc. She always went. During one of her travels, she was threatened by a Rwandan government military official who spoke to her as she boarded a plane to leave Rwanda. He told her that her life was in danger if she continued this work. She continued.

Before the genocide in Rwanda, people's identity card indicated if they were Hutu, Tutsi, or Twa. Alison convinced the pre-genocide Rwandan government to issue new identity cards without the ethnic classification and got a number of foreign embassies to agree to foot the bill. However, nothing happened. If this had been done as she had planned, I have always wondered how many more Tutsi would have escaped death during the genocide.

Human rights work was a new field in the early 1990's. The custom in the field up to that time was to say something like "a senior military official did..." Alison realized that it was necessary to state the person's name and the official position of anyone who was involved in human rights violations. This, of course, upped the consequences for the perpetrator, but also made the human rights worker more vulnerable to retaliation.

The genocide began on April 6, 1994 and during one hundred days of the genocide Alison did everything she could to stop it. During the genocide, I hardly ever saw Alison because she was a whirlwind of activity visiting diplomats and civil rights organizations all over the United States and Europe. This is how she described it for the Frontline documentary, "Ghosts of Rwanda," produced in 2004:

It's a blur of constant meetings, interviews, travel from one place to another; a lot of meetings here at the U.N., talking with Security Council delegates, particularly the Czech ambassador, the New Zealand ambassador, the Spanish ambassador, who became very concerned and very, very anxious to act to protect Rwandans; meetings in Washington with various people — the National Security Council people at the State Department, trips to Europe, meetings there with various government officials; coordination with colleagues in the NGO community, the non-government organizations; and lots and lots of time spent talking to journalists, trying to explain what was happening, to give some depth to the scenes of horror that were being portrayed.

At the beginning of the genocide, Alison was talking on the phone to a Rwandan human rights colleague named Monique Mujawamariya. Monique said that the *interahamwe* were entering her house and then the phone went dead. A few days after the genocide began; she had a letter to the editor on this incident, published in the *New York Times*, which aroused the interest of then President Bill Clinton. When Monique miraculously escaped, President Clinton lost interest in the unfolding Rwandan genocide. Alison took him to task about this on National Public Radio. When the NPR reporter, Neal Conant, asked her to sum up the genocide in one word, Alison gave him an earful. "How could such a tragedy be summed up in one word?" This illustrates how Alison had the guts to confront anyone. She continually challenged heads of states and high government officials about their lack of response to the genocide.

In July 1994, near the end of the genocide, some Rwandans organized a demonstration in downtown Washington, DC. I went and there were about twenty-five people, mostly Rwandans present. Alison was there also. It was a typical humid DC summer day with the temperature at noon near one hundred degrees. According to the rules that govern demonstrations, demonstrators have to keep moving on the sidewalk. To accomplish this they walk slowly around and around in a circle. Alison, who was clearly angry, walked in her usual fast gait, lapping the rest of us time after time. A reporter in a dark suit and tie was trying to interview her as she raced around the circle. He had to hesitate to write the answers to her questions and then had to run to catch up with her. I felt sorry for him but knew he was in the presence of a passionate and dedicated activist.

After the genocide, I continued to stay at the Des Forges' house with Roger but Alison was rarely there. She was determined to name the perpetrators and see that justice was served. Almost everyone she had worked with during her research in the 1960's had been killed during the genocide. Roger would tell me that he did not know when she would return home, yet she called home to Roger every evening.

When Alison and I did see each other after the genocide, we talked about her appearances in the various courts trying the *genocidaires*. Usually she would be questioned for up to a week's time. The defense lawyers would start challenging her, saying that she was not an expert witness and therefore was not qualified to speak about the genocide. In every case, they lost. They would then ask Alison the same questions over and over and over again hoping that she would lose her "cool," an impossibility, or make some inconsistency in her answers, not likely. For Alison, this was just part of what needed to be endured to bring justice.

In 2003, I wrote the following poem about the nonchalant attitude towards the death of the innocent.

A Missed Funeral

Once many years ago, I left for home on Route 45
Out of Lewisburg, Pennsylvania.
It was early Saturday morning in October
the sun rising in the blue sky,
the well-kept farms ripe with the labor of the year,
the old Dutch barns and farmhouses from a picture book,
the distant mountains close to heaven.
Alone in a car on a newly paved road.

Suddenly directly in front of my left wheel was a patch
of blood, guts, and fur of some unrecognizable creature
who, but yesterday, had been tending to life
with family, friends, or alone,
who, when crossing the road,
had been smattered by the lights of the killer car.

Should I swerve?
There was no danger of hitting an oncoming vehicle.
Should I keep going straight
and re-run over the mash of bright red and brown?

Many thoughts can pass in a few split seconds,
but not time enough for a well-considered decision.
I did not swerve.

By the moment the rear tire had run over the mash,
I regretted.
Sure, no one saw that I did not swerve —
except me — and God.
Sure, this was not a pet
to be buried with ceremony in the back yard.
Sure, I could not have brought the small creature back to life.
Yet, I had, so to speak, missed the funeral.
I had not shown my respect for the being,
that had been scurrying about on his or her life's work
but a few short hours ago.

As the years go by I reflect on that missed opportunity.
In the great affairs of the world and cosmos,

even in the material world of Route 45
this petty decision makes no perceptible difference

But it does.

When Alison was investigating the 1994 genocide in Rwanda, she drove up a grassy road to a church where a massacre had occurred. As she got out of the car, she stepped on the remains of a small child, flattened by numerous unsuspecting vehicles. She told me that this was the only time, after observing innumerable massacres, that she "freaked out."

In 1999, her book for Human Rights Watch, *Leave None to Tell the Story: Genocide in Rwanda*, came out and her period of frenzied pursuit of justice slowed down, although she continued her human rights involvement not only in Rwanda, but also in Burundi and North and South Kivu in eastern Congo.

One of the problems in human rights work is hyperbole, often overstating the number of people killed in a massacre. Sometimes this is politically motivated, but other times it is just guesstimations or sloppiness. Alison wanted exactness. When she could, she would count the bodies. I once asked her how she could see all those dead bodies and bones, clothes scattered about, and the other signs of massacres. She told me that you learn to control your emotions and numb yourself to the human condition of the victims as you have to stay calm and observant. I think that her power walks were her method of letting out built up anger and frustration.

One issue that Alison tackled was the number of people killed in the Rwandan genocide. Frequently the number given is eight hundred and fifty thousand or one million. On pages 15 and 16 of *Leave None to Tell the Story*, Alison shows why she thinks five hundred thousand is closer to the correct number. Her conclusion is the one I use in this book. This is based essentially on the fact that there were only approximately six hundred and forty thousand Tutsi in Rwanda before the genocide and about twenty-five percent of them, against amazing odds, survived.

It is ironic that Alison died in the first fatal commercial plane crash in the United States in two and a half years. Alison lived her life dangerously. Plane crashes are much more frequent in Africa and as she investigated some massacre the possibility of an "accident" such as being run off the road, i.e., an assassination attempt, was always possible. I knew that Alison would have no regrets. So many of the people she worked with and loved had been brutally killed and from her perspective, her life would be no more than those of the many bodies she saw. She treated everyone with the same dignity and respect, from the illiterate Rwandan peasant to the prime minister of England.

At the time of her death, Alison had twice been denied entry into Rwanda by the current Rwandan government. The Rwandan government was upset with Alison after Human Rights Watch published her criticisms of current judicial processes in Rwanda and her campaign to have those from the current government who committed atrocities during their conquest of Rwanda during the genocide brought to the International Criminal Court in Arusha for trial.

The press reports about the crash that killed her say that there was ice on the wing and turbulence in the air right before the plane crashed. This, I believe, is a metaphor for Alison's life — icy fearlessness in some of the most turbulent conflicts of our time.

❀ ❀ ❀

Cassilde Ntamamiro and Felicite Niyonzima

As I go around the United States giving talks, I frequently meet people who say that they have no intention of leaving their comfort zone. Because of this, they view me as some kind of "hero." I find this strange because I am doing what I am led to do. After so many years in Africa, I am accustomed to living here. I have become well used to the spartan living conditions.

My definition of a hero is slightly different. Cassilde Ntamamiro and Felicite Niyonzima are my heroes. I met Felicite in early 2005 when anti-retro viral (ARV's) drugs needed to keep an HIV+ person alive were not available in Burundi. Consequently, in order to stay healthy, HIV+ people had to eat, sleep properly, and not do any of those vices like drinking or smoking. Women also should not become pregnant since the gestation of the baby would be taxing on her body.

In 2005, I visited the Kamenge Clinic in Bujumbura, Burundi during the day set aside for the monthly nutritious communal meal. In its first year, the clinic had registered about seventy mostly women who were HIV+ in their program. According to their meticulous records, five of these had already died. Approximately thirty of the HIV+ clients attended the gathering. Most were young women, four had small children with them, and five were men who were mostly older than forty. The clinic is for women, but they do not turn down working with men who are HIV+.

When we arrived, the women were preparing a substantial meal and Cassilde, the founder and director of the clinic, showed us around the clinic: the large waiting room, the consultation room, the small store for selling items to the public, the hair cutting business on the side of the building, and the storeroom and medicine room. She also showed me three unfinished rooms on the side which she wanted to complete. She had a bed in one of the rooms for patients who needed to be under care.

Cassilde, on the left, showing me the store at the clinic. The man in the front is the storekeeper. The small number of consumable items on the shelves in common for stores in the region.

As people were gathering, the first activity was a public meeting that was education, organization, and advice. The topic was mostly about the importance of good nutrition. Various varieties of vitamin pills, including that for children, were displayed to the clients.

The organizational part consisted in discussing a method so that all the clients, who come from a rather large catchment area of Bujumbura, could be notified of the clinic's gatherings. Almost half of the possible clients did not attend. If they had, I do not know where they would have sat since the room was filled almost to capacity. There was also discussion of electing a committee for the group. It was decided to postpone this until everyone could be informed. Those who were able were asked to pay 200 francs — less than 20 US cents — per month to the association. These funds would be used for taking someone to the hospital and for their funeral costs. Cassilde wanted the members to "buy in" to their organization so that it did not seem like complete charity.

One man said that he was afraid to go upcountry to tell his wife that he was HIV+. The group counseled him to bring his wife to Bujumbura where he would tell her, bring her to the clinic to be tested, and they would help advise her according to the results of the test. I do not know if this happened or not, but it demonstrates the kind of help that such a clinic can provide.

The most shocking thing for me was the story of one of the women clients who had brought her husband to the clinic. His first wife had died of AIDS, his second wife had died of AIDS, his third wife had died of AIDS, and now his fourth wife was HIV+! It seemed that men lived much longer than women did when they became HIV+. Cassilde explained to me that the reason for this is that the men had more access to meat, milk, and medicine. With better nutrition, they lived longer.

A student at the Great Lakes School of Theology, named Fidele, had died a few days previously. Cassilde knew he had died of AIDS but he did not admit that he was HIV+ and had postponed going for testing until it was too late. The previous year his wife had died of AIDS. As Burundi Yearly Meeting was growing rapidly, by 2005 it had about fifteen thousand adult members. Probably one thousand five hundred to two thousand of these were HIV positive. Cassilde lamented the fact that there was not one member who was willing to publicly stand up in church and tell people that she or he was HIV+. Denial of AIDS runs deep in Burundian society since any member who admitted to being HIV+ was admitting that he or she or his or her spouse had "sinned" since no one could become HIV+ unless one of the couple had premarital or extramarital sex.

The clinic also sees regular patients who are sick with malaria, intestinal problems, etc. Their log showed that they had received about one thousand five hundred visits in less than a year and a half. During the time we were there about ten people came with these types of conditions. They go into the consulting room to meet with the nurse who prescribes the appropriate medicines as necessary.

It was moving to be in a room full of people who otherwise were destined for an early death — many so young, including teenagers. I had read that people in Africa died much more quickly than those in the US. If a person is HIV+ and follows healthy living habits, he or she may continue with a normal life for many years. But with neglect and poor nutrition, the HIV+ person dies quickly. This is why the work the Kamenge clinic is doing is so important.

Cassilde asked me if I would stay for lunch and eat with the clients. Everyone was served with lots of rice, beans, greens, and a piece of meat. No doubt everyone had enough to eat for that meal. The clients were then given two pounds of rice and a one-pound of beans to take home with them.

Later I went sixty miles up-country to Gitega with Elie Nahimana, General Secretary of Burundi Yearly Meeting, and Adrien Niyongabo, Coordinator of the HROC program. Here we met a woman named Felicite Niyonzima, a member of the Friends church. She told us that she was HIV+ and would be willing to speak publicly about this. When we asked if we could take her picture, she declined.

As we listened to her, she spilled out her story, as those who have had traumatic experiences tend to do the first few times they tell their story. She was married with two children and her husband died of AIDS in 1998. It took her a year to be

Felicite Niyonzima

33

tested before she found out she was HIV+. She was the assistant to the Gitega provincial educational inspector. She quietly told her family and her employer. Clearly, she had the means to continue with healthy living and so, although seven years had gone by, her viral load level was still too low to require medicines.

She said that a man had come to ask her to marry him. She declined. He came a second time. She again declined. When he came a third time, she told him she was HIV+ and he never came again to ask for her hand.

When I asked her what she expected would happen when she spoke out publicly in the church, she replied that she expected many people who were HIV+ would come to her for advice and support. I thought that she would quickly be overwhelmed by the number of people approaching her. Elie immediately invited her to come to speak at the next Burundi Yearly Meeting pastors' meeting.

When our conversation ended, she agreed to have her picture taken with us. Elie asked Adrien to arrange a meeting quickly between Felicite, Cassilde, and the person responsible for AIDS awareness in the yearly meeting, to discuss how to support and help Felicite in her forthcoming witness.

Two days later, on Saturday, as we drove back into Bujumbura from Gitega, we saw two pick-up trucks full of people. The first one was carrying a decorated cross in front. Elie honked and waved to the people in the trucks. This was the funeral for Fidele, the student who had just died of AIDS. Later in the day when we were leaving the church compound in Bujumbura, Adrien pointed out seven children, dressed in their Sunday best, walking down the street. Their ages were approximately five to seventeen. These were Fidele's orphans.

Felicite Niyonzima is my hero. She defied the conventional wisdom that being HIV+ was a sinful, secret activity and spoke out publicly to the possible approbation of everyone in her church; she challenged and overturned the conventional wisdom. She has guts.

As Felicite predicted, as soon as she announced her HIV+ status, many women came quietly to her to tell her that they were also HIV+. Through the Healing and Rebuilding Our Community program, they developed a special workshop for these HIV+ women. For not only did they have the trauma that everyone else in Burundi had after twelve years of civil war, but the additional trauma of being HIV+ and being rejected by Burundian society as soon as they showed any obvious signs of sickness.

Heroes are not necessarily those who travel to distant lands and help folks, but rather those who live in their community and take on the responsibility to do what needs to be done, regardless of the opinions of the prevailing society.

Odette Nahayo

On March 17, 2009, I received an email from Burundi that Odette Nahayo had passed away.

A few years back, in her blog about her time in Kenya, Sandy Grotberg, an AGLI volunteer, commented that the major difference between Kenya and the United States was that people died, frequently, from many causes. The life expectancy in the US is about 78 years while in the African Great Lakes region it is in the 50's. The difference in the rates is also related to the number of people who die young. Odette was thirty-eight years old.

Let me relate Odette's life as I know it. Odette was born in 1971. In 1972 there was a coup attempt in Burundi by the Hutu members of the military or a fake Hutu coup attempt organized by the Tutsi military in order for the Tutsi military to seize power, depending which side is telling the story. I prefer the second explanation as

Odette on her graduation from college on December 19, 2008

the Tutsi military ruled Burundi for the next thirty-three years. At that time, the Tutsi military killed all Hutu who had any education or were leaders in their communities. This was approximately fifty thousand Hutu. Odette's father was a teacher and, thus, was killed. Her mother was pregnant with Odette's sister, Alexia Nibona, now a doctor and the head of the Friends Women's Association's Kamenge Clinic described in the previous section.

After a few years, Odette's mother remarried and the two young girls were given to their mother's younger sister, Cassilde Ntamamiro, founder of the Kamenge Clinic described above, to raise. Cassilde raised her two nieces until they completed high school. In November 1993, Odette met Adrien Niyongabo, now Coordinator of the HROC program in Burundi. During the violence after the death of the Hutu president, Adrien was targeted because he was a Hutu (see page 241 for details). He decided to find refuge in Kamenge, a Hutu majority suburb. He knew a family there that was housing other young people. One of these was Odette. Odette and Adrien fell in love and married in 1997. Adrien told me that the wedding was not elaborate because the conflict was still intense at that time. Odette brought Adrien into the Friends church.

I first met Odette in May 2001 when I went to visit Adrien and his family during my rounds to various AGLI projects throughout the Great Lakes region. The couple then had two children, Kasia and Jonathan. I went with Brad Allen who was one of the AGLI volunteers in Burundi at that time. Adrien later told me that in hierarchical Burundi a "boss" would never visit the family of one of his "employees" so they did not really know how my visit would turn out.

When we got there, they asked us if we would like a soda. When we said, "yes," they pulled the sodas out of their cupboard. Later they asked us if we wanted tea and *mandazi*, African style donuts. Again they pulled them out of the cupboard. Then they asked if we wanted dinner and it was pulled out of the cupboard all prepared. In short, they were cautious about our visit and were taking the steps of hospitality one at a time. It was a wonderful evening, particularly being able to see their wonderful closely-knit family. As the years went by, each time I was in Burundi, it became our custom for me to visit the family.

I watched the children grow and two more boys, Joshua and David, were born. I found that their home was a drop-in center for many of their neighbors, particularly members of Kamenge Friends Church. The couple also lived with and supported Odette's younger siblings from her mother's second marriage and other relatives, most of who were studying in Bujumbura.

Odette began attending college at Great Lakes School of Theology and, when it closed, she transferred to Hope University, a newly opened Free Methodist college in Bujumbura. It was at this time that she began speaking to me in English rather than the Swahili that we had formerly used. In November of 2008, Odette received her BA degree. She had begun working with the Friends Women's Association leading peace-making/trauma healing workshops for women. Odette had a calm, quiet, strong presence. She was always interested in the people who came to visit the house and had a nice sense of humor with a wonderful smile.

Her biggest contribution to Burundian society and her Friends church was the "Circle of Sisters." It began in 2001 following a visit by Rachel Fretz, clerk of AGLI's Working Group, our decision making body. Once a week at 4:00 PM, the women of Kamenge Friends Church would meet at the church under Odette's leadership. Since the Circle of Sisters was self-supporting, I really did not realize that it continued. Six years later, Adrien mentioned it and so I asked Odette about the group. Odette told me that the most popular topic was "How to deal with your husband" when up to fifty women would attend. The second most popular topic was "How to deal with the in-laws." Other sessions were more practical — how to sew children's clothing or prepare a more nutritious kind of food. It had continued on a weekly basis for eight years, essentially as a women's support group.

Odette died from complications of pregnancy. Adrien had written to me that Odette, whose first four pregnancies were relatively easy and normal, was having difficulty with this pregnancy. When she was about seven months pregnant, she was feeling badly and they took her to the hospital. There she had a miscarriage and never regained complete consciousness.

This was the third woman I know in Africa who has died of complications from pregnancy in the previous two years. In the United States, I have personally never known any woman who has died from complications during pregnancy. After a nurse in Michigan read my report on Odette's death, she emailed me that in Kenya the rate of death due to complications from pregnancy was five hundred times higher than in the United States. This is the only statistic that she could give me, but the rate in Burundi is probably even higher.

Adrien had lost his wife, the four children, then between about three and eleven, had lost their mother, the Circle of Sisters had lost their leader, Kamenge Church had lost a stalwart member, and the community had lost a wise, calm leader. May her soul rest in peace.

Gakemba

In 1964 when I was teaching in the refugee camp in Tanzania, a famine set in when the government and the United Nations High Commissioner for Refugees cut off rations. Justin, one of our students, came to tell us that an old man across the road in his village of Muyenzi Juu needed some food because he was too weak to walk. Randy Kehler, my co-volunteer, and I gave him the usual pound of rice that we handed out and really did not think much more about it. We fulfilled requests like this every day.

Three days later, Justin came to tell us that the old man wanted us to come to the village as he was still too weak to walk to the school. He wanted to thank us. That afternoon after school, we went to Muyenzi Juu to meet with him.

We learned a little about the old man. His name was Gakemba. Unlike most of the refugees, he had no family in the refugee camp and people did not really know much about him. He lived a few huts over from Justin. He came in slowly, leaning bent over on a long stick, and wearing a wrap-around cloth instead of trousers. He greeted us warmly and then thanked us. He then said something that affected me even to this day, "I thank you for the help you have given to me, but I have nothing to give you in return. God will bless you for what you have done." I guess it was the simplicity and sincerity of his response that so affected me.

We then became great friends with Gakemba. He was approximately seventy years old and he could remember when he was a young boy and the Europeans first came to Rwanda. He was somehow attached to one of the royal courts and as a boy had learned the songs, poems, and stories of the court. He said that he had to recite a passage word for word without making a mistake and he was hit if he mispronounced even one syllable. This is, I guess, how Homer's epics were passed down from generation to generation before they were written down. We had a small reel-to-reel tape recorder and we recorded some of his songs and poems. When we asked our students to translate the poems for us, they did not know the words he was using in Kinyarwandan, the language of Rwanda. He had to define the words for them. The poems in particular were mostly about how beautiful the long-horned Ankole bulls were. This was all metaphors about the history of Rwanda and the various *mwami,* kings. Everything was so complex with hidden meanings that it made Shakespeare seem simple.

Gakemba had a great sense of humor. He, for example, would come to the school, hide in such a way that I could not see him, but the students could. He would then mimic me. The class would start breaking up in laughter until I figured out what was going on. Once he had gone down to get a pair of shoes that the United Nations High Commissioner for Refugees was distributing. He tried on many, but none would fit him because after walking barefoot his whole life, his toes had spread apart and there was no shoe that would fit his feet. His comment was, "My soles are better than the shoes anyway because they never wear out." He was illiterate, but once patted his stomach and said, "This is my book of agriculture. When I get hungry, I go and cultivate." We always enjoyed his coming around so much.

I did not find him like the Africans of the old ways as depicted in so many novels written by Africans and others. He did not yearn for the good old days, fighting for tradition over the new ways. Although he said he had no desire to learn to read, he was clear that this was the future for the young people and so they had to go to school. In other words, he approved of our teaching the Rwandan students. He was not a Christian, he said, but had no animosity to those who were. He was sure of himself even if that world he grew up in had passed away and there was a newer, different world in front. He was comfortable with himself and his life.

We never learned why he was alone.

Section 2

Understanding the Cultures

Until recently, my father-in-law, David Okwemba, kept wild quail.
In each of these little baskets are two or three quail. At the time of
this picture, he has put millet on the ground under the baskets and
the quail are eating it. He catches more quail in a trap where the
captured quail squeak and this attracts the wild quail. When they
enter, the trap closes. The birds are then eaten as a delicacy since
one bird is enough for only one person. I have eaten my share of
his quail including the first time I went to his house to meet him.
Surplus quail are sold to neighbors for special occasions.

Chapter 3
Cultural Adaptation

Some Cultural Miscues

When I travel from Kenya to the United States, I cross an invisible line somewhere over the Atlantic Ocean. Usually I am fast asleep and never notice that I am now closer to one place than the other. The ease in which we can travel today is so breathtakingly fast and so mind-bogglingly disorienting that the airlines have installed maps in the seat in front of us to help us locate our place in the world as we hurl through space. Unfortunately, we have not yet developed a map that helps us navigate cultures. This chapter includes a number of stories that indicate cultural differences.

Some people are much more attuned to culture. When I toured four African countries with my daughter, Joy, in 1995, I was amazed at how quickly she was able to recognize customs and adapt accordingly. I remember by the second day in Zanzibar, she was able to blend right in with the crowd — not only in dress but also in understanding the proper way to pay and board the local bus system. During the same trip, when we visited her grandparents in Kenya, Joy's grandmother asked her to serve the food. Joy started by serving her grandfather, then me, then her uncles and aunts, and lastly her various cousins. Later I joked, "Why do not you serve me like this in the United States?" knowing that her actions in Kenya seemed to go against her usual feminist stance. Her reply was quite sensible — it would have been extremely rude for her to refuse her grandmother's request. Since the custom in Kenya was to serve the oldest man first and continue down the line, she felt that she should do what was expected. Nevertheless, she jokingly made it clear that I should not expect such service in the United States.

A number of years ago I was at a seminar on cross-cultural issues and the presenter opened the seminar by asking, "In which country do American businessmen have the most difficulty negotiating and completing contracts?" The first answers were the obvious ones such as China and Japan whose culture is different from American culture. This was not the correct answer. The next set of responses included America's "enemies" such as Russia and Cuba. Again, this was wrong. No one guessed the right answer, Australia.

Americans know that China and Japan are different so they take seminars to learn and accommodate those differences. Businesspeople are extra conscientious in dealings with "enemies" so their contracts with Russia or Cuba are closely scrutinized. Americans incorrectly think that Australians are just like Americans, not realizing that they have their own cultural characteristics.

If one marries the girl next door, one expects that everything is the same when it may well not be so. There is an advantage of marrying someone of a clearly different culture. One is prepared for the unknown, accommodating to the differences, and is ready to adapt.

The biggest cultural misunderstanding I can remember in Kenya occurred, not between a Westerner and an African, but between differing ethnic groups at the school where I was principal. A certain amount of tension developed at the Mua Hills Harambee Secondary School and everyone was unsure why. In most of Tanzania, the younger person greets the older person first with "*Shikamoo*," a greeting of respect in Swahili, while the older person responds with "*Marahaba*." These greetings are based on age. I once saw President Julius Nyerere of Tanzania, after giving a presentation to some farmers, walk pass an elderly man with a stick and blanket. Nyerere nodded his head and said, respectfully, "*Shikamoo*." The fact that he was president of the country and the other was just an old man made no difference. In Tanzania, where Swahili is widely spoken, if a person passes a school just as the students are going home, each one will say *shikamoo* requiring the response of *marahaba* hundreds of times until one is hoarse.

Our school was located in Kenya in the area of the Kamba people who have the exact opposite custom. In the Kamba tradition, the elder person must greet the younger person first. The elder says, "*Wachaa*" and the younger one answers, "*Aah*." I always thought that this was quite clever since even a very young child can say the word, *aah*. I was in Kenya with Tommy, my then one-year-old son, and while shy at first, he learned to shake hands and respond *aah* with everyone. When he returned to the United States, he waited for adults to greet him. When they did not, he held out his hand, as he learned in Kenya, to shake it with people he met. Unfortunately, only one elderly man ever shook his hand and greeted him. After a short time, he forgot the custom he learned in Kenya and stopped putting out his hand for his elders to shake.

This is essentially the same cultural difference that was occurring in the school in Kenya. The Kamba students were waiting for their teachers and elders to greet them, while the non-Kamba students were waiting for the Kamba students to greet them. The result was that the groups — each waiting for the other to greet them — felt that the other group was unfriendly and rude to them. Unfortunately, these ingrained cultural norms were hard to break and even after we understood the root of the problem, it was still difficult to bridge the friendship gap between the two groups.

I was once in Burundi and, as a guest to the country and her foreign "boss," one of the local AGLI staff members asked me to dinner along with an American volunteer. The American complained to me that, after being in Burundi for more than a year, this was the first time her co-worker had invited her to dinner. Later I heard from the Burundian that the American volunteer had never stopped by for dinner. Clearly, a cultural miscue — the American was waiting to be invited, while, according to Burundian custom, a person should just drop in for dinner.

Visiting

The custom in Kenya is that relatives and others visit our house all the time. In most cases, we do not even know that they are coming as they just show up. One day there was a woman who came to our house. I asked Gladys who the person was. She responded that the woman was her cousin. I asked how long she planned on staying. Gladys did not know, but she indicated that according to Kenyan hospitality she was welcome to stay as long as she wanted.

Most of the people who visit us are female. The reason for this is that men are tied to their property, livestock, fields, and possessions. For instance, when Gladys's father comes to visit us, he does not want to stay because he has to get home to see how his two cows are doing. When he was younger, he would spend three hours getting to our house, stay for three or four hours and then return home, another three-hour ride. Women move to the husband's house, but since this is not their property, they do not feel as attached. Consequently, they visit each other more often, particularly their sisters and other female relatives.

How can we handle all these guests? When a female guest comes, she frequently will be coming with some kind of food, usually something she has just harvested from her plot. After normal greetings, she may go to the kitchen and help with food preparations. This might include picking through greens for the evening meal. In this case, all the women will sit outside together, pick the greens, and discuss whatever is on their mind. Usually there is a lot of expressive talking and considerable amounts of laughter. Consequently, the visitor is not treated as a guest but rather as a member of the family. One thing that really amazes me about all this is that no one is asked to do anything as the visiting woman just pitches right in without any authority figure giving commands.

Cooking, washing clothes by hand, and other household tasks in Kenya are extremely labor intensive. Any woman who has a job — a teacher, for example — needs to have household help to take care of these task while she is at work. This domestic worker is treated differently than those in American or European homes' or ones in the homes of foreigners living in Kenya. The American or European sees the domestic worker in class terms, as a subordinate who does certain necessary but mundane tasks. The live-in domestic worker sleeps in a room outside the house and does not eat with the American or European family. A Kenyan, at least those who have not been influenced by Western classism, considers the domestic worker to be part of the family, which in fact she frequently is. She sleeps in the house with the rest of the family and eats at the table with everyone else. A stranger to the household might not be able to tell the domestic worker from other relatives visiting in the household. I know many cases where the "domestic worker" is a young relative who, in exchange for helping with domestic chores, is supported to attend further schooling.

Consequences of a Young Society

One overlooked attribute of African society is the effects of a high birth rate. Let me give personal examples. I have three siblings. Gladys had nine; three died in childhood. Her father, David Okwemba, had a second wife and Gladys had another eleven half-siblings through this union; again, three died in childhood. Of the fifteen remaining children, the father has already outlived four. This means that of his twenty-one children, only eleven are still living.

I have six first cousins. Gladys has eighty-six first cousins; these are only the ones who survived to adulthood. Most of these relatives are married, giving connection to another large family, and they have children. Some of these children are old enough to have the next generation so we have uncountable numbers of grand-nieces and grandnephews, cousins once removed, and so on. More-over, here in Kenya, people consider second and third cousins as "cousins." This exponentially increases the number of relatives. At times when Gladys says, "Meet my cousin" and I ask her how this person is related to her; she has to think hard to untangle the rela-tionship.

Furthermore, if one looks at generations — her father's, hers, her children, and her grandchildren — the number of people in each generation increase multifold. In other words, as the demo-graphic statistics always point out, there are proportionately more young people than there are older people. I read in a recent report that 81% of the Kenyan population is under thirty-five years of age. The result is that there is always a niece or nephew, grandniece or grandnephew around to do whatever needs to be done. Manual labor is not nearly as challenging for the society here as in the United States because there are so many young, vigorous hands to do the manual work.

When a woman here gets older and her sons are married, the older woman becomes the matriarch of the family and begins to stop all those arduous duties that strike Americans as so menial. The older woman has her daughters and daughters-in-law, and then later her granddaughters, to do this work for her. As you might ex-pect, one of the biggest intra-family problems here in Kenya is the relationship between the mother and her daughter-in-law who is living in her compound, although in a different house. The mother-in-law is commanding her daughters-in-law in all those household chores and the daughters-in-law may resent this. In American soci-ety, the son breaks away from his family, including his mother, to set up a separate household with the new wife. Here the son does not break away from the orbit of his mother.

In Gladys' case, there was an additional problem. Her father and mother had no sons survive to adulthood — the two sons died when they were children. Normally, it is the oldest son who be-comes responsible for his parents as they get older. Or rather it is the duty of the wife of the oldest son to take care of her parents-in-law. Under Kenyan culture, Gladys should take care of my parents. This is something she did when we lived in St. Louis from 2000 to 2005 to help care for my mother with Alzheimer. Gladys liked being in St. Louis partly because, according to her Luhya culture, she was doing what she was supposed to do. In 2005, my mother passed away. Gladys' mother died the following year and we moved to Kenya partly to look after her father who was then eighty-four years old. This should have been the duty of the eldest son, but since there was no son, Gladys has taken over this responsibility.

In Gladys' role as "eldest son," she has taken care of not only her father and mother, her six sisters, but in many cases their children. This meant their education, particularly secondary school and university. Sickness is the next most important aspect for which the eldest son is usually responsible. In Gladys' case, she supported her family by working overseas. In this she was no different from many Kenyans — almost 10% of the Kenyan adult population is overseas earning money to send back to support their families. Repatriation of earnings is the second highest income source of foreign earnings in Kenya. The United States, Britain, other English speaking countries, and the Middle East are the largest recipients of Kenyan migration. Many of these immigrants, particularly those like Gladys who leave their families behind, do return to Kenya when they have earned enough. In the past, it was mostly educated sons who went overseas, but in the last ten to twenty years, it has included middle-aged women who go to provide for their children. Nursing homes in the United States and England are filled with middle-aged Kenyan women.

Children are Decision-Making People

When Susan B. Anthony and others in the women's rights movement began to labor for the rights of women, they neglected the rights of children. Before the US Civil War, women and children were the property of the husband or father. After a long, bitter struggle, women were freed from the bondage of their husbands, but children continued to be possessions of their parents. When the parents are decent parents, this is no problem. When the parents fail their children, this brings anguish and bitterness to the children.

Traditional Kenyan society does not share this American concept that children are possessions of their parents until they reach the magical age of an adult on their eighteenth birthday. In Kenya, a child is allowed to make personal decisions from the time he or she is born. For example, the day I wrote this paragraph Gladys gave her two grandsons each a hen. The boys, aged 6 and 8, will decide what to do with the hens — eat them, keep them for eggs, or keep them to hatch more chicks.

Once our five-year-old niece, Gloria, decided that she wanted to stay with us; so she came to reside at our house. After about a week, her mother came to visit and asked Gloria if she wanted to return home. Gloria said, "No" and she continued staying with us until she felt like returning home a few days later.

Wire toy trucks such as this one are common in the region. This elaborate truck has a steering wheel. On the back axle is a device that makes a sound when the truck is pushed. Here the boy is carrying a stone. I have seen boys drive their trucks to the store and have their trucks carry back a pound of rice or sugar.

This picture was taken outside of the Kamenge Clinic in one of the poorest sections of Bujumbura in one of the poorest countries in the world. Notice the cracked, plastered wall and wooden shutter in the background.   (continued on next page)

I have seen much simpler toys. Naturally these toys are easily broken, but then the child can easily fix them again. Soccer balls are made from old pieces of cloth or discarded plastic bags. I have seen a whole toy plot with house, trees, and animals elaborated constructed with sticks, grass, stones, and parts of various plants. Another common toy is a bow and arrow made from sticks and string.

I would suspect that the person who made such a fancy wire truck. was the boy's father or other relative. What is the difference between a toy made by oneself or a parent or other relative versus a toy manufactured as sold in Toys R Us? I think that those Toys R Us toys convey the subtle message that promotes the passive, consumer society. To buy something gaudy and unbreakable is better than something handmade and home-made. For the boy who makes his own simple push toy or soccer ball versus the store bought variety, the difference is between being an active participant in creation and a passive consumer.

Use of Tools

One time I was with my first wife, Rodah, and I picked up an ax to chop a piece of wood. She quickly took it from me and chopped the wood herself. In Africa, the women collect the fire-wood and chop it into appropriately sized pieces. Therefore the ax is seen as a female tool. In America, chopping wood is considered a male duty and therefore the ax belongs to the man.

My first father-in-law, Wilson, was unable to cut wood with a handsaw. When he needed to cut a piece of wood, he would ask me to do it. I do not really understand why he could not cut the wood with the saw, but somehow he had not learned to use the tool cor-rectly. One day we went to visit one of Rodah's relatives who was a Kamba wood carver. These are the people who make the carvings of antelopes, giraffes, and other animals that are so common in the curio shows in Kenya. One of the workers picked up a block of wood and then with an adze — one of the first tools invented — chopped away. Chop, chop, chop. In just twenty minutes, the block of wood had turned into a giraffe, needing only sanding, polishing, and varnish to be complete. So, I picked up a block of wood and tried to make a chop with the adze. All I did was make a dent in the wood. I tried a number of times with the result being only more dents. I did not understand what I was doing wrong any more than I could understand why Wilson could not saw a piece of wood.

48

Personal Space and Privacy

Americans value privacy very highly, but in Africa, there is little privacy. In order to create a private space, Africans do many things differently. People of the same sex sometimes hold hands, not because they are homosexuals, but as an indication that the two people want to discuss something privately. For an outsider, it acts as a "Do Not Disturb" sign. On the other hand, in most cases people of the opposite sex, even if married, do not hold hands or show other displays of affection in public. Because of this, it is often difficult to tell by behavior who is married to whom. One has to be told.

There are other methods of being private. In a society where everyone is shaking hands with everyone, if I am in our living room in Kenya reading a book, an entering guest will not greet me, as he or she will not want to invade my privacy. If I am in my study, they will not come to the door of the study which I always keep open. In America, an open door is a sign that anyone can come in to say "hello." With the African custom, I must go out to the living room to greet them. When my mother used to entertain guests in St. Louis, she had to talk with them constantly. Africans on the other hand are willing to sit, wait silently for a long time, even hours, without talking. Americans consider this rude.

Kenyans, like many people in the world, stand much closer to each other than Americans. Kenyans can stand so close to each other, in a line for instance, that they will be touching the person in front or back. In a presentation once, I was able to make an American move backwards all around the stage as I tried to be as close as Kenyans sometimes are during a conversation. As I moved closer to him, he felt uncomfortable and moved back a step. A Kenyan might interpret this unwillingness to be close as unfriendliness.

After all these years, I do not have any problem with this closeness except for one issue. Drivers in vehicles, particularly motorcycle drivers, drive much closer to pedestrians and other vehicles than is done in the United States. Even after all these years, it still scares me when they drive so close to me.

Africans also do not have the possessiveness of Americans. Where a person sleeps depends upon who is in the house that evening. For instance, when my stepson lived with us in a two-bedroom house in St. Louis while going to graduate school, if we had a guest, he would — without being asked — move to the living room couch so that the guest could have his bed and bedroom.

Americans guests felt that they were putting him out when they were offered his bedroom and bed. African guests considered this only normal politeness. We can have up to ten guests in our house in Lumakanda. As people come and go, each night the guests will rearrange themselves according to who is there.

Cooperation

As I mentioned above, when women and girls come to our house, they immediately join in with whatever task is at hand. Recently the acre plot of one of the relatives visiting us needed to be planted and all the other women of the household at the time, including Gladys, one sister, one niece, one grandniece, and Nancy, our helper, went to assist. Two year old, Junior, went also, but I doubt he was of much help. In all these activities, there is no "supervisor" as we seem to need in America. Everyone just pitches in. No one gives directions, no one supervises, and everyone works as an equal. This does not mean that someone might not ask for assistance if needed. For example, if the women are planting, someone might ask another to bring her more seeds.

I saw this same cooperative spirit when I was principal of the Mua Hills Harambee Secondary School. Like anywhere else, the school had a Board of Directors and the rules included a majority vote. Not once, in more than two years I was principal, was there ever a divided vote as all votes were unanimous. People discussed issues without getting hung-up on which side they were one until there was complete agreement by everyone at the meeting. Since starting a high school is not an easy task, this cooperation was extremely useful to me as I got the school off the ground.

My friend, Mary Kay Rehard, whose husband was the principal of Friends Theological College here in western Kenya, told me an interesting observation. She had decided to go to medical school in Eldoret. There were about twenty students in the class and rather than compete to see who was the best student, they wanted to make sure that everyone passed. As a consequence, any student who was weak in a certain subject was encouraged and tutored by the better students until that student mastered the material.

Most Americans think that nothing can happen, that nothing can be accomplished, unless there is someone with authority given responsibility to see that the goal is accomplished. This implies a hierarchy with one or more persons assigned to supervise the activity. Under this arrangement, there is a lot of interpersonal conflict. In the case of paid employment, this often brings out the passive resistance of those who resent being ordered about. This dynamic is missing in the local Kenyan context. It also proves that the hierarchical system is not a prerequisite for accomplishing a task. Let me illustrate the difference with two incidents, one from the United States and one from Kenya.

I was at a Quaker meeting in the US that, like most meetings, had workdays to spruce up the grounds and building. There was a person responsible for the workday and he developed a list of tasks to be done. This included raking the many leaves. He divided up the grounds and gave each person a section to rake.

On October 26, 1968, the not yet opened Mua Hills Harambee Secondary School had a *harambee* (self-help — "let's work together") day. The task was to dig the foundation for the first four classrooms. The masons had set out the lines for the foundation. When the people arrived, they formed a line, started a little dance step, sang a call and response song, and dug the foundation in unison. The lead singer made up the song as she went along. One verse was to thank me for coming all the way from America to help them start the secondary school. One elderly woman, who was no longer capable of physically digging, got into the line, did the dance step, and pretended that she was digging.

In the American case, efficiency — getting the work accomplished — was the primary objective to a workday. In Kenya, working together, having fun, singing and dancing were as important as completing the task.

Gender Roles

Gender issues are quite different in Kenya. We have a gas stove in our inside kitchen. If I go and try to warm up some tea on the stove, every female in the house, except Gladys, comes running to my rescue because, as a man, I am not supposed to cook. Although I cook some in the United States, with breakfast being my specialty, in Kenya I rarely go in the kitchen except to take my dishes off the table after eating, as my mother taught me to do.

Enmeshed gender roles are still strong here in rural Kenya. One hardly ever sees a woman riding a bicycle. Women almost never build. Carpentry, masonry, electrical work, and so on are all completely male occupations. Once AGLI held a work camp in Burundi and my daughter, Joy, was a member. At first, the masons there would not let the women do anything except carry the bricks. Joy got tired of just being a gopher and she just started laying bricks. Since she was inexperienced, she did not do it very well, but as she said, "I knew that the masons would have to come over and show me the correct way if I was doing it incorrectly." Soon all the women, including the Burundians, were laying bricks correctly.

About ten years later, the building Joy worked on had developed many cracks in the walls. The local Burundians said it was because women helped with the construction. This is what is said in the village and the story is used as a cautionary tale. Never mind that one of the international work campers who witnessed the construction of the building observed that the masons had not dug a sufficiently deep foundation.

Gender roles are well defined, but this was the same in the United States in the 1950's when I grew up. My mother never taught me how to cook, although I was required to wash and dry the dinner dishes. She had her own set of specific gender roles — the girls set the table and the boys took the dishes off the table after dinner.

Yet I think that the real division is that Americans are taught to do things for themselves, while Kenyans are taught to do things for each other. I remember in 1964, the first time I walked to the school where I would be teaching. All the students wanted to carry my bag, but I wanted to do it myself. Looking back, I see that I was rude because, for the students, this was just a common courtesy.

Yet a custom can be controversial depending upon how one sees it. Since most houses in Kenya do not have running water, before and after eating someone brings around a basin and a jug of water for people to wash their hands. Frequently this is done in the order of seniority based solely on age — older people are served first. I get no special privilege because I am an *mzungu*. Normally this has no real special significance and anyone can hold and pour the water for anyone else — sometimes one holds for a second person and then the second person returns the favor.

I was once at a Friends church where a group of us, peacemakers, was making a presentation. This included two other *wazungu*, one from England and one from South Africa. After the presentation, we went to the home of one of the leaders of the church for lunch. The wife, who was a secondary school principal, held the basin and water for all the guests, Kenyan or foreign as is the customary tradition. My two *wazungu* guests considered this to be demeaning to the woman as her husband ought to have been the one to do this. I explained that for this family having all these guests including the foreigners was an important event. The wife undoubtedly felt honored to hold the basin and water for people to wash their hands. If her husband had done it, she would have considered it inappropriate. I failed to convince my colleagues that in Kenyan culture this was completely normal and proper and should not be looked at as a sign of gender inequality.

Being an Obvious Foreigner in Kenya

As far as I know, I am the only resident *mzungu* in Lugari District, which has a population of around 250,000 people. The nearest towns — Eldoret, Webuye, and Kakamega, each thirty to fifty miles away — have lots of *wazungu*. As a result, whenever I walk around where I live in Lumakanda, the little kids call out, "*Mzungu, mzungu,* how are you?" I reply, "I'm fine. How are you?" Sometimes when we are together, Gladys gets annoyed that the kids do not even notice her. Kenyans are extremely warm, welcoming, hospitable people and so I always have felt welcomed.

In 1963, when Alison des Forges came back to the US from Tanzania — where she had lived in a tent with another American volunteer while she taught Rwandan refugees — people would exclaim, "You lived there all by yourselves!" This was as if the thousands of refugees surrounding them did not count as people. I have observed that those Americans who are uncomfortable with Africans — probably due to the racial tensions between whites and blacks in the United States — are those who are most resistant to accepting the warm welcome of the Kenyans.

As I become older here in Kenya, something interesting is happening. To be elderly in Africa is to be respected. In Swahili, the term given for this is *mzee*, which is translated as "old man" or "elder." Elderly men are called this all the time and accept it as a sign of respect. Adults who do not know me are no longer calling me *mzungu*, but rather *mzee*. At first, I was a little taken aback since where I grew up in America, to be elderly was to be looked down upon as one who had outlived his usefulness. With time, I have accommodated to this newfound respect.

Customs Surrounding Dying and Death

Perhaps the greatest cultural difference between Kenya and the United States concerns dying and death. After my mother died, Gladys commented, "You [Americans] do not have any customs."

My father, Richard, died in January 1999 when I was on an AGLI delegation in Rwanda. My sister placed my mother, Helen Jane, in a nursing home because she was in the middle stages of Alzheimer and could not take care of herself. Physically, she was still quite active. After we moved to St. Louis in May 2000, we started bringing my mother to our house for dinner four or five times per week. I would take her to the park to see the children play or walk around a lake and whatever activities I found that she could do. This went along fine until January 2003 when she had a severe stroke on the left side and became confined to a wheel chair. It was no longer feasible to take her out or to bring her to our house for dinner. So almost every evening I would go to the nursing home at dinnertime to feed her and then take her for a ride around the nursing home for "sightseeing." Only a few family members came regularly to visit. The vast majority of the patients never had anyone visit except on the big holidays like Christmas, Easter, and a fall picnic day. Even on these days, many of the patients did not have anyone visit them. In America, people die alone.

In Kenya, people die surrounded by family, friends, and neighbors. In September 2006, Gladys talked with her sisters in Kenya and they told her that her mother, Selina, was not eating. Gladys and I traveled from St. Louis to western Kenya and found her mother in the hospital in Eldoret. She had esophageal cancer and could no longer swallow. Since esophageal cancer is usually due to smoking and she never smoked, I suspect it was due to all the smoke from the firewood in the kitchen during eighty-one years of cooking. She was living on IVs. Gladys talked with the doctor who said that he could operate on her and put a tube in her stomach and that she might live somewhat longer, perhaps a few months. Selina would have none of this. "God did not want me to be cut open. If He says it is my time to die, then that is His will."

The medical staff there wanted to keep her in the Lumakanda Hospital because they had to give her the IVs twice per day. After one night, Selina refused. We brought her to our home and put her in one of our bedrooms. Her younger sister came and stayed with her, sleeping in the same bed with her as they probably had done when they were children. The house was a constant stream of visitors from near and far away. Many people stayed overnight until our small house was crowded with people sleeping everywhere. She was visited by people who had moved to Lumakanda from her home town of Viyalo and friends and acquaintances of ours, particularly people from the local Friends church. The Medical Officer-in-Charge and the nurses from Lumakanda Hospital would drop in. These were not only old people; even the youngest of the adult generation and older children came to visit. There was not much to say as Selina was not talking too much herself. Everyone greeted her, shook her hand, and spent some time with her.

I had to return to the United States, but Gladys continued to stay with her mother. As Selina declined further, she decided that she wanted to return to her home in Viyalo. Gladys hired a vehicle and took her home. There, even more relatives, neighbors, and people who had known her for years visited Selina at her home. She died in the midst of her loving community.

At ninety-one years of age, my mother continued to decline. She was not taking in enough water — either she was not drinking enough or her stomach was no longer able to absorb the water. About once a month, she would need an IV for rehydration. After doing this many times, it was no longer possible for the nurses to find a vein that could be used. Gladys and I, my sister, Arlene, and her partner, Zulemya, were at her side when she slowly died.

A few days later, we had the funeral. Negotiating with the funeral parlor was an experience. While there was the basic funeral, there were innumerable add-ons. The purpose of many of these add-ons seemed to be for people who had not visited their elderly relatives, felt guilty, and bought them as indulgences. The funeral at the funeral parlor was rather straightforward and perhaps fifty people came, including family members. Later, we had a memorial service at a nice arboretum. The family members all got a chance to give short eulogies and then anyone else present who wanted to make a presentation could do so. Classical music, which my parents liked, was played. Since this was an arboretum, the place was filled with flowers and plants. Since my parents were not particularly religious, there was no overtly religious nature to the memorial service. I personally found it much more satisfying than the funeral.

As I mentioned above, I was unable to attend my mother-in-law's funeral because I had returned to the United States. I have attended a good number of other funerals in this part of Kenya including that of my sister-in-law, Rose, providing me with an understanding of Kenyan funerals.

Gladys and I disagree about what happens to us when we die. People in western Kenya cannot conceive of cremating the body as my parents had done. Kenyans must bury the body. If Gladys happens to die in the United States, I would have to transport her body back to Kenya for burial in the front yard of our plot in Lumakanda. If I did not do this, her relatives, including her children and grandchildren, would consider it sacrilege. When we lived in the United States and a Kenyan died, there would be a *harambee* to send the body back to Africa. Gladys would always contribute to this, while I, not having this value system, did not because I did not think it necessary. If I die in Kenya, I am certain I will get the Kenyan treatment and be buried in the front yard of our house. If I were to die in the United States before Gladys, since the cost of sending the body back to Kenya is over $10,000, I would prefer the funds to be spent on doing some more peacebuilding workshops. Then, it will be up to Gladys to decide what to do since I would not be around to protest her decision. I know of a Senegalese man who was dying of AIDS. When he was on his deathbed, rather than die in the US, he took the plane to Paris where, due to his deteriorating health, he was hospitalized for a week. When he gained enough strength, he proceeded to Senegal. He returned to his home village, died a few days later, and was buried by his mother. Thus he saved his family thousands of dollars.

If a woman dies, a white cow must be slaughtered. If a man dies, then a black bull must be slaughtered. What is the significance of the color? No one has been able to explain this to me. When the person dies, a drummer comes and drums throughout the night. When I hear this drumming in the night, I usually ask Gladys who has died and most of the time she can tell me who it is. The funeral, which is usually on the following Saturday, really begins the previous day and night. Gravediggers are brought in to dig about a five foot deep hole. A coffin is bought and they are getting fancier and fancier as the years go on. A small observing room made out of poles and banana leaves is built and the coffin is placed there with the head part open and a small plaque with the person's picture, name and dates of birth and death. During the day prior to the funeral, many people come and pay their respects. They will go to the coffin, say a prayer, and perhaps sing a song of good-bye. There will be a continual stream of people coming by. People will be cooking, gathering firewood, erecting a tent for the honored guests.

This is a picture from Selina Imali's funeral, Gladys' mother.

Relatives from afar will arrive and spend the night in the compound. People will stay up all night or doze off wherever they are sitting. A *isikuti* band will play from about 11:00 PM to 3:00 or 4:00 AM. This is a group of about six or so men who dance and sing traditional songs to a lively beat. They will have a drum or two plus the ring from the engine of a vehicle, which makes a pleasant sound when it is hit. Many people bring a gift, usually a consumable item like a hen, some corn, or beans. These items will be used right then and there or the next day during the funeral.

If the person who has died is of note, or the father or mother of someone of note, a picture (black and white for the middle-class, colored for the wealthy) will be placed in the newspaper. People like Gladys read these pages and notice the people they know who have died. On the day I write this, for instance, the *Daily Nation* had four and one-third pages of pictures for fifty-six people. Gladys put in a black and white one for her mother and it cost about $200. With most funerals, there will be a program with the picture of the deceased on the front, and inside the order of service, and obituary.

The service, held in front yard of the deceased, is supposed to begin about 10:00 AM but will probably start closer to 11:00 AM. An average person will have five hundred to one thousand people attend, while a well-known person may have many more than that. The church to which the deceased belonged will conduct the service. There will be a lot of singing by the church's choir, usually thirty or more women dressed alike. A well-known pastor will give the sermon. A good deal of time will be taken up with testimonies, which start with neighbors, friends, other churches, and then move to family. The family testimonies begin with the in-laws in strict order of birth, starting with the youngest. For example, at my sister-in-law's funeral I was the last of the in-laws to speak because I am married to her oldest sister. Then comes the turn of the immediate family. One of Rose's half-sisters spoke too long and the master of ceremonies cut her off. Since Rose was not married and had no children, Gladys as the oldest sister was the second-to-last to speak. Her father was the last.

There is usually a long sermon because the church is using this as an opportunity to show off and attract more people. The sermon has nothing to do with the deceased or death, but is just a usual Christian sermon. Then the burial starts and they do something touching. The pallbearers pick up the coffin and with the choir and some family members behind them march out of the compound and then turn around and re-enter for the symbolic last entrance into the home. The coffin is placed next to the grave. After prayers, the coffin is laid in the grave with ropes that are then pulled out. Another prayer is given and a small shovel of dirt is thrown in. Then some men fill the grave. As I saw long ago in the movie, *Doctor Zhivago,* the first shovelful of dirt hits the coffin with a loud thud. For some reason this is the point where I realize that that life is really over. Members of the family usually dance and sing in a circle as the men fill the grave. After a final prayer, the service is over. Sometimes a concrete marker is placed on top of the grave, but others are just left to return to dirt

This is not all. A year after a person dies there is a memorial service. In this case, of course, there is no body to be buried and the turnout might be half that of the funeral. Otherwise, the service is much like the earlier one but shorter and the deceased possessions are then divided up.

Attributes of Culture

Over the decades, I have observed various aspects of African and American culture. I have realized that there are significant points in the discussion of culture that need to be kept in mind. Here are ten points that I have found.

1. Culture can vary between closely connected individuals. A few years ago when Gladys and I were in Bujumbura, Burundi, we were invited to dinner at the home of a Burundian couple. When we arrived we shook hands with the kids, but then, during our dinner and stay, they disappeared into the back rooms. The hostess told us that this was Burundian culture. When we left the children returned to bid us goodbye.

The next night we were invited to dinner at the home of another Burundian couple. In this case, the children went in and out and ate dinner with us. This couple was certainly as "Burundian" as the first couple was. So which custom is Burundian culture?

2. Customs can and do change all the time. When I was in the Rwandan refugee camp in Tanzania, I knew a young man, perhaps twenty-five who was married to an older woman. She had three young children. This was a case of "wife inheritance." In this region, it was customary that if a man dies, his wife was inherited by the oldest surviving brother. In the olden days, this clearly had its benefits, as no woman along with her children would be left uncared. Moreover, the family would stay united and the sons would still be part of the larger family.

Then the AIDS epidemic came along. If a man gave AIDS to his wife and then died, the brother would acquire AIDS from the infected wife and give it also to his first wife and so on. The result was that the adult members of whole families were dying out. As an anti-AIDS measure, governments and health organizations began campaigns against the practice of wife inheritance. In Kenya, there is debate if wife inheritance should be made illegal. In this case, the custom has mostly died out quite quickly because men were afraid of marrying their brother's wife.

3. When a custom does change, the change may have its own problems. The opposite of wife inheritance is wife disinheritance. I know of a Luhya woman who has five children between three and eighteen. When her husband died, her brother-in-law — the oldest who would have married her under wife inheritance — threw her and the children out so that they could control her husband's land, house, and livestock. She had to return to her father's home. She would not inherit there either as it would be her brothers who would inherit the father's property. While her daughter might get married off to a man with land, her sons would essentially be landless and homeless, making it difficult for them to establish a home and family. This woman's predicament is common in the region at this time.

4. Customs, culture, and tradition may or may not be followed according to the whims and wishes of particular individuals. When my mother-in-law died, she had seven surviving daughters. The traditional sign of mourning for such a close relative is for a woman is to shave her head. Some of the daughters did this, some did not, and others compromised by cutting their hair short.

5. What to do about a "bad" custom is not easily resolved. Let us turn to another tradition, female circumcision. Neither the Luo nor Luhya in Western Kenya have ever engaged in female circumcision. Most of the rest of the groups in Kenya do. Gladys has a friend named Jacinta who has an orphanage near Nakuru in the Rift Valley. When we visited once, she was "hiding" six Masai young women so that they would not be circumcised. There is a major campaign in Kenya against female circumcision, which is illegal, promoted most by women's groups and their non-governmental organization supporters. Actions that these groups have taken include safe houses during the time of circumcision, alternative initiation rites at puberty for the young women, and laws outlawing the custom. Every year it seems one or more circumcisers are charged with murder when one of the young women dies because of "the cut," as they call it here.

I know of no one who defends this custom except traditional patriarchal men and the women who perform circumcisions. Note that there is an economic advantage for the women who circumcise since they are paid in money, goats, honey, etc. for their work. It can be a substantial income for them during the initiation period.

6. When a custom needs to be changed, how is it done? Adrien Niyongabo from Burundi notes that the division of people in Rwanda and Burundi into Hutu, Tutsi, and Twa is a bad custom that needs to be eradicated. Rwanda and Burundi have taken divergent methods of dealing with this. In Burundi all positions in government, army, parliament, police, etc. are defined in concrete percentages. The police, for example, are half Tutsi and half Hutu. Therefore ethnicity remains a significant factor. In Rwanda, the use of the terms have been officially abolished so that everyone is now a Rwandan. Nonetheless, everyone knows, even if they cannot say it aloud, who is Tutsi and who is Hutu. The result is that no one is allowed to count the percentage of the minority Tutsi in authority in all the institutions of the country. It is therefore a method of ensuring continued Tutsi domination. Laws can lead the way but are ineffective if people resist them.

7. Customs and their rationale are sometimes strange only because of one's own assumptions and biases. Sharon Phelps, a board member of Friends Peace Teams, once wrote me an email in which she noted that years ago she had helped introduce ox plowing to an area in Africa where oxen were not used for plowing or pulling. The rationale for not using oxen to plow was as follows:

> They raised cattle for meat and could not imagine using them to plow or for other work, because they felt it would be wrong to eat an animal after it contributed labor to the life and wealth of their families.

This reluctance to use oxen for plowing is difficult for an American to understand. Africans, including people in Kenya, who use oxen for plowing, would also find this difficult to understand.

8. What may seem like a difficult way of life for a foreign observer might be rather easy for an African accustomed to doing it. Most Kenyan, Ugandans, Rwandans, and Burundians carry things on their head, while others (Kikuyu, Kamba, Meru, and Embu in Kenya and then some groups in South Kivu in the eastern Congo), carry things on their back with a rope that is placed on the forehead. I always wondered how the various methods developed and why one group does it one way and another group, another way. Here is a story from my time in the Rwandan refugee camp.

One day during my period off from teaching, I went to our house and opened the wooden shutter to grade papers on the dining room table. As I did this, I noticed two women talking outside the window. I knew them both. One of the women had a five-gallon metal tin on her head filled with water, which she had just drawn from the spring. The tin filled with water would weigh about thirty-five pounds.

Many times, I had walked to the spring with a tin to draw water. First long blades of grass are formed into a halo, which is placed on the head under the tin so that the weight is distributed more evenly on the head. It took me about fifteen minutes to walk uphill from the spring with the thirty-five pound tin on my head. I had two problems when I did this. The first was that my neck muscles were not strong enough to hold this weight for that length of time. However, as I did this every three or four days, my neck muscles became stronger and this was no longer a problem. My second insurmountable problem was that I could not balance the tin on my head without it falling. I had to resort to holding the tin with one hand. This arm would soon get tired and I would use the other one. This also would get tired before the first arm had recovered. By the time I reached home, my arms ached. Then with those tired arms, I had to take the tin off my head without dropping it.

As I watched the woman, I noticed that she never once put her arm up to stabilize the tin on her head. Whenever it began to fall to one side, she would deftly move her neck and head and rebalance the tin. Clearly, she did this without thinking because she just continued her discussion with the neighbor.

One time when I was going to draw water, I noticed about seven children, three to seven years old, near the spring. They had a tin can and they would half fill it with water, go to a part of the path, which was level for about fifty feet, and see if they could balance the tin can of water on their head the length of the straightaway. When they succeeded, they were all happy and excited and, when the can fell, they ran to get more water and try again. The younger children were totally unable to balance the tin, while the older children frequently succeeded. What was I doing when I was seven years old? Learning to ride a bike. A person needs to learn both of these skills when they are a child. At only twenty-one years of age, I was already too old to learn how to balance anything on my head without holding it up with my arm.

At the end of my forty-minute break as I closed the shutter to return to class, the two women were still talking. I could never have held thirty-five pounds on my head for more than forty minutes. The point is that when foreigners comment on how hard life is for Africans because they would be unable to do what the Africans have learned and are accustomed to doing, these seemingly hard tasks may not be difficult for the Africans themselves. In other words, in order to understand the Africans condition, you cannot just interject yourself into the situation because your experiences and conditioning may be different.

9. A person can adapt to culture quickly and change "culture" according to the context. In Africa where we live, the temperature is pleasant all year around. Consequently, families do not live in one house. Usually there is a separate room for the kitchen since it becomes full of smoke from the firewood. When a boy reaches puberty, he is supposed to build himself a small house/ bedroom and no longer sleep in the same building as his parents. This is usually a rather simply built one room ten foot by ten-foot structure, frequently built with mud, wattle and a grass roof.

The requirement that the son does not sleep in the same house as the parents was not one that I had considered. However, the situation was different for Gladys. When we got married, she made sure that her father built another house next to his so that when we visited him, we would not have to sleep in his house. In our own house in Lumakanda, when male members of the family, including her father, come to visit us, they would go to her sister's house to sleep. Since this was sometimes inconvenient, Gladys built two additional outside, detached bedrooms in which male members of the family could sleep. Gladys once got upset with her son-in-law because he had slept in our house when we were not there. This did not upset me at all because it seemed to me to be quite normal.

American homes are designed under one roof for the obvious reason that in the winter time a person could hardly be expected to go back and forth from one building to sleep and another to live, eat, and socialize. When we were living in the United States Gladys' son lived with us while he was studying for his MA. He slept under the same roof with us since we could not really expect him to live in a tent in the back yard!

10. Cultural influences come from many sources, not only from America or from Europe. Recently I was at a wedding in Rwanda with some Kenyan women including my wife. Rwandans are much more staid and stoic than the emotional, exuberant Kenyans. When the newlywed couple entered the reception room after the wedding, the assembled well-wisher oohed and awed much as we do in the United States. In a Kenyan wedding when the couple enters everyone is singing and dancing, with the women ululating (trilling with their tongues) making a joyous noise. At the Rwandan wedding, my female Kenyans could not restrain themselves and made their joyful Kenyan noise to the stares of the Rwandans sitting near us. After the wedding, I could not help jokingly accusing the Kenyans of being cultural imperialists trying to bring Kenyan customs to Rwanda.

In summary, we must see customs, culture, and traditions not as a fixture carved in stone, but as living, breathing entities that are open to continuous change and various interpretations by different people. Some customs may not be beneficial while changes may also have their pluses and minuses and there is a likelihood of a great variation even between close family members and neighbors.

Chapter 4
Culture, Tradition, and Change

"Where are You From?"

In the United States, as an icebreaker when talking to a person we have just met, we sometimes ask the question, "Where are you from?" Usually we respond with the city where we spent our formative years. My response, "St. Louis," quickly turns the conversation to the Arch or the Cardinals baseball team.

In Kenya, I have met numerous people who were born in Nairobi or outside of the area where their ancestors originated and who have lived their entire lives there. Yet, when I ask, "Where are you from?" it is the area their ancestors came from that they name.

The cultural construct is that each person has an "ancestral home," a place where his or her paternal ancestors originally lived. Let me describe how this works using the example of my grandson.

My grandson, Matias Zarembka's, turned four in 2011. Little does he realize that his ancestral home is Golina, Poland, where in 1886, his great, great, great grandfather, also named Matias Zarembka, was living. Young Matias' other fifteen great, great, great grandfathers and his sixteen great, great, great grandmothers do not count in this determination, even though they came from Kenya, Japan, Argentina, the United States, Italy, Germany, Spain, and perhaps other countries. Golina, Poland, is also my "ancestral home." .

In 1979, with my parents, brother, and sister, I visited my "ancestral home" in Golina where my father was born. It was a small town with perhaps five thousand people. We stayed with my father's cousins and one of his aunts who was ninety-six years old.

If Matias came from an area that believed in the concept of an ancestral home and a conflict occurred that would cause him to be expelled, he would return to Golina, Poland. People in Golina may not even know of his existence, but they will welcome him back as a long, lost relative. Unfortunately, after he, with all his other relatives, has been there for a few months, the welcome will become stale and Matias and his family will have to survive as best they can under the circumstances. Perhaps the Polish government will offer some support for re-settlement. Since Matias is still young, he will probably be able to pick up Polish quickly. I, on the other hand, would not be so fortunate.

It is impossible that this will happen to my grandson, but if he had been living in some areas of Europe outside of Poland in 1945, he would have been repatriated to Golina. Today, in some parts of Africa, this is quite common. One of the most absurd cases I have heard of is that of Kenneth Kaunda who had been president of Zambia for twenty-five years. Later, when he attempted to run for president again, the government declared that he was not a "Zambian" because his parents had been born in Malawi. This was taken to court and Kaunda's citizenship was restored for him to contest the election. He lost.

Since people from the United States seized most of the country from the original Native Americans, the concept of ancestral land does not resonate in American culture. Rather we assume that anyone can move anywhere in the country in order to pursue the best opportunities available. In order to understand this mindset in Africa, one must understand the concept of a people who have a homeland, their personal Garden of Eden which they have left, but to which they will return if necessity ordains. They know that, when they return, they will be welcomed as one of the community.

On a personal level, when I was attending a HROC workshop in Byumba, Rwanda I was paired with a young woman named Chantel because she was the only one who knew Swahili. In 1998 during the Congo War, when she was a teenager, her family fled from Kasai in the Congo. Kasai is about seven hundred miles from Rwanda. They had lived there for generations. Yet, because they were Kinyarwandan speakers, they were sent to Rwanda. Her mother had no idea where they came from in Rwanda and had no known relatives there. They were put in a temporary repatriation village outside of Byumba which seems to continually receive Rwandans expelled from other countries.

When the Europeans divided up Africa beginning in 1884, they did not have much knowledge of the interior of the continent. Boundaries were drawn for exterior reasons rather than putting ethnics groups together. One example is how the boundary between Kenya and Tanzania — then German East Africa — curves around Mt. Kilimanjaro because Kaiser Wilhelm thought that Germany should get one of the tallest mountains in Africa as Britain was already getting Mt. Kenya.

Tanzania is known for being more welcoming to refugees than other countries in the region. Nonetheless, in 2006 and 2007, Rwandan refugees in the West Lake region of Tanzania, bordering

Rwanda, were pushed back into Rwanda. AGLI has been working with these returnees in their new settlement camps. Here is a description and a testimony from an AGLI report by Emily Higgs and Nyatomba Emmanuel, *To Love My Country without Fear: Evaluation of Alternatives to Violence Workshops in Rwandan Resettlement Camps.*

The Tanzanians made no distinction between the refugees from 1959 [Tutsi] and 1994 [Hutu], and suddenly turned on anyone who was, or ever had been, Rwandan. In 2006, the Rwandans were chased out of Tanzania, and those who did not flee fast enough were beaten or killed. Most were forced to leave behind all of their belongings and property, and some even had to leave children or family who were not at home in the moment of forced removal. The Tanzanians responsible for chasing out their neighbors took everything left behind as their own, indicating that perhaps land shortages and poverty also contributed to the suddenness and ferocity with which the removal was carried out. The majority of these refugees — some of whom identified as Rwandan, but many of whom identified as Tanzanian — fled to a camp in northeastern Rwanda called Kiyanzi.

Jane, a Rwandan expelled from Tanzania reported:

I was born in Tanzania — my parents went there in 1959. We came here recently, chased by Tanzanians who said we were not citizens. Before that, we had considered ourselves Tanzanians and we even had citizenship. Then they took our property, beat us, and chased us away. We came here without anything — we left everything behind.

Though my grandson is never going to be repatriated to his ancestral home, it is a possibility for anyone living in this region of Africa who is not in his or her ancestral home, the status of an increasingly large percentage of the population. Many more wars and internal conflicts are going to start because of this mindset which is so easily manipulated by chauvinistic demagogues. When the international community tries to negotiate settlement of the various conflicts, it should confront head-on the absurdity of this assumption.

Concepts of Land Ownership

Hundreds or thousands of years ago, people were few and isolated while land and wilderness were plentiful. In these circumstances, people moved to new uninhabited areas when their old homes became populated or due to famine, drought or conflict. For example, here in Kenya, there is a story of two brothers in south Marigoli who got into a fight. The losing brother then moved his family and clan to north Marigoli on the other side of a river. My wife comes from north Marigoli.

In much of East and Central Africa, a person does not "own" land but has the use of the land. The government of Tanzania has the right to repossess any land that is not being used and lease it to someone else who will use it. Moreover, land was not held by an individual, but by the group. When there was much vacant land, each person was given land sufficient for his or her needs. Land was cultivated until it "wore out" and the farmers moved to a new plot while the old plot lay fallow to renew its fertility. This is called shifting cultivation and was still common but overstretched when I arrived in Africa in the 1960's. Now that there are more people than land, this system is no longer prevalent in the region.

Foreigners who come with concepts of land ownership see this community used land as "empty." This situation allowed the British settlers to remove people from about one third of the arable land in Kenya and make the area into the "White Highlands" where British setters had enormous estates and were given title deeds to the land they secured. Like the enclosure movement in England, violence was needed to push Africans off the land and resistance, bloodshed, and death from exposure resulted as people were driven out.

Traditional and Modern Life

In the late 1950's, Colin Turnbull wrote a book called *The Lonely African*. His thesis was that Africans were a mixture of the old traditional culture and the newer western culture and therefore were "lonely" because they did not know who they were. His examples were mostly from Rwanda and I read his book at the time I was teaching Rwandan refugees in 1964. To me the refugees did not seem to fit Turnbull's description at all.

For example, one of the teachers at the primary school in the Tanzanian refugee camp got married. With his bride in a nice white wedding gown, he went to the Catholic church where there was the usual Catholic wedding (Western culture). Later the bride's family brought the bride and all her goods from her village to the groom's village, singing as they came (traditional culture). When I asked the teacher about this, he did not see the situation in these terms at all. He was a Christian so they had the church wedding, but the bringing of the bride from her village to his was a nice custom, too. In essence, he had integrated traditions from the two cultures into something new that satisfied him. It is only Turnbull who in traditional Western mode of thinking analyzed everything into "western" or "traditional."

I have found that many Americans are like Colin Turnbull when they visit this region of Africa. They analyze everything into either old African traditional culture or western culture which in their minds creates a division. Such people tend to be reluctant to impose any of their western values on the Africans because they believe that they might be destroying the traditional culture.

Identity

In order to deal with the mass of humanity humans encounter, they seem to have a need to label people. I do not know if this is genetic or a learned behavior — clearly the details are very much learned — but it is the root of many of the problems in East and Central Africa and perhaps many other parts of the world. Most people, Africans as well as Americans and Europeans — to use some identity labels — assume that my last name, "Zarembka," is an African name. This has led to a number of humorous incidents. When a Kenyan Quaker was picking me up at the Nairobi airport in 1999, he held a sign saying, "David Zarembka." I went up to him and said, "Hello, I'm Dave Zarembka." He looked at me and said, "No you're not!" as he was expecting an African. I was taken aback and the Kenyan quickly realized his mistake. Another time, I gave a workshop on the African Great Lakes at a peace conference at George Fox University. Later, in Bujumbura, I met one of the conference attendees who told me that she was so disappointed that I was not an African that she did not attend my workshop. Ironically, since my children, Joy and Tommy, have a Kenyan mother, they are half-African together with that African-sounding Polish name.

Now "Zarembka" has also become an African name. It is the custom here in Kenya that, when giving a child their African name, the names of the grandparents are used. Gladys has a daughter, Beverly, and when she gave birth to a son, they gave him the Christian name of "Danson" and an African name of "Zarembka," after me. If Danson Zarembka happens to have many children and then male grandchildren, in fifty or so years, there could be a number of Zarembkas here in Kenya.

Once I went to visit my daughter, Joy, who was attending Haverford College. I found her watching a co-ed rugby game. She pointed out one player to me and asked, "Is that player a male or a female?" It was difficult to tell — deciding one way and then the other way. Joy's comment was, "It does not make any difference which gender you think that the player is, but you are uncomfortable until you make the decision one way or the other." She then commented that in America, after determination of gender, the next crucial determination is race.

In her book, *Pigment of Your Imagination: Mixed Race in a Global Society,* Joy discusses the differences in mixed white/black couples and their children in England, Kenya, Zimbabwe, and Jamaica. During the 2008 election, Barack Obama was seen in the United States as "black" and much has been made of the fact that he is the first African-American US president. He was labeled "black" and his racial "identity" has little to do with his upbringing because he was brought up completely by the "white" side of his family. If he had grown up in Kenya, he would have been labeled "white." This is because the word *mzungu,* which is used even in English, to denote "a white person," in fact means "stranger." Someone who is racially mixed is therefore unusual and acquires the label "*mzungu.*" Frequently people with racial mixture are called "point five" as in ".5," meaning they are half-and-half.

In Kenya, race is not the determining factor it is in the United States. When Joy was interviewing people about "race" in Kenya, they frequently talked about "tribe" and "ethnicity." One's ethnicity counts the most. One can usually tell the ethnic group of a person by their African name. This ethnicity is passed through the fathers side only, so there cannot be "mixed" people even though a large number of people are actually "mixed." In Kenya, Obama is seen as a Luo regardless of the fact that he barely knew his father and has visited Kenya a total of only a few weeks. The Thursday after the US election of President Obama, Kenyans got a holiday to celebrate the success of one of their own.

The labeling of identity has little relationship to reality, but puts the masses of people in the world into narrow, connecting boxes. Most of the Quakers in Kenya live in Western Province and are a group called the Luhya. However, this is a simplification. There are actually fourteen, or sixteen, or twenty-one sub-groups among the Luhya. They were not even considered a group of their own until 1940 when they organized together to increase their political clout, beginning by giving themselves the new name "Luhya." Nevertheless, among the Luhya, people immediately determine which sub-group other people come from. As can be expected, these sub-groups all have their stereotypes. As we drive around the countryside, I ask Gladys where the boundaries are between the different groups and it is usually a road or a stream. I wonder how people who are, say, on opposite sides of a stream, can be all that different from each other. Lugari District, where we live, is not the home area of any one of these groups so that people from the various groups have come to live here together. Still, everyone identifies from the area he or she came from. There is a tremendous amount of inter-marriage but children follow the designation of their father.

If an ethnic group is defined by language, then the Luhya are not a tribe or ethnic group since the Maragoli, the southern most group, cannot understand the Bugusu, the most northerly group near Mt Elgon. Ethnicity and tribe are such ill-defined concepts that they can include substantial ambiguity.

Frankly, I am irritated by these subdivisions, although by now I can frequently tell which sub-group a person is by his or her name or where he or she comes from. It seems so trivial, yet real. As much as I dislike this labeling of identity, to ignore it is impossible if one wants to understand what is going on. At one of my talks in England, the brother of a Kikuyu politician who was on the Orange Democratic Movement side, i.e., not supporting the Kikuyu Kibaki side and therefore opposing the "Kikuyu identity," noted to me that during the election campaign where he was helping out his brother, he was continually attacked as a "traitor" to the Kikuyu. I think, he felt physically in danger. Those who do not wish to conform to their supposed identity frequently have a tough time.

In Rwanda and Burundi, since everyone speaks the same language, has the same culture, and lives intermingled, there is no "ethnic difference." but labeling as Hutu and Tutsi has made it deadly so. I will explain the origins of this at length in Chapter 7. Again, the system works only because there cannot be mixed people in the center who are not of one side or the other. I know the family of a Burundian who was half Tutsi and half Hutu. In 1993, the Tutsi military invaded her secondary school and asked her, to move to one side if she was Tutsi and another side if she was Hutu. She decided not to choose, but to stay in the middle. She was killed.

However, the result is clear. We live in a murky world of make-believe identities, which are important only because they are used to control who has power and have such negative, even deadly, effects on people's lives.

Is Barack Obama an African-American or an American? Is he "black" in the US and "white" in Kenya? Is he a Luo? Is he an African?

Women Solidarity

A number of Americans who have visited the region have mentioned how difficult the lives of people seem here, particularly the women who have to do so much work. These Americans wonder how they could cope in a similar situation. Clearly, the African women do cope. How do they do this?

The first thing I noticed is that the women's greatest handicap has been turned into an asset. This is the concept of "patrilocal" which means that when a woman marries she goes to live at her husband's homestead. Family and neighbors from the bride's village carry all her personal property to her new husband's house. This is both a concrete and symbolic move. As a stranger, she is thrust into an already firmly established social setting. Since she is not directly related to anyone and most everyone else is directly related, she has no family or social network at the new home to support her.

In Kenya, marriage is mostly exogamous, meaning that a person marries outside his or her immediate family. Incest in Kenya is defined much more broadly than in the US — marrying a cousin or even second cousin is considered incest. This also results in a high rate of inter-ethnic marriages.

How does the young bride cope with this situation? As I noted above one usually marries outside one's clan. When she marries, a woman retains her clan affiliation which she got from her father. Clans are controlled and run by women. In Ukambani, the area of the Kamba , clans are extremely well organized and strong. When I moved to the area to start the secondary school, I did not belong to a clan so I was immediately put into one. When I learned that the taboo food for members of my new clan was liver, I knew that I had been assigned to the correct clan. Ester Kyule was my clan mother. Whenever there was a fundraising event to build a new school including my secondary school, Ester would come by and collect 3/- (then 43 US cents) from me. At the fundraising day, all the money collected by my clan would be donated together. The clans competed to see who would donate the most. At the *harambee* day organized for my secondary school, we raised $700, which together with a donation of $1,000 from the US Peace Corps was enough to get the school up and running.

Ester was the lowest member of the clan organization, which reached up until the whole area of the Mua Hills, and then the whole of Machakos District was included. Each clan had an area leader and then all the clans together had a supreme leader. The leaders were not "elected" in our sense of the word but chosen because they were good leaders dedicated to their clans. Each clan had its own dress color with the supreme clan leader having a dress with all the clan colors. The clan members would sit together at meetings and ululate — trill their tongues, something most people cannot do unless taught when young. When something good was said, the women ululate. This was amazingly effective. Nothing is as powerful as the dead silence when the women disapprove and do not ululate. If a politician wanted to win an election, he had to have the blessings of these clan leaders. I knew a man who did not get their blessing and he received exactly seven votes. People remarked that this was not even enough to include all his wives and children. The winner had over ten thousand votes.

My first mother-in-law, Priscilla Mateta, of the Kamba ethnic group was steadfastly involved with her clan. Eight to ten of them got together and formed a group called a *mwethia*. These women would work together. About 8:00 AM, they would come to my mother-in-law's plot to weed the corn. As they hoed, they would all talk, laugh, sing, gossip, and sometimes just be silent. About noon to 1:00 PM, i.e., a four to five hour workday, my mother-in-law would provide lunch for the group. I used to joke with her that there was no work being done, but only fun. Yet a large part of the plot would be weeded. The next day they would go to someone else's plot and do the same. And so on as they went around the group. Nevertheless, this was not their only function. If one of the women got sick and could not work her own plot, the group would respond by doing the work for her. In other words, there was group solidarity, caring, and sharing.

Forty years later, here in western Kenya, the arrangement is somewhat different as it is not based on clan, but serves the same function. The organizing group is the Friends church which has a strong United Society of Friends Women (USFW) chapter in every church. The women of Lumakanda Friends Church meet every Thursday. Gladys attends when she can. It is a prayer meeting, usually with one of the women giving a presentation or sermon. However, the real issue is group solidarity. They have started what is called a "Merry-Go-Round." Each of the forty-five members puts in a certain amount of money and this money is used for some common activity or for a particular person if she has some disaster in her family. Almost every women's group has this practice.

The women, in one fashion or another, join together for support, caring, sharing, socialization, and solidarity. I see no evidence that the men in Kenya behave in the same way.

Bridging the Traditional and Modern Worlds

This section a long involved story that shows how the traditional and the modern, in this case Christianity, can intermesh and how people use various aspects for their own benefit.

On Tuesday, February 17, 2009, Gladys and I accompanied four members of Lugari Yearly Meeting, to which Lumakanda Friends Church belongs, when they went to visit a man in Sugoi, fifteen miles from our home. The man wanted to donate a small plot of land to start a Friends' church there.

The potential land donor was a man named Mutai and his wife, Ester. The plot is a few hundred yards off the main road to Uganda in a flat area next to the railroad line that heads towards Kampala. The couple had a normal sized house that, by the amount of rust on the roof, was built about twenty-five years ago and was quite habitable yet in need of repair. As usual, there was a small thatched roof kitchen next to the house.

When we arrived, Mutai was across the railroad tracks herding his cows. He had about fifteen nice cows and a big bull plus a few sheep. We were told he also had many goats that were being herded elsewhere. He told us to go back to his house where he would greet us properly. He called his fourteen-year-old daughter to take over his duties of herding the cows.

We sat next to his house in the shade and had a most entertaining time as he described major events in his life. Mzee Mutai was eighty-three years old. As such, he is from the older, more traditional, generation. He has that old-fashioned story-telling cadence that is going out of style in the younger generations. As he told his story, there were many hand movements. He would stand up to emphasize some critical event, and he would go into his house to get props. For example, at one point he brought out an impala's horn which he blew. One of Lugari Yearly Meeting members tried to blow the horn and could not get a sound. The Mzee picked it up and blew a tune to show how it was used. At another point, he brought out a $1 U.S. bill and a $100 U.S. bill. The $100 bill had "fake" written on it. He gave them to me and told me to take them to America to determine if they were fake or real — later I took it to the bank in St. Louis and it was obviously fake.

Interestingly enough, Mzee Mutai is Tugen, a small Kalenjin ethnic group that comes from farther north in the Rift Valley near Lake Baringo. As a youth, during World War II, he had been a member of the Kenyan Army. The Tugen are traditional cattle keeping people whose value system included the concept that there was nothing wrong with stealing cows from others and that a real man protected his cows from theft by others. In 1953, he had stolen seven cows from a British settler. As he said, "The *mzungu* had many cows and I only took seven." He was put into jail for one and a half years in Nakuru. When he was released, he had to walk more than a hundred miles back to his home in Baringo. As he walked, he thought that he could not really return empty-handed so he stole four more cows near his home — this time he stole them from an African and was not caught. At another time in his presentation, he described how he would get up at night to check that his cows were okay. His spear was stuck in the ground as a prop. Once someone had come at night to steal his cows and he had used his spear to pursue the man to the road. Even at his age, he was still the warrior.

In Baringo, he had a wife and at least three sons. He indicated that he had educated them and that one was in the army, another was a policeman and a third in the navy. The British colonial government tended to recruit military and police from smaller tribes like the Tugen because they would not be as likely to become a threat to the colonial power. As per the custom, he had divided his land in Baringo among his sons. Somewhere unknown to me he had a second wife who had died and his children with her were given his land there. He had then bought the plot in Sugoi, which had a title deed, and married Ester, his third wife, in a common law marriage. They have two children, a girl about fourteen and a boy about eight. Ester is fifty years younger than Mzee Mutai, approximately in her early thirties, the age of his grandchildren.

The team from Lugari Yearly Meeting was quite judgmental about this age discrepancy. Yet I realized that Ester's job was to take care of the old man — the Kenyan equivalent to an assisted living facility in the United States. We were told nothing of how their relationship developed, but seeing them interact indicated that they had a warm relationship.

They had decided — and I think this was mostly Ester's idea, but clearly with the Mzee's blessing — to give the plot to the church. This is a common arrangement. Gladys's father, David Okwemba, has a plot in the shape of an isosceles triangle and had given the part at the point for the building of a church. The group of us went to the field from which they wanted to give the plot and marked off the boundaries. It was approximately one-quarter of an acre, more than enough to build a church. The idea was that the new church would also lease the three acres of surrounding land so that Ester would have enough funds to send her two children to school. Leasing of land is a common practice in the area and, if the church decided to grow corn or some other crop on the three acres, they would recover the rent and some surplus to help with the building and upkeep of the church.

I asked Jotham Nwongesa, the general superintendent of Lugari Yearly Meeting, if a church were built on the property, would there be people who would attend. In other words, would it become a functioning church? His reply was "definitely, yes" because already a group including Ester was meeting for worship. The nearest Friends church was far enough away that people from Sugoi would have to take a mini-bus to church and back each Sunday which people could not afford. Thus, some Luhya who lived in the area and had previously attended Quaker churches were now attending other closer churches. They would be more than happy to return to the Friends church if there was one in the community. A viable Friends church could develop quite quickly.

However, the couple had some further restrictions, namely, that the Yearly Meeting, if it took the plot, had to commence to build the church. Ester even suggested that in April the church could get a tent and hold a "crusade" on the plot. This would have involved an extensive event, usually at least a week long, where there would be a lot of singing, preaching, etc. This is a major draw in a community with no television, movie theater, or other forms of mass entertainment. The focus of this crusade would be on reconciliation so that it would draw people from all ethnic groups. One of the reasons that I was supportive of this whole enterprise is that the Sugoi Friends Church would not be a mostly Luhya church, but one including numerous ethnicities, a quality which I see as necessary for a peaceful future in Kenya.

This was all well and good and papers were drawn up detailing the agreement.

Now let me explain to you what I think was really happening. This incident is an obvious example of a rather elaborate and bold method of how women cope with their situation in a paternal society. If one conceives of women in Africa as passive victims of the extremely patriarchal system that prevails, then one must despair. Nonetheless, the women do not see themselves that way and are quite creative in working the system to their advantage.

Here is the problem. What happens when Mzee Mutai dies? Do not think that the land, house, and animals will go to Ester. That is not the custom. The custom is that everything will go to the sons of his first wife. If this land were in the traditional Tugen area near Baringo, Ester would have no chance of remaining on the land. When Mzee Mutai died, his sons would evict her from the property as she and her children would become nomads, surviving by any means they could. This was not traditional land since Mzee Mutai had bought the plot himself. There probably were few other Tugen close by. Nonetheless, Mzee Mutai's sons, on his death, would come and evict Ester from the plot, probably sell the animals and land, and keep the inheritance for themselves. As a young woman, a generation younger than Mzee's sons, she would have a difficult task to hold on to the land.

If there were a church on the land with three acres being leased and Ester is a member of that church, then her position is decidedly strengthened. Those church members, particularly the women, will be on Ester's side and will oppose the sons, who are not members of the local community, obtaining the land and selling it off to the highest bidder. Mzee Mutai said that he was a Christian once for ten years but then stopped. He did not indicate why, but he did indicate that he would be attending the new Friends church. When he dies, it will be the church that will bury him. For a respected elder like Mzee Mutai this is going to be a major occasion, probably lasting for days. All his children, grandchildren, and great-grandchildren will attend. However, the church members will be in charge of the funeral and this will greatly strengthen Ester's position. Ester was straightforward in indicating her uneasiness about what will happen to her when her husband dies. If an active church is on the property and the sons realize they are in a weak position, they might not even challenge Ester's right to the property. If this happens, Ester will live happily ever after on the plot as her son will inherit it fifty years later when she passes away.

I was much intrigued by my conjecture of the real reason for this plan. I think that if the church is built, Ester's plan is likely to succeed. Clearly, Ester is no passive female victim of a patriarchal society. Rather she is building a brave new world based not on ethnicity but on a new, shared voluntary commitment.

Frequently in the United States, I have heard from those who oppose the Christian influence in Africa — their belief that Christian missionaries to Africa destroyed the native cultures in their Garden of Eden-like existence by imposing a foreign ideology and value system that disrupted that blissful state. The Kenyan tourist industry, with their promotion of the native Masai, fulfills these expectations. Members of the Friends church in Kenya do not subscribe to this mythology. They are thankful for the education, health-care, Christian value system, and women's liberation that the Quaker church has brought to them.

In this case, I have emphasized the traditional nature of Mzee Mutai — he is not much different, in his cattle stealing days, from those traditional Masai. Yet he is clearly supportive of Ester's scheme to use the church to allow her to keep the land after he has died. This is a specific, stark case of traditionalism versus Christianity with Christianity being the excuse, the cover for Ester's needs.

Unfortunately, this plan failed. In November 2009, Mzee Mutai died. As predicted, one of his sons came, beat up Ester and drove her off the property. She became depressed and died. I wonder if this is a euphemism for suicide. Although the congregation had been meeting weekly under a tree on the plot where they were going to build the church, by November no construction had occurred. The church was kicked off the property and the members are now trying to find another site to build the church.

Men and Agriculture

In the countryside of Rwanda and Burundi, few men are cultivating. Rather women and children, frequently in groups of up to ten, are working together. Where are the men? Some of them are making bricks and building houses which is tough manual work, but many are just standing around the roadside doing, well, nothing. During the time I was in the Rwandan refugee camp, I heard men state that they would never use a hoe to cultivate. That was women's work. Real men took care of cows.

This is not the case in Kenya. Men are in the fields working alongside the women. In Kenya, for instance, when it is time to plant (and early planting is one of the major requirements of a good yield), everyone — men, women, children, young and old — are all out together planting the corn which is the major crop in this area. When it is time to plant, almost everything else stops, including our AVP workshops. The planting is then accomplished in a few days.

Kenya is much more prosperous than Rwanda or Burundi — three times, five times, nine times more prosperous depending upon how you look at it. The major reason for this, in my opinion, is because the Kenyan men are involved in farming. It is naive to think that the women who are already collecting firewood, cooking, taking care of children, the elderly, and the sick, can single handedly produce a bountiful crop.

Why are Kenyan men involved in farming? Because in Kenya the plowing is done with oxen and, as noted above, cows are men's work. I have never seen any ox plowing in Rwanda or Burundi. In Kenya, almost everyone has access to oxen for plowing. If they do not own oxen themselves, they can borrow or rent oxen from their neighbors. Since Kenya has become more affluent, oxen plowing has in some places been taken over by tractor plowing, which again is done by the men.

When oxen are used, there are many advantages. The fields can be plowed much more quickly and consequently can be larger. Ox plowing also turns the soil better than cultivating with a hand hoe called a *jembe*. The result is a higher yield. Plowing with oxen must be done on the contour as an erosion control measure — in Burundi, in particular, people cultivate up and down the steep slopes and the erosion is everywhere as Burundian soil is filling up Lakes Victoria and Tanganyika.

The fundamental issue is that men then become stakeholders in the farming. Men in this region have the money. When they are involved in agriculture, they are willing to put their funds into farming because they can see the profit from the results. In Kenya, when people go to Nairobi or some other town to work, they invest in their rural home. Some of the houses on farms around us here in Lugari District are much nicer than the house Gladys and I built. When Kenyans retire, they return home to their nice house and farm that continues to sustain them. In Rwanda and Burundi, on the other hand, there is little investment in the countryside. Agricultural practices are at a subsistence level and nice housing is rare in the countryside. The elite build their nice homes in town. I surmise that this difference is due to the fact that since the time of independence, when Africans began to have significant income to invest, there have been many periods of unrest in Rwanda and Burundi. Consequently, Rwandans and Burundians have been reluctant to invest in the countryside where nice housing would be destroyed in the next round of violence.

The culture in Kenya is extremely different from the culture in Rwanda and Burundi. Culture can have a profound difference on the prosperity of a society. If I tried to get men in Rwanda and Burundi to cultivate with oxen, I would be trying to make a considerable change in their culture. Culture is not a static abstract that needs to be preserved as it includes changes that leads to the improvement of people's lives.

Lynching

When I was at the dentist's office in Nairobi in 1968, I watched a mob run after a "thief." They ran out of my view before I could see what happened. Later in 1969, I heard President Jomo Kenyatta speak in Machakos in eastern Kenya and he said that people ought to push the faces of thieves in the mud. I was appalled at this promotion of vigilantism. When Joy, my daughter, was in Kenya in 1994 researching her book, she knew a young man in her neighborhood who had been killed by a mob because he was a suspected thief. In our training for work campers, we advise them (a) not to interfere with a lynching because they might be beaten or lynched also and (b) not to shout "thief" if someone steals something from them because they then might be accomplices of a murder.

Page 34 of the January 9, 2009, *Daily Nation*, the leading Kenyan newspaper, has this headline: "Four cattle thieves lynched: Mob cornered them as they tried to steal the animals from a Siaya village." The article also says, "In Nyamira, a 35-year-old man on the police list of most wanted criminals was beaten to death by a mob." Every two or three days there is an article in the paper about a lynching or attempted lynching. The man about to be lynched is lucky if the police arrive in time to save him. Moreover, the normal punishment for the crime supposedly committed, stealing cows for instance, is not execution.

Lynching is of course against the law but, as in the US's lynching days, it is extremely difficult to find those who have done the lynching, prosecute them, and punish them. Police frequently ask for help in identifying the lynchers, but I rarely see any follow-up on these requests. Lynching is done with impunity.

What surprises me most is that I have never yet seen any politician condemn these lynchings. Even more surprising is that I have not heard any church condemn them either. Where are the Kenyan Quakers and other religious leaders? Where is there someone in the human rights community who is tracking the lynchings and investigating the facts of each?

One of the reasons I think that an anti-lynching campaign is extremely important for Kenya is that it is only a small step from the mob violence of lynching a suspected thief to the mob violence of attacking another ethnic group as happened in the 2008 post election violence. If life is sacred or, as the Quakers say, "there is that of God in every person," then life should be respected in all cases. I myself am opposed to the death penalty because in taking away a person's life, the possibility of remorse, redemption, and rehabilitation is also eliminated. When a society breaks that respect for the sacredness of life, it can easily be turned into a "Reign of Terror" as happened in the French Revolution. If a person can be beaten to death because he is a suspected thief, the same lack of respect for human life can be used to attack and kill people of another ethnic group, religious group, or political party.

In Kenya, I would estimate solely from newspaper reports that at least two hundred and fifty people are lynched by mobs each year. Much work needs to be done.

Robin Dunn is an Australian who has been in Western Province of Kenya for a number of years. One time he was in Kakamega when a crowd was chasing a "thief." Robin went to save him, got him bleeding, and dazed from the experience. A nice picture of him supporting the man on the way to the hospital was in one of Kenya's major newspapers. I sent this out on my "Reports from Kenya" and was criticized for doing this because it was an example of a white person saving a black person. I have three reactions to this criticism. First, the Kenyan newspapers thought that this was newsworthy. Second, it does not reinforce the normal stereotype which is how whites abuse blacks rather than saving them. Thirdly, he saved a life, something I have not done in my life and I am a good deal older than Robin.

Later I received a report about one of our HROC workshops where a man named Ndirangu not only saved someone from a lynch mob, but also then employed him. Here is his testimony:

> HROC is of so much important because on my side, it helped me heal and it has taught me tactics on how to live with others. I also remember one day I met a crowd which was beating up a young man because he had stolen. I took up the stand and defended him. I asked him to be sentenced to thirty days community service but I took him and he helps me work on my shamba [small farm] for a fee [daily wage]. Were it not for the teaching I got about reaching out to the good part of everyone, I could not have stood up for him and I could not be selling a lot of vegetables thanks to an extra strength.

Chapter 5
Visit the Great Lakes Region

Fear of Africa

I recommend that you visit the African Great Lakes region. If you wish to visit the tourist attractions such as climbing Mt. Kilimanjaro (hard) or Mt. Elgon (easy), lying on the beaches of the Indian Ocean, and/or observing the acclaimed wild animals, that is fine. My recommendation, though, is that you visit the people and their communities. As my favorite John Woolman quote indicates, *It is necessary to dwell deep, that thou mayest feel and understand the spirit of people.* This chapter will give some ideas, considerations, and advice on visiting the Great Lakes Region.

Some Americans fear coming to Africa. A few years ago, a college student applied for one of the AGLI work camps. She had a wonderful application, which showed a good grasp of motivations for wanting to attend the work camp — I always find that those who emphasize what they hope to learn during their visit to Africa are more impressive than those who indicate that they are going to do charity work. Shortly thereafter, she informed her parents. They "hit the roof," declaring, "How can you make us worry so much about you when you are in Africa?" Since she did not have the support of her parents who were paying her college costs, she had to withdraw and not go to Africa. I felt quite sorry for her and sent her an email that said that obviously this was not the right time for her, but she had a long future ahead of her where she could implement her desires.

I have to bless my mother for her encouragement and support when I first went to Africa in 1964. When I applied, I was still only twenty years old and, at that time, the age of maturity was twenty-one so I had to have the approval of my parents. I wrote them a letter outlining what I wanted to do. In response, I received the most positive, encouraging letter from my mother giving her approval. My father did not protest, although he made it a condition that I promise to return for my senior year at college, which I did.

Frequently I have had to speak with parents who are nervous about their adult child going to Africa. I have learned how to soothe their concerns. "Almost two million tourists visit Kenya in a year." "Our African partners are extremely cautious about the security of the people coming from overseas." "We allow the work campers to go off the site only with other adult African members of the team and that they must obey the advice of their hosts." Once, a father who was going with his family kept asking me about all kinds of problems — security, health, water, climate, etc. In the end, I told him that if he was afraid to take his family, then he ought not to go. The last thing I would want is to have an extremely nervous participant in the work camp. He ended up going and he and his family had a wonderful experience in Kenya. He later laughed at his previous nervous hesitations.

When people ask me if I am afraid, my answer is, "The most fearful part of going to Africa is the turn-off from the Washington, DC beltway and the need to cross four lanes of speeding traffic on the Dulles Toll Road in order to get to the airport access road." I have always assumed that people in Africa would be just as friendly and helpful as people in the US are. With some visitors to Africa, I notice that they are hesitant in their interactions with Africans — there is a holding back, a certain cautiousness. I attribute this not only to the inexperience of Americans in dealing with foreigners, but also the poor state of race relations in the United States.

If you have fears about traveling to Africa, you need to question where these fears come from. Is it due to worry about the unknown? Is it due to hesitancy about how Africans might treat you? How much is due to the stereotype in the United States that blacks are violent? Are there other unexamined fears lurking there in the background? If you have these fears, how much is this reinforced by the negative projections about Africa from the American media? If you have fears about visiting Africa, please try to uncover the reasons and roots of those fears.

US State Department Travel Warnings

If you look at the US State Departments travel advisories, any fears you have might be reinforced. As I am writing this, there are thirty-nine countries on the travel advisory list. Thirteen of these are in Africa including the Democratic Republic of the Congo, Burundi, and Kenya. I will go through each one.

The Democratic Republic of the Congo is clearly still in a state of civil unrest and potential war, particularly in the east and northeast of the country. This could be considered the equivalent to Iraq, Iran, and Afghanistan which are also on the travel advisory list.

With Burundi, the travel advisory admits that the last rebel group signed a cease-fire in 2006. Yet it does not reflect any return to normality that has occurred since that time. It seems that once a country gets on the travel advisory list it is difficult to get off the list. Both positive and negative developments occur all the time and the US travel advisories should be revised frequently according to the latest conditions.

Since 1999, I traveled to Burundi one or two times a year. Many of these trips occurred during the time when a travel advisory clearly did apply. During that time, we also continued with projects in Burundi. When I visit a war zone or unsafe area, I depend upon the local people with whom I am working to help me with safety. I go only where they say it is safe for me to go and I always go with them. I am always cautious and prudent. In 2002, during the height of the fighting in Burundi, I went up-country to the town of Gitega on a mini-bus — something the travel advisories indicate you should never do. I did this because I went in the mini-bus owned by Burundi Yearly Meeting of Friends so that the driver, Vitol, a member of the yearly meeting, would look after me and insure my safety. Because of my long history of living in out-of-the-way places in Africa, I am more accustomed to the situation and thus have less fear than someone who is visiting for the first time.

In the old days, before cell phones were common, as we approached an area, we would stop and ask the local villagers if all was well ahead. We would go a few miles and ask again, proceeding cautiously on. These days with cell phones, this is no longer necessary. When violence breaks out in an area, those who live there quickly notify everyone else by cell phone through calls or text messages. This is why I always have felt safe and secure.

Let us now turn to Kenya. In 1998, the US Embassy was blown up in Nairobi and in 2003 a hotel owned by Israelis was bombed and a missile was shot at an Israeli airplane in Mombasa. The chaos in Somalia also impinges on the situation in Kenya. I suspect that the well-known corruption in the Kenyan police force is a contributing factor since a "terrorist" would quickly buy their way out of jail. On the other hand, almost two million foreigners visit Kenya each year for vacations and one hundred and twenty-three thousand Brits live in Kenya. Why is there still a travel advisory? Many countries, including the United States, England, Japan, and Spain have had equally serious terrorist attacks and they are not on the travel advisory list.

Part of the advice in all these travel advisories is the danger from theft and robbery, particularly in the major cities. This I find most interesting because Washington, DC, Los Angeles, and most major US cities are hardly crime free. I would think that almost anywhere in the world one has to be careful about robbery and theft. Again simple precautions count for a lot. Once I knew two Russian women who were visiting Nairobi and decided to walk somewhere at twelve o'clock at night. Fortunately, the police saw them and took them back to where they were staying. I never go out to at night without being accompanied by a local person who knows the territory. We advise people who go to the region not to take any valuables or items of personal importance with them. Not only is there the danger of them being stolen, but the continuous concern to keep the items safe detracts from the experience of the visit.

Unfortunately, for AGLI, these US travel advisories present a difficulty. Any university that is receiving funds from the United States government cannot use university funds for travel to countries that have travel advisories. Other organizations have adopted this same policy. For AGLI, this means that people, frequently students, who are receiving financial assistance for their time in the region, can only visit Rwanda and Uganda, but not Kenya, Burundi, or the Congo.

Empathy

I suspect that most foreigners who visit Africa from the US, Canada, Australia, or Great Britain have given much consideration to the dichotomy between wealth and poverty, advantage and disadvantage, race, nationality and social class. Much of AGLI's in-service training for work campers has to do with how to handle the dilemmas that arise. Yet this, I think, is the main benefit of being an AGLI work camper/volunteer. It requires that the person step out of their comfort zone and interact and relate on a personal level with those whose situation is so different.

Sometimes I myself have a difficult time understanding American culture. Why do we put so many people in jail? Why do we believe in the "American dream?" Why are we so afraid of the "other"

— the definition of which changes through the years? Why do we substitute consumption for community? For more traditional Americans, why do we put the fork to the left of the plate, the knife, and the spoon on the right side? When I was a kid this cutlery setting was an important cultural attribute, but today do kids even know it exists? Exposure to a different part of the world is extremely useful in seeing our own culture from a new perspective.

It is difficult to understand another person. Sometimes it is even difficult understanding oneself. However, understanding others — finding that of God in everyone as Quakers say — is critical for a more peaceful world. Empathy is the skill of putting oneself in the place of another. To do so successfully one needs to let go of one's own culture, predilections, narrow-mindedness, and prejudices. This is difficult to do, but is well worth trying.

Cultural Differences

In the United States, we have two words, "guest" and "stranger." These have different connotations, as the first is someone welcomed and entertained, while the second is treated with suspicion. In Swahili, there is only one word, *mgeni*, for both "guest" and "stranger." In other words, strangers are treated like guests. For this reason, Americans find Africans especially warm and friendly.

In the United States, guests are to be given a lot of attention. When we had out-of-town guests, my mother would devote 100% of her attention to entertaining them. Since she lived in St. Louis, she had taken innumerable guests to go up in the Arch. Yet when they left, she was dog-tired and secretly glad to see them go. In Africa, guests are not necessarily entertained by the host, but expected to settle immediately into family life. There is a Swahili saying that a guest must pick up a hoe on the third day — in other words, they have to get to work. Once when I was hosting a Rwandan in my house in St. Louis, which I was repairing at the time, he insisted that he help.

This difference, of course, can lead to funny misunderstandings. We had a situation once where an African was coming to visit in the United States and a potential host said that his family could not accommodate the African because they would not be home much during the weekend he needed to be there. The African response was, "Are they afraid to let me stay in their house?" In another incident, some Americans were at the house of an African who left them in the living room while he finished a number of duties that he had to do. The Americans were offended because they thought he was ignoring them.

Here is our advice to the AGLI work campers:

There is little privacy in the lives of most Africans. Many people live close together in small spaces, and you will get a direct experience of what this is like. For some people this can be a stressful part of the work camp experience because we are often used to lots of privacy and physical separation from people in our lives. People, particularly children, are curious about everything — your skin, your eyes, your hair, your voice tone, your language. They seldom see foreigners. Be aware that Africans do not live with the same kinds of background noise that we do (traffic, heavy machinery, electrical appliances, etc.). As a result, their hearing is exceptionally good. Be sensitive about anything you say in public and in what may seem like private. Never assume that they cannot understand you because they do not speak English. Many Africans understand English much better than they speak it.

The local people are forgiving to a guest who makes a mistake. They just figure that the guest just does not know any better, which is true. Many Americans have that go-get-it attitude which sometimes leads them into minor mistakes. I find that a better method is to just be patient and see what the Africans do and then copy them.

I remember a case in Burundi where I was attending an official function with a young woman from the US who was in her early twenties. At the function, she had the choice of sitting with the dignitaries like me because she was an America or she could play the role of a young female by serving the people food as all the African young women were doing. In this instance, where she could adopt one of two identities, she chose the role of the young woman and served the guests. The Africans were quite surprised to find themselves being served by a white American. Foreigners and guests, I often say, are given an extraordinary amount of respect which they have neither earned nor deserved. This is one of the reasons many foreigners leave with such positive feelings when they visit this region of Africa.

How Not to Behave

In 1968, when I was in the Mua Hills of Machakos District, just east of Nairobi, I was involved in a case of how not to behave in Africa. The high school was being built on the site of an old farmhouse of a former British settler. The house had a nice system of gutters that went into an open cistern right below the house. During the rainy season the cistern, which was about fifteen feet across, would fill up with water. The local people would come and draw water for drinking and cooking from a tap at the bottom of the cistern. There was a college aged American staying at the old farmhouse. One day, he decided to go skinny-dipping in the cistern. After his dip, he put a towel around his waist and walked to the local shop about half a mile away.

I did not see any of this, but the local people told Sub-Chief Mativo about this incident. Mativo came to see me and asked me to speak to the young man and inform him that this was unacceptable behavior as he was fouling the drinking water of the people. He also asked me to tell him that he should not walk around near naked. I approached the young man and told him of his "misdeeds." He was totally surprised since he did not realize that people were using the water for eating and drinking. He somehow had never noticed people coming to draw water at the tap.

An interesting aspect of this story is that if a person does something really wrong, the approach in Africa will be to find someone close to the offending person who will be asked to talk with the offender. In this case, I was considered "close" because we were both Americans. In 1999 at the first AGLI work camp in Bujumbura, Burundi, some of the work campers did some offensive behaviors. Two separate people, both *wazungu,* were sent to me to say that if the work campers did not behave better, they would not be welcome. Neither informant knew what the work campers had done wrong. It was left up to me to guess. I had some strong suspicions and drew up a list of "expected guidelines" for work campers.

Also, note the comment about the towel. Many Americans think that Africa is the bush so that they can dress in torn, dirty clothes, wear little, not shave, walk barefooted, and think they are camping in the wilderness. All of this is offensive to Africans. They expect people to dress in nice, clean clothes including shoes or sandals. Women and men should not show too much skin. I myself dress better when I am in Africa than when I am in the United States. This only shows respect. Walking to town with a bath towel around the waist is a sure sign of disrespect.

Asking for Money

There is no greater difference between Americans and Africans than the customs around asking for money. In the United States, if a person asks for money for personal use from a friend or stranger, this is interpreted negatively. Certainly at best, the person is not a rugged individual able to care of himself or herself. More than likely the person is an alcoholic, a drug addict, or mentally unbalanced. In East and Central Africa it is quite acceptable to ask people for money or possessions and is done all the time. This disconnect between the two cultures is sufficient enough that AGLI had to ask all the AGLI supported Africans not to ask any AGLI supporters, volunteers, and visitors for money for personal use.

Since in Africa there is no stigma in asking for money, the request is in fact a method of developing a bond between the asker and the asked. Unlike Americans, the Africans are not offended when the request is turned down. Of course, if the request is successful, then a bond has developed between the one who is asking and the one who is giving. In Africa, someone may be at one time a giver and another time a receiver. This practice holds an African extended family or a local community together. This asking and receiving not only includes asking for money, but borrowing salt or "fire" from the neighbor, getting a drink of water, escaping from a downpour in a neighbor's or even a stranger's house, taking someone to the hospital, and on and on.

When westerners visit this region, they are always asked by numbers of people for money or other goods. Some *wazungu* get really upset by this frequent asking. They assume that they are being asked because they are wealthy *wazungu*, but they are wrong. Africans also do this with each other all the time. Gladys is a Kenyan and she gets many more requests than I do. It is made even more difficult because the askers are family members. In the United States one is infrequently asked for money so people do not know how to say, "No." They feel guilty if they refuse. Africans, on the other hand, are not at all negative when the answer is "No."

Sharing something nice has a high value. I once read about a non-violent society in Malaysia that considered the desire to possess things as the root of violence. Nobody owned anything as everything was used by everybody as needed. Or as my favorite Quaker, John Woolman, wrote, *May we look upon our Treasures, and the furniture of our Houses, and the Garments in which we array ourselves, and try whether the seeds of war have any nourishment in these possessions or not.*

The culture of possession is one that needs to be taught. The culture of sharing can also be taught. In a poor society, the culture of sharing is necessary for survival. When famine occurred in the Rwandan refugee camp where I taught in the 1960's, I was amazed that, when people obtained food, the first thing they did was share it with their neighbors, particularly the elderly and single mothers. Rather than hoard food for the next day, it was given away.

Here is an example of the connectedness that I have found in Africa. In late 1964, half way through my time in the Rwandan refugee camp, the United Nations High Commission for Refugees and the Tanzanian government decided to end the rations for the refugees since they were supposed to be self-sufficient. But they were not, so hunger stalked the people of the refugee camp, including my students in primary school.

An older student, Frederic, who had finished secondary school in French in Rwanda, would come most days after school to learn English from us. We would talk, review the essays we gave him to write, and listen to his stories about Rwandan culture, the current situation in the refugee camps, and many other interesting topics.

Then one day we learned that he had not eaten for three days. We immediately asked him to dinner. He turned us down! We were amazed and could not understand how a hungry person could turn down food. He later told us that he was living with his sister who had a number of small children under the age of six. He did not feel that it would be right for him to go home on a full stomach while he listened to the young children cry from hunger. He agreed that, when there was food at home for his sister and the kids, he would come and have dinner with us. He did so a few days later.

Yet I have had the same kind of dilemma. As I describe on page 38 in my story about meeting Gakemba, a few days after we had given some food to him, we visited our student's house to meet him. His mother was roasting some Spanish peanuts on the fire in the hut. There is nothing tastier than freshly roasted hot peanuts. She put them on a plate for us to eat. The family was badly off and I did not need to eat the peanuts. However, to not eat the peanuts would have been rude. So what should I do? In the end, I ate a few peanuts, but left most of them for the family.

The result of this sharing in the refugee camp was that only a few people — seven that I heard of — died of hunger. If people had hoarded their food, many more people would have died, particularly the elderly and children, while the able-bodied people who could more easily obtain food would have eaten well. The system works because the next day if those who had been the recipients now received some food, they would share it with those who had formerly given them food. It is awesome when you see it in action.

One of my favorite testimonies from a HROC workshop occurred in Burundi where the good life is to have a cow that gives a big glass of milk to drink each morning. One man who attended a HROC workshop lived contentedly with his cow and daily glass of milk. After the workshop, he looked around his village and saw a small, emaciated boy in his neighborhood. He asked himself how he could be happy drinking the milk every day, knowing that this child was malnourished? Therefore, each day in the morning he sent a bottle of milk over to the boy. If everyone in the world did as this man did, hunger would be abolished.

Here are some question AGLI asks its work campers and volunteers who go to Africa on its programs:

- When you consider giving a gift to a person in Africa, are you aware of how others in Africa may become jealous or feel slighted?
- When you feel the desire to give a gift, are you considering the others on your team and how this might affect them?
- Are you considering the long-term effects that the gift giving will have on team members who come to the work camp in future years?
- Have you considered ways to give that may benefit the larger community, the project, or AGLI rather than just one or two individuals or families?
- Have you first spoken about your gift-giving ideas with other members of your team in a group meeting setting? What feedback do they have for you?

• Does giving gifts to your host family feel different to you from giving gifts to African workers, or others in the community where you are staying? Why or why not?

What is most interesting is that this American trait of reluctance to ask for funding is one of the major impediments for people wanting to go on our programs. AGLI has up to twenty-five work campers and extended service volunteers participating in our programs each year. Due mostly to the high airfare, the trip is not cheap and each work camper needs to raise at least $4,300. This includes airfare as well as $1,200 for building materials on the project plus funds to subsidize an African work camper. We prefer that work campers and other volunteers ask others for the funds since this is an excellent method of publicizing AGLI and our African programs.

Because Americans are reluctant to ask others for donations, AGLI makes it easier by having the donations go directly into the AGLI account which becomes a tax-exempt donation. In addition, since a considerable amount of these funds is not for the individual, but the particular project, this helps the person get over the fact that he or she is asking for personal help. We have found that those who conduct fundraising are surprised at the generosity of their family, friends, neighbors, acquaintances, and even those they barely know or do not know at all.

Time

The sense of time is different in Africa. The Western emphasis on being timely is not so prized. "Time is a stream I go a-fishin' in" perhaps best describes time in Africa. Until recently, few people used watches and many people still do not. Time is much more elastic and the foreigner has to learn to go with the flow of the stream of time. Sometimes things that have been arranged never happen, but then again things that are not arranged just pop up. Visitors have to learn to not be upset by the former and to be quick to grab opportunities that develop with the latter. It is necessary to become more flexible.

In Swahili and many African languages, the hours follow the Muslim custom. The time of day starts with sunrise rather than noon. Of course, since these countries are on the equator, each day is the same length and the sun rises and sets about the same time all year. This means a six-hour difference. 7:00 AM in our time becomes 1:00 AM in Swahili time. Once I arranged for a visitor to meet me and forgot I was using Swahili time. I was disappointed when he did not show up in the morning as I expected, but realized my error when he showed up six hours later in the afternoon.

There is another dimension to time, which I will call "speed." Americans tend to be in a hurry, wanting to get things finished "on time." Africans are much more willing to pace activities with little rush. For instance, at our work camps, Americans tend to work hard until they tire themselves out physically. This is not only a comment on a day's activity, but sometimes an American has to take a day off from the work camp because he or she has overextended. If you watch the Africans closely, you will notice that they work diligently for a few minutes, then rest for a minute or so, and then go back to work. In other words, they pace themselves. As a result, they seem to be able to continue with physical labor for a much longer time and do not burn themselves out.

Another aspect is that the Africans seem to be much more patient than Americans. I attribute this to the fact that most Africans have had to herd cows, goats, and/or sheep. People herding animals spend the vast majority of the time doing nothing but watching the animals graze. For a cow to become full takes hours so the herdsman must be patient. I think that this carries over into other activities. When things do not happen as they should, Americans tend to become anxious, even upset, while Africans go into their patience mode. Once in the United States I was giving a ride to a woman from one of the pastoral groups in Uganda. When the vehicle broke down and needed towing and repair, she quietly wrapped herself in her *kanga* (a large shawl-like piece of cloth used by many traditional women) and withdrew into a quiet patience. The interruption of the journey did not seem to bother her at all. An American might have fretted, looking at her watch, calculating how late she would be.

African Perceptions of *Wazungu*

The Africans have their own concepts of *wazungu*, foreigners. For example, fruit is common, good, cheap and eaten a lot by the

Africans, who do not think this common food is appropriate for foreigners. These fruits include pineapple, mangoes, oranges (bitter), papaya, guava, passion fruit, many kinds of bananas, avocados and other fruits whose English name I do not know. In the US, there are only one or two varieties of bananas. In Africa, there are so many different varieties. One that I like best is a reddish banana that has a pear taste. Because Africans assume foreigners would not want a common food, it may be necessary to ask for fruit.

Africans also think that *wazungu* cannot do any manual labor. I have no idea how they think all those tall buildings in New York City were constructed. The origin of this belief was that the colonialists and white settlers lived like royalty, having innumerable servants to do everything for them.

In the summer of 2006, AGLI organized a work camp in Bujumbura to build the Kamenge Clinic. The work camp had three American females and one Kenyan male plus a large number of Burundians. Here is what the leader of the work camp, Cassilde Ntamamiro, reported:

> Initially the presence of white women was a puzzling idea for local people. Many people in Kamenge did not understand why we have to make whites work so hard instead of giving the poor, local people an opportunity to make money. Men, women, and children would come around and ask how much one white woman is paid in order to come work in the mud and carry heavy rocks and bricks. They insisted on answers.
>
> As they continued to ask, I took one morning hour to educate people, explaining the role of *wazungu* and other work campers as volunteers. I recalled the ancient time when we Burundians went as a whole village to help cultivate or collect the crops for one family or help carry a sick person to the hospital, or build a hut for somebody whose house caught on fire. I showed the community the similarity between the two activities.
>
> I told them the importance of joining our strength as Burundians and any other things we have in order to develop ourselves and especially leave the fear of the past wars behind by coming together, freeing ourselves from any type of ethnic prejudice. If people came all the way from America and Kenya to help us, it is because they are encouraged by

the progress we make in peace, so we should feel encouraged to rebuild the community.

Not every African has a great desire to go to America. Some are afraid. They have heard how in America if a person is in a long gas line, he or she can be shot and killed. If there is a dispute with someone over a girl friend, one can also be killed. Politics in America is no different than in Africa. John F Kennedy, Robert Kennedy, Martin Luther King, Jr., and others were killed just like politicians in Africa. The brother who is governor of the state of Florida, just like elections in Africa, manipulates the outcome of the votes there to give his brother the presidency. They have no understanding of why America fought the war in Vietnam and now the wars in Iraq and Afghanistan. The problem here is that I myself cannot give satisfactory answers to their questions.

The local Africans, therefore, may have as many misperceptions as the visitor. Their experiences may make it hard for them to understand conditions in the United States. Try, for instance, to describe a terrible ice storm to someone who has never seen ice. Or the Washington DC beltway to one whom at most has experienced a potholed two-lane highway.

Philosophy of AGLI Work Camps and Extended Service Volunteers

One can best feel and understand the spirit of people by living and working with them. This is the reason that we assign work campers and extended service volunteers to a specific program with specific purposes. If a person is building a structure with Africans, he or she must work together and this working together is how a significant relationship is formed.

The African Great Lakes Initiative requires applicants to have a clearness committee. Here is our advice:

This committee should consist of three to six persons with whom you will be comfortable speaking about sensitive topics. The clearness committee should include both youthful and mature members; and ideally, at least one person who has lived in a third-world country. The committee may be appointed by your Friends meeting or church, or, self-constituted. One person should be appointed as clerk (chair) and it is best if that person invites the other people to be part of the committee. If needed, AGLI will try to help you find people for your clearness committee. The committee should meet with you one or more times to discern your clearness to go to Burundi, Kenya, Uganda, or Rwanda as a member of a work camp peace team.

Interestingly enough, some of the best clearness committees have been those during which the whole group, including the applicant, decided that he or she should not go. In one case, the person's health was the deciding issue. In another, it was lack of family support. In a third, it was that the person was too afraid to go to Burundi when the conflict was still going on. In each of these cases, I was thankful for the insights, care, and concern of the clearness committees as they discussed the situation with the applicant. Nonetheless, in most cases the applicant is "cleared" to go.

AGLI's application and clearness process is much more taxing than many other programs. The general feedback was that the process made sure that the others go[194] were taking the prospect seriously, that it was not going to be just a joyride, an exotic adventure.

We have found that it is best to limit the number of foreigners in a work camp to only six. We then add six local Africans to make a total team of twelve. This is still the size of a viable work group. As work campers labor together with the Africans, they will see what the Africans do and how they do it. They will be teachers to the international team members. Work campers also experience the usual African frustrations. For instance, one day, there may be no piped water to mix with the cement so bricks cannot be laid. Then someone might try to get a pickup to bring water in forty-four gallon barrels. This may or may not work out. Since neither the international nor the African work campers will be skilled masons, masons will be hired to see that the work is done properly.

Each work camp has an African leader. At one time, people wanted me to be part of the work camps but I declined because without me the work campers have to solve whatever small or large problems that arise. I would not be present to be the go-between, the mediator, between the work campers and the Africans. For some this may be difficult but it forces the Africans and foreigners to interact even in problem situations — all is not laughter and fun.

This relationship between the Africans and the international team members is tricky. Some foreigners do not want to be under the direction of the African leaders — sometimes this is just part of the anti-authoritarianism of Western culture and sometimes, I hate to have to admit, it is due to racism. On the African side, the problem is that the Africans, being too hospitable, do not want to offend their guests. One good example was when the work campers met a soccer team on the airplane and one of them asked to stay an extra day in the capital in order to watch the game rather than go up-country to the building site where people were waiting for their arrival. The director of the work camp agreed to let them stay and watch the soccer game. If I had been there, I would not have allowed this since I would consider it rude to make all those people who were expecting the work campers up-country wait an extra day.

When it is possible, we like the foreign work campers to live in local homes. This allows them to get a better feel for everyday life in the community. In order for this to happen in a household, someone has to give up their bed. As I described above this is a normal custom in the region, but the work camper frequently feels that they are imposing on the person who has been moved to another bed.

Our work camps last about five weeks including travel time and a one-day orientation. I think that this is necessary because it takes that long to become comfortable in the new setting.

If a work camper goes to Rwanda, he or she loves Rwandans. If to Burundi, Burundians. If to Kenya, Kenyans. And if to Uganda, Ugandans. This is to be expected and encouraged. In a successful work camp experience, the work camper comes to identify with the people with whom he or she has been working. This shows that the relationship has matured.

We find that unless the work camper has had other African experiences, the work camp experience is nothing like what he or she envisioned before coming. In such cases, the experience is profound because it substitutes vague generalizations about Africa with concrete experiences.

For the person visiting this region of Africa, my advice is that it is useful to assume nothing, and be curious about the culture of the area being visited without being judgmental or analytical. During the time in Africa, the visitor will just scratch the surface of what it is like to live there.

Americans are taught to be analytical — this is the goal of a good education. Yet when a person first comes to Africa, this analytical outlook can get in the way of the experiences which have to be seen, felt, heard, smelled, and tasted. If the person is trying to analyze every new aspect — and since this is a new environment there are literally thousands of them each day — it gets in the way of observing what is happening. I suggest that the visitor revel in the impressions at hand in order to fully live them. Then after the returning home, he or she can begin to analyze and put together the month of experiences. Some of these may be ambiguous or difficult to interpret. This is part of the learning process that makes going overseas so worthwhile.

It is not the role of the visitor to try to change everything or anything about the world he or she is visiting. Rather he or she should immerse himself or herself in it, observe it, and enjoy the differences. It is helpful to let go of notions that American ways of doing things are better. There will be things that may surprise, shock, or disturb the visitor. The person may miss his or her home, but there will also be things that he or she will envy and desire, as they are missing from his or her life in North America. This is a different culture with different values and beliefs. The visitor may learn a great deal about others and himself or herself if he or she can stay open and welcoming to the experiences while visiting

The Mennonite Central Committee sends volunteers around the world with a three-year commitment. I was once speaking with one of their volunteers in Gitega, Burundi, and he commented to me, "After I have been here for a year and a half, I am just beginning to understand things." I have had requests from people who want to parachute into Rwanda for a few days or a week, interview victims of the genocide, and think that they can understand what happened. This, I feel, is naïve. .

Some visitors have problems. There was one shy person who felt uncomfortable as numerous children watched her every move. Another was unhappy eating the same food day after day. This made me realize that one of the "luxuries" of American life is to have a choice of food — pizza today, Italian tomorrow, Chinese the next day, and so on. Another common problem is aggravation on the part of the foreigner when things that were supposed to happen do not either happen or take an inordinate amount of time to accomplish. Some work campers like learning to wash clothes by hand and other find it a nuisance.

If you have had interesting, challenging, and/or unusual time while in Africa, it may be difficult to convey this to others when you return home. When I first was going back and forth to Africa, I found that returning to the United States was a bigger culture shock than going to Africa. Once when I returned, I was at my cousin's house. He took a plastic milk jug and smashed it with his hands. I almost responded, "Do not do that! People can use the jug to draw water." However, I realized that there was no way I was going to get an empty jug from the US to Kenya. After the work camper has lived simply in Africa for more than a month, it is hard to return to a world where so much is wasted or to describe experiences in ways that others can understand. At a deeper level, it is difficult to reconcile the differences in living conditions between Africa and America.

Extended service volunteers (ESVs) have even a greater chance of a deepening experience. We now ask that ESVs go for at least three months. The ESV is placed on his or her own because usually he or she are the only foreigner in their work assignment. They are not assigned to a construction project, but to a part of one the ongoing programs of our African partners. Frequently, the role is in publicity, fundraising, grant writing, or program development, depending on the skills and background of each ESV. If the volunteer is flexible, there is always something that he or she can do. Some of the volunteers have stayed one, two, or more years and have had meaningful experiences.

Chapter 6
Poverty and Wealth

Definition

In the United States, being financially poor is associated with many negative connotations whereas being financially wealthy is linked to positive implications. A quick search on the Internet quickly proves this point. The first definition of "poor" on Google is "hapless: deserving or inciting pity." The second for "wealth" is "the quality of profuse abundance."

I rarely hear of Africa being wealthy. Yet, there are millions of people living "wealthy" lives. They are financially poor in comparison to most Americans but one of my favorite Henry David Thoreau quotes is *A man is rich in proportion to the number of things he can afford to leave alone.*

When Western visitors come to Africa, many often first notice the region's financial situation compared to the material affluence of their societies. Many foreigners who come are shocked by the financial poverty of the Africans. After my experience of living one year in a refugee camp in 1964-65, I looked at the same "financially poor" Africans and saw how "wealthy" they were. It all depends upon your frame of reference.

Lack of Money

In the United States, labor is expensive so we do many things ourselves — get cash from ATM machines, pump our own gas, take our groceries to the car, and so on. The situation in the Great Lake region is the opposite as labor is cheap and abundant. Since I know the economics of rural western Kenya best, I will focus mostly on examples from there, but the other countries in the region have even cheaper prospects. The details of the situation in the cities and towns are somewhat different.

In western Kenya, a person can be hired for a day's work for $1.33 plus lunch. If a nice lunch is not provided, a person will be reluctant to or even refuse to work. $1.33 buys only ten pounds of corn flour or two and a half pounds of sugar, so it is very little. For this payment, the person can do agricultural activities — plowing the field by hand using, planting, weeding, harvesting, drawing water, or any other type of unskilled, manual labor.

With labor so cheap, no one can afford to invest in laborsaving devices. Muscles work more than machines. This can lead to ironic situations. Cutting edge technology of optic-fiber cables are being laid throughout the region alongside the major highways. They are buried about three feet in the ground. How are these trenches covering hundreds of miles dug? The work is done by men with picks and shovels, similar to what could have been done at the time of the Roman Empire when the aqueducts were built.

Alexandra Douglas, an African Great Lakes Initiative volunteer in Burundi wrote this comment when she was working with the Kamenge Clinic (Blog, *Sustainable Peace by Peace,* October 27, 2009):

In the United States, we are driven by the Puritan work ethic. The capitalist mode of production emphasizes efficiency and the elimination of forces which do not quantitatively benefit surplus (cost-benefit analysis — weighing the total expected costs against the total expected benefit). We believe, or even if we do not believe in it, we are acculturated into a system that says our work/time should result in profit/benefit. Time is money. Anything that costs us time, costs us money. Therefore, we get impatient.

But this system, this culture, says almost nothing about the survival strategies — the daily realities — of people living in poverty.

On Friday, I was sitting in a staff meeting at the clinic where we were discussing the priorities of our work and we came to the subject of the restaurant run by the clinic. The restaurant was started by grant seed money with the idea that the restaurant could, for one, provide employment to some of the clinic's HIV+ patients, and secondly, provide seed money for micro-credit loans to other HIV+ patients with the profit earned. This sounds fantastic in theory and the clinic staff was chatting excitedly how much money was being earned and how to organize the group of women who were engaged in the restaurant project.

You can imagine my shock when I was told that the monthly revenue of the restaurant was (in a good month) around $46.

Now, in Burundi, this sum covers both the restaurant's staff salaries, the cost of food, and still leaves a (small) net profit which is being contributed to the micro-credit fund. However, that equation does not account for the staff time that is given to the restaurant in terms of overall management, organization, and accounting.

The voices of my finance friends went off in my head... and for once, I thought I agreed with them: "Not efficient."

But as I listened to my colleagues speak and later spoke with a few more personally, I realized what an important role the restaurant plays for both the clinic and its beneficiaries. It provides jobs, it provides income, it provides seed money. It also provides an organization in which HIV+ people are able to meet and support one another. It allows for basic survival.

While I with my Western mind see a lot of work with little gain, it is the privilege of having many other options that gives me this perspective. Sometimes the costs outweigh the benefits, but when the benefit is survival, what other choice is there?

Too frequently, foreigners in Africa express amazement and criticism of the extent and inefficiency of the manual labor. In the United States, a person can buy mortar mix by the bag and just add water. Here people have to buy cement and sand separately, mix them together, and then mix with water, all by hand. Since someone can be hired for so little per day, it makes no sense to get a cement mixer as the gasoline alone to run the cement mixer would be more than the pay of the human mixer.

Manual work can be done on a grand scale. During the civil war in Burundi, the World Food Program (WFP) had a food for work project up-country where a hillside was leveled and a stone retaining wall was built — the wall is about fifty feet high. This required a tremendous amount of moving soil and stone. A bulldozer could have leveled the whole place in less than a week. The WFP had at least a thousand people — both men and women — working day after day carrying thirty-pound loads of dirt and rocks as needed. Since the people needed food, for them, it was a good deal.

Yet there is a flip side to this cheap, abundant labor; namely, a person can do many things that earn him or her more than $1.33 per day. The newspaper reported that sixty percent of Kenyan women participate in petty trading. The result is a very strong, vibrant informal economy. One of Gladys' relatives works for the Kenya Revenue Authority, the tax collection arm of the government, and she lamented this strong informal economy. Why? Because the government is unable to tax the informal economy. In the formal economy, Kenya has a 16% value added tax (VAT) on everything that is purchased.

According to Wikipedia, "the **informal economy** is the part of an economy that is not taxed, monitored by any form of government or included in any gross national product (GNP), unlike the formal economy." When I go to the store and buy something it is in the formal economy because it is regulated and taxed (unless tax-exempt). If I buy a chicken from my neighbor, it is not in the formal economy because it cannot be taxed or regulated.

I suspect that here in rural Kenya, more than half the monetary exchanges are in the informal economy. For example, when we built our home here in Lumakanda as I mentioned in the introduction, almost everything came from the informal economy. The only things that were purchased in the formal economy were cement, nails, the corrugated iron roofing sheets, and materials needed for the electric and plumbing systems.

My brother-in-law, Samson Kemoli, front on left, and our nephew, Johnston Musolitsa, front on right, with the five workmen from the neighborhood who were building our house before we moved to Kenya.

So many people have self-employment because it is easy to earn more than $1.33 per day. Here are some examples:

A person will have a garden to grow greens, tomatoes, onions, or other common vegetables. Income will depend upon the scale of the garden, the fluctuating price of the vegetables, and the quantity available in the market.

Along the road throughout the region, there are women and teenage girls sitting on the roadside selling items. The smallest of these have only a few tomatoes, onions, and other vegetables. Others will have sweets, small packages of washing soap, and other small consumer items. Some women will build a small shelter for their items. The largest stalls have a great variety of produce, while others have consumer items. The profit for these enterprises comes from buying a large quantity. For instance, five pounds of tomatoes for $1.33 and then selling them in very small quantities at $.13 to $.27. They might be able to sell the $1.33 of tomatoes for $2.67 giving them the equivalent of a day's labor.

If a person can obtain a bicycle (a new one is about $100, but a used one could be bor-

Linnet Maleya and her son Moses sit in front of their house near my father-in-laws' house. She only does this in the afternoon for a few hours as she sells small quantities of consumable items — soap, salt, matches, peanuts, tomatoes, and onions. While she obviously cannot make much per day from these items, it must give her some income. She also watches children and adults go up and down the road. I admire her layout because it is always so neat, simple, and useful.

Here is a more substantial business. Gladys is thinking about buying a cabbage from Ezinah Kazira, who goes to Kipkarren River about three miles from Lumakanda on market days, Thursday and Sunday. She buys in bulk and then resells in small quantities. She sells tomatoes, onions, scallions, beans, dried corn, a small sardine-like fish from Lake Victoria, dried tilapia, mangoes, and cabbage. She is able to make a good business out of this because hardly anyone has a refrigerator so people have to come to buy perishable items every few days. Her stall is next to the butcher shop so that when people drop in to buy meat, they can come to her stall to buy vegetables and other items.

rowed or bought for much less), he can become a bicycle taxi driver called a *boda-boda* in Swahili (a shift of the English term, "board-board" as in boarding a train). They carry not only passengers but also goods. For example, when we buy cement from the shop in town, the *boda-boda* driver will get $.27 to bring each bag to our house. He will carry two at one time, walking next to his bike due to the weight. I estimate that a *boda-boda* driver can earn $4.00 per day. These *boda-boda* drivers, who are all male, are everywhere.

When we moved to Lumakanda in March 2007, there were no motorcycle taxi drivers at the junction, one and a half miles from the town center. Three *matatu* carried people to town for $.27 each trip. Then all of a sudden, there were more than fifty motorcycles. They were charging $.40 per trip. Soon they put two of the *matatu*

Motorcycle taxi drivers waiting for customers in Lumakanda

out of business with the remaining one taking people who did not want to get on a motorcycle or had too many small children or too much luggage to get on a motorcycle. Motorcycles are extremely dangerous. In less than one month, Gladys and I passed two accidents in which motorcycle drivers were killed. Since a motorcycle cost over $1,000, the young drivers are unable to purchase them so they rent them from owners. The biggest owner of motorcycles in Lumakanda is the teachers union. They rent them out to the driver for $6.67 per day, returning their investment in about six months. The drivers supply the fuel at about $1.33 per day so they need to make $8.00 to break even. I calculate that the driver may make nothing to perhaps $30.00 on a good day. If they average $15.00 per day, they would make $4,500 in a year for three hundred days work. Now the problem is that there are over one hundred motorcycles here while the clientele has not increased so it has become harder for the driver to make a decent income after expenses

Once we were waiting at Malaba, at the Uganda/Kenya border, for a minibus to take us to Lumakanda. A boy about twelve years

107

old was selling hard-boiled eggs. All he had was a plastic bucket, perhaps three dozen eggs, a saltshaker, and some hot sauce. He was selling the eggs for $.13 each. I bought two for myself and two for Gladys. He, or rather, I suspect, his mother, was buying them for $.07 apiece so he was making $.06 on each. If he sold forty eggs in a day — and I watched him sell some to other people — he would have netted $2.40.

The one that made the most from hawking, as it is called, was the pineapple man. I bought a pineapple slice in Eldoret and watched him sell three other pieces in a few minutes. The hawker had an old wheelbarrow full of ripe pineapples, a sharp knife, and some plastic "napkins." He would take a large pineapple and cut it into sixteen pieces which he sold for $.13 each. I can buy a pineapple for $1.07 so I suspect that he gets them in bulk for $.80. Therefore, he makes $1.33 per pineapple. By looking at the shavings from the pineapples in his wheelbarrow and the number of pineapples he had remaining, I would estimate that he sold twenty pineapples per day for a net income of $26.60. If he did this three hundred times per year, he would have yearly income of $7,980 — no bad at all.

I could give many other examples like this. People in Kenya are extremely energetic about finding ways to make money. Everyone

Douglas Donyi is working at the *jua kali* furniture shop in Lumakanda where we bought our living room furniture.

is doing something. There is also the *Jua Kali* sector. I have always liked the term very much because it means "hot sun" and refers to those people who work outside making things. They make amazing amounts of things. In our house, the windows, metal outside doors and windows, wooden inside doors and molding, most of the furniture, and many other items were all made by *jua kali* workers in our little town of Lumakanda.

People living in Nairobi depend much less on the informal sector, but most people in Kenya do not live in the cities. While Kenyans all look for those nice salaried jobs, in the meantime people set up their own small-scale methods of earning some cash income.

Criticisms of Micro-Credit Organizations

The first reason I am critical of NGOs promoting micro-enterprise endeavors in the region is because frequently they are only setting up another person to do the same activity that many others are already doing. While that person might make an income and return her — most micro-credit loans are to women — loan, this in only because she has cut into the income of other women doing the same thing. How many women can sit by the roadside selling exactly the same tomatoes to people passing down the road? At some point the local economy is saturated with women selling tomatoes so that none makes a decent living.

A second issue that I have with NGOs is their approach to micro-credit schemes. I question if NGOs are destroying African society under the guise of trying to save it. We live in a patriarchal world. This system is based on self-seeking personal advantage, competition, hierarchy, and the profit motive.

In African societies, the male and female worlds are quite separate. In most cases, certain activities are the responsibility of males and others of females. While people are aware of the obvious ones — women cook while men take care of the cows — others vary from society to society. The most interesting one to me is who thatches the roof. In some cultures this is women's work, in others men's work. In still others, the women cut the grass but the men thatch the roof. The important distinction here is that the roles are set in each culture. As I explained in the previous chapter, women in Africa structure their society very differently from the male

These women all trying to sell tomatoes to passengers alighting from our pickup at a major junction. Notice that they are all selling exactly the same item, although one has the tomatoes in a bucket which, if you purchase her tomatoes, she will put them in the plastic bag she is holding. You can say, "*Ongeza*," which means "add more" and the woman will add two or three more tomatoes to your purchase. The price is the equivalent to twenty-eight cents per pound.

model. Women work together rather than individually. They depend upon each other for all kinds of activities.

Many women would rather set up a cooperative business with other compatible women rather than the individualistic enterprise promoted by the micro-credit lending organizations. The micro-lenders ask the women to form small groups to be responsible that each one repays her loan, but the loans are given out to individual women. The women realize the insecurity of their world. They can build up a nice enterprise, but then they get sick, are out for a week, and the enterprise collapses. Perhaps it is one of their children, a parent, or some other relative who gets sick and needs attention.

In 2002, I met with a group of about thirty women in Bujumbura connected with the Friends church. As a group they had rented a plot in the rice growing scheme on the plains north of Bujumbura. They were so proud because they had earned sufficient income to pay for the school fees of all of their children. As I looked at them, I noticed that most of them were barefooted and only a few had cheap flip flops. I am not even sure if the micro-credit organizations would have agreed to lend funds to these women in their individualistic way. But as a group working together, they had met their goals, even if they were quite modest one of paying for their children's school fees. This group continues to rent the rice plot almost a decade later.

Another issue is that if a woman is working individually, there is little chance of her developing a business that is more than just a one-person enterprise. The type of activity, such as selling tomatoes, is a long-term dead end. A group of women can make larger, more significant businesses that can grow and expand if successful. NGOs would be much more innovative if they worked with groups of women to develop larger scale businesses. A value added project would also be more important than just re-selling already produced products. Wealth is added when something is made or produced which would then help the whole local society rather than just dividing up the small income into smaller pieces. The rice growing scheme described in the previous paragraph is an example of this as the women have cultivated and produced rice.

Consequently the NGOs which promote individualistic micro-credit enterprises are destroying this feminist system of mutual support and substituting the male oriented system common to the Western world. There is a lot of criticism that the early missionaries in Africa destroyed traditional culture by being unknowledgeable, insensitive, and disparaging of it. Many NGOs promoting micro-credit seems to be doing the same thing.

The Lesson of the Tin Can

As I mentioned in the introduction, I originally went to Africa to learn how people in another part of the world lived. One of the lessons I learned was how little people need. This situation that happened the first time I was in Africa brought home this point:

> When Randy Kehler and I were living in a Tanzanian refugee camp, we ordered a two hundred pound bag of Irish potatoes and the Catholic mission we were working for dropped them off on the road in front of our house. It was

about fifty yards to the house. I was thinking how I might get the two hundred pound bag from the road to my house, when one of my neighbors offered to carry it to our kitchen. For payment he asked for the two-pound Blue Band margarine can that he saw on our table. I told him that we were still using the margarine in the can. He said that was fine as he would wait and get the can when we finished the margarine. I thought it was a good deal so I agreed. Two other men put the two hundred pound bag on his shoulder and he quickly carried it with shuffle steps — it was clearly heavy — and dropped them on my kitchen floor. He would then come by every day or two to see if we had finished the margarine and when we had, we gave him the can.

When I told my students about this incident, their reaction surprised me. They told me I had been ripped off. For that tin can, I could have asked the man to work for me for the whole day — washing, cleaning, yard work, cooking, or anything else we wanted done. A tin can I would have thrown away at home was worth a day's labor.

A big adjustment I had to make in the first year I lived in Africa was changing my perception of what was essential to daily living. While I had considered a washing machine to be a necessity, I realized it was a luxury. Items such as the tin can which had no value to me in the United States, suddenly had value in the refugee camp. While a telephone seems a normal item in America, there I lived where there were no telephones.

How Do People Live?

Wikipedia indicates that the average Kenya has a per capital income in 2009 of $938 per year, a statistic I'll analyze below. I will show in this section and the next how people do live on such little cash income.

Most Africans have some land, a *shamba*, as it is called in Swahili. In Western Province of Kenya this can be anywhere from less than an acre to up to thirty acres. If a person has more than ten acres, he or she is considered part of the middle class. If a person has more than a hundred arable acres, he or she can be classified as part of the elite. There is less than one acre of arable land for each person in Kenya.

The house above was built by our nephew, Geoffrey Muhalia. This is called a mud and wattle house. There are poles stuck in the ground and small sticks tied across. Then it is filled with mud and plastered with mud on both the inside and outside. The roof is thatch which can be obtained at the river. He told me that he had spent about $50 on this house and, with the help of family and friends, built it in two days.

If a person has a piece of land, no matter how small, he or she has a place to build a livable house at little monetary cost. Therefore, there is no rent to pay and no land taxes so housing is essentially taken care of at no recurrent cost. In contrast, the average American is supposed to spend 30% of their income on housing, but many spend 50% or more. I was amazed to read an article in the *Washington Post* of a couple who made over $150,000 a year but were living month to month due to their mortgage.

Most of the land produces some kind of income. For instance, my father-in-law, David Okwemba, with less than an acre of land has two cows. Almost everyone with some land has at least one cow. If you look at the benefits, you can quickly see why. Each cow will give milk for nine months of the year. Most of the cows in this

This is my father-in-law's house. It is thirty feet by twenty-five feet or 750 square feet. This house is also a mud and wattle house, but it is plastered with cement on both the inside and outside making it much more permanent. There are four rooms. The thatched building in the back is the fifteen foot square kitchen. Both were built about twenty years ago. To build this house today would cost about $750.

area are half local Zebu cows and half European breed cows and give only two quarts of milk per day. Since a quart of milk is worth $.33, that cow will give milk worth $237.60 per year. Most of this milk will be consumed at home as part of the tea that is commonly drunk in Kenya. If there is extra milk, it is easily sold to neighbors whose cow is in the "dry" period before the new calf is born. The cow also gives a calf. Depending upon whether it is male or female and how long the owner wishes to keep it before it is sold, this is also nice additional income. If it is a female and kept for a year, it could be sold for $200. Thus, one cow is worth more than the basic wage of $1.33 per day. The newspapers have great success stories of people with only one acre and a few high-grade European breed cows who earn up to $10,000 per year on their sale of milk and calves. This is unique enough that it makes the newspapers.

Most people also have chickens which give eggs, chicks, and meat. A grown hen or rooster ready to be eaten is worth about $4, an egg about 8 cents. At the moment I write this, my wife, Gladys,

This is our house in Lumakanda. It has a living/dining room, four bedrooms (one which is my office) a small kitchen with a gas stove, a full bath and a half bath. It is about 1500 square feet. There is also a bigger kitchen outside where firewood and charcoal are used for cooking. Outside there are two more bedrooms , a latrine, and a chicken/sheep house plus a dog house for our two dogs. The house has electricity with a back up solar panel for lights and my computer. We have piped water, but also have two tanks which collect rainwater from the roof. If both of these water systems fail, we can go next door to a well — this has only happened once in four years. We have banana trees, an avocado tree, sugar cane and a vegetable garden full of collard greens. We have spent about $30,000 on this property including the $1,500 for the lot.

has twenty-five hens or roosters and thirty-five chicks with two hens sitting on eggs which will soon give us another ten to twenty chicks. We have more eggs than we can eat. Most everyone has chickens, although not always as many. They are frequently given as gifts when visiting someone. One hen can have three broods of ten chicks per year. With an average price of $4 per grown chick, one hen can "produce" $120 of income per year. Again, most of the offspring will be eaten by the family or given away as presents. If the hen just lays an egg for three hundred days a year, at eight cents each, it generates the equivalent of $24 per year.

Some people may also have goats, sheep, pigs, ducks, turkeys, or rabbits. Each animal has its economic benefits. AGLI has a goat program in Burundi, which gives one goat to two women who share the goat's manure to fertilize their exceedingly worn out soil. This, I estimate, triples or quadruples their yield. Then when the goat gives birth to a female, it is given to the other person so that each now has a goat. Then the second person must give her first female goat away to the next woman in line.

Some farmers might have a team of oxen. The team will plow his land, be hired out to plow fields of people without oxen, and perhaps, pull an ox-cart. Other people have donkeys. Just a few days ago, Gladys bought seven two hundred pound bags of corn and they were brought to us in two donkey carts. A town nearby has a market twice each week. On market days, I have counted over fifty donkeys that had carried goods from the interior to the market on the main road. On World Donkey Day, the newspaper reported that there are six hundred thousand donkeys in Kenya.

I have not yet begun to calculate what a small plot can produce in crops. There are two growing seasons in this region. We live at the edge of the "corn belt" of Kenya which produces thirty million two hundred pound bags of corn in a normal growing season, mostly eaten by people. On the average, each person in Kenya eats one bag of corn per year, mostly as a corn mush called *ugali*. Small scale farmers usually interplant the corn with beans and sometimes squash that is similar to summer squash in the US. An acre of corn can produce ten to thirty bags if done well. Corn is presently selling for $30 per bag so one acre can yield $300 to $900. People also have banana trees for cooking bananas called plantains. One plant can give four to six big bunches per year worth about $5 per bunch.

In addition to corn, beans, and bananas, farmers grow sweet potatoes, Irish potatoes, squash, millet, sorghum, sunflower seeds, Spanish peanuts, tomatoes, onions, greens of various kinds, and other vegetables. They also grow various fruit trees and vines including avocado, mango, orange, tangerine, guava, passion fruit, papaya, and others, the names of which I do know. When bearing fruit, a large avocado tree can produce over a thousand avocados. This is more than the farmer can eat, sell, or give away to family and neighbors, so the remainder might just be fed to the cows. Once when I was in Uganda, yellow bananas were so plentiful that people, complete strangers, just gave them to me for free.

In other words, the cash income that a person makes is used only to buy things that cannot be produced at home; sugar, tea leaves, wheat flour and its derivatives such as bread, cooking oil, kerosene for a lamp at night, medicine, washing and hand soap, and like consumer items. If there are no funds to buy certain of these items people go without them.

No one individual farmer grows all of these crops. Rather there is an extensive system of mutually cooperation. It is not barter because a farmer with a surplus of a certain crop (e.g., avocados mentioned above) will just give it away. At another time, he will be given something else. The other day, one of Gladys' aunts met us on the road and gave us a big bag of delicious, freshly harvested beans that had not yet become dry. I asked Gladys why her aunt gave them to us and Gladys responded, "That's just what we do."

Here is a comment by Laura Shipler Chico who spent twenty months as a volunteer with AGLI in Rwanda:

> The way Rwanda works is that people with more give and people with less ask. Usually what people give is short-term; it is not sustainable and cannot be counted on. But usually things come back around — they are a part of a large patchwork of giving and receiving that lasts for years and generations. The generosity can be staggering — our landlords routinely give half of what they make each month to people who need help. Our house worker, now that she has a job, has taken in a battered woman she barely knows along with her sick infant. Our neighbors used to feed our house worker and her children when she was starving and out of work and now that they do not have that burden they bring us milk each week from their cows and refuse to be paid. This is how people survive, and it is beautiful to see.

How do people obtain clothing? In order to buy a new dress for Christmas, women will go out and work at the $1.33 rate per day until they have earned enough, according to Gladys, to buy the material for around $10.67 and to have it sewn by the tailor for $6.67. Of course, women with more income will have more dresses and probably buy cloth that is more expensive and have a more elaborate design.

Ironically, I can buy a T-shirt in Kenya for much less than an American can buy the exact same T-shirt in the US. I once paid $.67 for a new T-shirt in the second hand market. It had the three times marked-down price tag with it — the lowest price was $3.99. No one in the US wanted it so it was given to Goodwill, shipped as part of a five hundred pound bundle of used clothes to Kenya where it made its way to the nearby city of Kisumu. There is no lack of good used clothes here in Africa. It no longer surprises me to find Kenyans in rural areas wearing Green Bay Packers shirts. I often tell Americans not to consider bringing dirty or worn clothes to give away when they come to the region as there is a sufficient supply of good, clean clothes available at bargain prices. The downside of this is that the influx of used American clothes has crippled the local Kenyan cotton and textile sector.

Almost every adult in Kenya has a cell phone. There are twenty million cell phone subscribers in a population of nearly forty million where children comprise half of the population. The cheapest new cell phone costs $15 and I am certain that a used cell phone can be purchased for much less. The important point is that only the dialer is charged when a call is connected. The receiver does not pay anything. A poor person can have a phone and rarely, if ever, be charged if he or she only receives calls. This has led to the custom of "flashing" (30% of the calls) where a person rings a hopefully wealthier person with one ring signifying that he or she wants to be called back so that the one flashed is the one to pay the phone charges. The receiver looks at the number and decides if he or she wants to return the call or not.

A recent innovation is sending money through the cell phone in a system called "M-Pesa," meaning "mobile money." This began in 2007 by Safaricom, the biggest cell phone provider in Kenya. It already has thirteen million subscribers in Kenya who can send or receive funds through the cell phone. The latest upgrade is to use the cell phone as a bank account with no minimum balance, no fees, with access wherever the client happens to be.

Let me now summarize. People in the countryside, still the majority of people in this region, survive because their cash income is only a small part of their total "income" which would have to include the proceeds from their plots of land and the mutual sharing. Much of the food is homegrown. Housing can be built very cheaply if necessary. Clothing from the affluent nations, whether new or secondhand, is inexpensive. Phone and basic banking can be done at low cost and can be kept to near zero if one does not have money. Mutual sharing and support is the "social security system" that works fine since everyone is willing to be a giver and a receiver as needed.

The Rich and the Poor

What I have described above is the average person with a small one to ten acre plot of land. Many Kenyans are much richer.

If a person has more than ten acres of land, he or she can easily produce much more than the basic necessities for his or her family. Many of the farmers around Lumakanda have more than ten acres. Some have tractors, pickup trucks, cars, nicely built permanent houses, electricity (solar, if necessary) and in no way can be considered poor by Kenyan standards.

Others have permanent jobs that pay better — teachers, medical professionals, government employees, shopkeepers, and business people. I would estimate that at least 20% of the Kenyan population is in this middle-class category, although probably less than 10% in the rural areas.

At the end of the nineteenth century my great-grandfather, Matias Zarembka lived and worked in the United States for eleven years before returning to his family in Poland. In those days, he could just come and go as he pleased. His intent was to make some money to support the family back home in Poland. My grandfather, Frank, came alone to the United States in early 1914, just in time to escape from being drafted into the Russian army. I think my grandfather planned on earning some money and then returning to Poland, but when the war destroyed much of Poland, he decided to have my grandmother and father come to the United States.

This is exactly what almost ten percent of the adult Kenyan population is doing, going overseas to earn income in order to send funds back home to support their families. Remittances by Kenyans living overseas are the second to largest method of foreign exchange earnings in Kenya. Those who have family working overseas have a nice additional source of income.

Then there are the truly wealthy elite who compare favorably with the wealthy in the United States. Many of these have business and political connections that have allowed them to become rich. When the British left Kenya in 1963, many of these wealthiest people bought up the large estates of departing Brits at bargain prices. Frequently these estates would be three hundred to one hundred thousand acres. Most of the remaining nine million acres, which belonged to the British settlers, changed hands from the British elite to the newly wealthy Kenyan elite. This is almost one third of the arable land in Kenya. Was this progress? I doubt it as Kenya, like the United States, has one of the greatest disparities in the world between the wealthy and the poor.

Then there are the poor. I think there are essentially three classes of poor people.

Only 20% of Kenya is arable land. Most of the north and northeastern sections of the country are grassland unsuitable for farming. The people living in these areas are pastoralists. They are not necessarily poor. That Masai so loved by the American media with one hundred head of cattle cannot be considered poor. At $250 each, those cows are worth $25,000 and multiply at a much faster rate than any bank account. When the rains fail, as they did in 2008 and 2009 in some parts of Kenya, many of the cows, goats, sheep, and camels die. My own impression is that Kenya is over-stocked with grazing animals. Everything is fine when the rains are good, but when they fail, there is not sufficient grass and water for all the animals and some die. These are the people who needed food aid during the 2009 drought.

Alcoholism is the second main cause of poverty. There is a lot of very cheap booze called *chang'aa*. Made from molasses, it is amazingly potent. The street children in town are frequently the offspring of alcoholic parents — one or both of them — who cannot feed or cloth their children and other relatives dispossess these children because of the parents' alcoholism.

The last category is the landless. If you read my description of how people survive, you will notice that much of this depends on having a piece of land to build a house and grow some or a lot of food for personal consumption. It is very difficult for a person to live on a $1.33 per day if he or she has no land to grow food.

Many landless are given a small piece of land where they can build a house by some kindhearted soul or relative. At other times the "squatters," as they are called here in Kenya, just use a vacant plot without permission. Their existence is precarious as they cannot build anything but the simplest home since it might not be a permanent home. Those who do own land dislike them and consider them the thieves and thugs of the area. Some of these are the ones who end up in the enormous slums in Nairobi and other major Kenyan towns. In the rural areas nearby, squatters are estimated to be 5% of the population.

How Wealthy are Kenyans?

The Sunday before I wrote this was the day for thanksgiving at Lumakanda Friends Church. The harvest was almost complete and members of the church were bringing in an offering of corn. More than ten two hundred pound bags of corn filled the front of the church. People brought in between an eighth of a bag to a full bag each. Gladys' comment was that this was very little. In the old days, a person could bring in as much as ten bags of his or her hundred-bag harvest. This led me to the question, "How wealthy are Kenyans?"

As I have said, Wikipedia indicates that the Kenyan per capita income in 2009 was $938. Economists have developed the concept of purchasing power parity (PPP) which adjusts the per capita income for the fact that so many things are cheaper in Kenya than the United States. For instance, five pounds of tomatoes in the United States would cost more like $10 than the $1.40 it costs in Kenya. But then again electronic devices are much cheaper in the United States. When these differences are all added and subtracted, the PPP per capita income for Kenya is stated as $1,732. As I noted above I think that the informal economy is at least as large as the formal one. This would double real income to $3,464.

Yet there is even another economy, the non-monetary economy. Whenever a person goes for a visit, he or she will take something as a gift Most people from Gladys' family bring something when they come to visit us. Once we had so many "gifts" of beans that we were hard pressed, even with many guests, to eat them all. Since we do not have a farm, when we visit someone, Gladys usually buys some sugar, one of the few mass consumption items that is in the formal economy, as her gift. Frequently, not including the obligatory meal, we are given something back, a hen, for example.

Then there is the subsistence economy I described above. Economists pooh-pooh this economy, but for the well-designed and functioning homestead, the local plot can take care of most of the food budget including eggs and milk for a family. How much does this add to the per capita income? A lot. If locally produced food adds $5 per day per person to income, our total per capita income is now $5,289 plus gifts. The per capita income and the purchasing power parity in the United States, by definition, are the same — $47,701. While this is nine times more than Kenya, it is a big difference from the original $938.

Then we can look at what the Kenyans do not have to spend that Americans do. For me, of course, the most important is that Kenyans do not have to support the bloated US military budget. Here in Lumakanda, we do not have to worry about heating, cooling, or insulation. In Kenya, 87% of the people own their houses, even if somewhat simple, and most of the renters are people living in the cities. People, who do own their own house, do not have a mortgage since people build houses slowly as they get the funds to complete them. Health care here is much cheaper than the US — I estimate 10% or less of the cost for routine care in America. When a young relative of Gladys' was slashed by a machete and needed eight stitches at Lumakanda Hospital, the charge was $5. The bicycle taxi, motorcycle taxi, mini-bus, and bus system of transportation are amazingly efficient, if not always pleasant, and one can get around anywhere quite cheaply. For us the trip of about thirty miles to Eldoret costs a little over a dollar each way. A person can easily get around without a car.

In Kenya, most people's net worth is small but on the positive side because they have no access to loans which would put them into debt. While this is an old statistic before the recent recession, I once read that the net worth of over half of adult Americans is less than zero. If they sold everything to pay off all their debts, they would still be in debt. Over 60% of Americans die with nothing to leave to their children as much of what they had has been spent for medical treatment during their last year of life. Only 2% of Americans die with more than $1,000,000. How much does the average American pay in interest? As became clear in the recent financial meltdown, they pay too much. When will Americans realize that the "American dream" is a mirage to keep them working at "lives of quiet desperation" as Thoreau once said? Is the average Kenyan really that much worse off than the average American?

If this is all true, why do not Kenyans look more prosperous? The first answer is that Kenyans do not live in the consumer society. In fact, they live in an anti-consumer society. Africans are very generous to help people who fall into difficulties.

When someone is sick, visitors not only bring gifts as outlined above but also may donate towards the recovery. Our friend who lives nearby, Elizabeth Imbale, had kidney failure while attending the Friends United Meeting Triennial in Des Moines in 2005. She could not raise sufficient funds in America for a kidney transplant as it was too expensive. Gladys and I were asked to contribute and we did. Eventually she came back to Kenya on dialysis where she did more fundraising until enough funds were received for her to have a kidney transplant in India. She is now doing well.

There is another side to this custom of helping people out. Unlike the US where people look really well off, but are almost in bankruptcy, as they cannot pay off their loans, in Kenya people want to look poorer than they are so that other people do not expect too much from them. In other words, people hide their wealth. Looks, both of prosperity and poverty, can be so deceiving.

My best example comes from when I lived in Tanzania. I was in a small market town and there was an elderly man. This man had on old shoes, pants, and shirt, a blanket over his shoulder and carried a long stick which was much more common in the old days. While he looked healthy enough, he was thin. I was thinking I should buy him lunch at the local restaurant. He was there to buy a cow and calmly took a wad of bills out of his pocket to purchase the cow he was negotiating for — he paid the equivalent of $250 in cash. He was not poor at all.

Another example occurred one time while I was at my father-in-laws. One of my nieces, Jacquelyn, who was then in high school, wanted $1.33 to go to a book fair the next day with her friends. There was a $1.33 admission fee usable towards the purchase of a book. The group of them would then use their $1.33 each admission fee to buy a biology book that they thought they needed. I considered this a good idea. I could have easily produced the $1.33, but I had learned that I needed to keep my money in my pocket. Besides her grandfather, three of her aunts were at the table. No one gave her any money at that time. I do not know what happened but the next day I met her going to the book fair with her friends. Where did she get the $1.33? One of her aunts? Her grandfather? I suspect that she had the money all along. However, if she could have gotten that $1.33 out of one of us, then she would still have her original $1.33.

In Kenya, the elite decision-makers live in the cities and have arranged things so that food consumed in the cities is cheap. One of the things they fear is urban food riots. Furthermore, the rural areas are taxed to pay for improvements in the city centers. If rural farmers were paid appropriately for the food they grow and export to the cities, they would be much better off. Fewer of them would then have to move to the city slums to try to eke out a living by day labor. I hope that the price of food does increase relative to everything else, as this will do more for the majority of rural Kenyans than the "industrialization" which has been pushed by economists since the time of independence in Kenya in 1963.

In summary, looks can be very deceiving. When Americans come to Kenya, they may perceive themselves as much wealthier than the Kenyans with whom they are interacting. But are they? If so, in what way? Greater access to credit? Willingness to display their wealth rather than hide it? Guilt at the overabundance of possessions that they have?

I have many friends in America who in the 1960's and 1970's were back-to-landers because they rejected the everyone-for himself or herself competition of the American rat race. They tried and in many cases have succeeded in developing communities which mirror more the way of life here in Africa than normal American middle-class, consumer society.

Even though economics have been trying for decades, material wealth is an abstraction so that it is difficult to compare disparate parts of the world. While it is clear that the average Kenyan does not have the material goods that the average American has, it is also clear that the average Kenyan is wealthier than the cursorily comparisons made by foreigners.

As I see it, the goal of the global community is to ensure that everyone in the world has the basics of food, shelter, medical care, and education and then any excess can be used to enhance people's lives. Unfortunately, to date, the world has failed in that distribution to cover basic necessities so that many have too little and others more than enough.

Chapter 7
The Mirage of Tribe in Africa

Definition

While the word "tribe" is used in East Africa rather than "ethnicity," the word "tribe" to most Westerners has negative, "primitive" connotations. Why are Native Americans considered tribes, but Italians or Poles are not considered a tribe? What is the difference between the Scottish "clans" and tribes? Since language is often what separates one tribe from another, why are not the Welsh considered a tribe as they have their own language? When did the Angles, Saxon and Norman tribes that conquered England stop becoming "tribes" and become English?

The So-Called Exploration of Africa

For my undergraduate college thesis, I wrote on the divergent traveling techniques of two "explorers" of East and Central Africa — Joseph Thompson and Henry Morton Stanley. While these men are credited with "discovering" parts of Africa, they did not discover anything that was not already known by the local Africans. But in the nineteenth century, the knowledge and experience Africans possessed did not count in history books written by Western authors. These two men explored Africa in completely different styles.

Joseph Thompson was a Scottish geologist who led expeditions in East Africa in the 1880s. He was a scientist who observed the plants, animals, geology, and natural surroundings. He was the first European to pass through Masailand in Kenya; the Masai were considered warlike and vicious. Thompson would explore with a small band of porters who carried the luggage needed for the trip. Thompson had guns only to kill wildlife for either protection or food. He was noted to walk alone ahead of his porters investigating the fauna. He recorded his observations as a scientist should. He "discovered" Thompson's Falls in Nyaharuru in the Rift Valley, Kenya. Thompson's gazelle is also named after him. Thompson prided himself on never having a confrontation with his porters or the people he met. He claims he never had to kill an African nor lose any of his porters to violence. His motto was *He who goes gently, goes safely; he who goes safely, goes far.* He died of pneumonia when he was only thirty-seven.

The same cannot be said for Henry Morton Stanley. Stanley, was born in Wales, and immigrated to the United States in time to fight on both the Confederate and Union sides during the Civil War. He began writing and was hired by the *New York Herald* to find David Livingston who had been missing in Africa for the previous few years. He found Livingston in 1872. Two years later, the *Herald* assigned him to travel the length of the Congo River from Lake Tanganyika to the mouth. Out of the three hundred fifty-six men who started out with him on this expedition down the Congo, only one hundred and fourteen survived. Later he worked to secure much of the Belgium Congo for King Leopold II of Belgium. His expeditions were military campaigns of looting, destruction, and death. He is quoted as saying, *The savage only respects force, power, boldness, and decision.* The barbarity of his last African expedition in 1886 (to "save" Emin Pasha) tarnished Stanley's reputation. Stanley's armed forces looted and destroyed villages, killed any Africans whom he did not think were cooperating with him, and left a trail of destroyed societies as he passed through their territory.

Through all this destruction, or rather because of all this destruction, Stanley became quite famous and his books were very popular. He later entered parliament in Britain and was knighted as Sir Henry Morton Stanley.

On his last expedition, one of Stanley's British companions, unbeknown to Stanley, bought an eleven-year old girl and offered her to cannibals to document and sketch how she was cooked and eaten. Those places named after him — Stanleyville, Stanley Fall — had their names changed to African ones after Congolese independence. Interestingly enough, recently, there has been a campaign to sanitize his name. The claim is that he overemphasized his cruelty to his porters to pander to the prejudices of his American and British audiences. If this is correct, fulfilling racial stereotypes were seen as more important for these audiences than the facts.

Unfortunately, most of the "explorers" were much more like Stanley than Thompson. To be an African "discovered" by an explorer was frequently not a pleasant event for those who were "discovered." In 1884, the Scramble for Africa began and exploration took on an imperial aspect. The purpose became not to find out about formerly unknown parts of the world, but by hook or crook, to put them under the colonial rule of one of the scrambling powers. Stanley helped King Leopold to secure the Congo and Thompson failed to secure Kitanga in now the Democratic Republic of the Congo for the British.

For the Africans, this period began great upheavals that are still being felt today.

The Commonality of Genocide

In 1995, my daughter, Joy, and I traveled from Dar es Salaam, Tanzania, through Lusaka, Zambia to Harare, Zimbabwe. We took the Tazara Railroad from Dar es Salaam. The train passed through one hundred miles of the wilderness of the Selous Game Reserve. In 1905, this "wild" area was full of prosperous villages. From 1905 to 1907, the villagers revolted against the German rule of then German East Africa in the Maji-Maji Rebellion. The Germans responded with a brutal genocide. They attacked the villages, killing people and livestock and destroying homes and fields. Their method of obtaining subjection of the people was induced "famine." Those people who had been living in the Selous Game Reserve either perished or moved elsewhere. The area became depopulated and the tsetse fly moved into the newly growing bush. Tsetse flies bring sleeping sickness to both people and cows — even today, there are large sections in Africa that are uninhabited because of the tsetse fly. As the tsetse fly moved in, people were unable to re-establish their villages, farms, and communities. The bush thrived, the wild animals returned and multiplied, and Selous Game Reserve is one of the biggest reserves in Tanzania, larger than the better-known Serengeti Plains.

This is only one of the many genocides in Africa during this time. A prior one had occurred in German Southwest Africa, now Namibia. The Herero and Nama tribes revolted in 1904 in what is now considered the first genocide of the twentieth century. These groups revolted after German settlers had taken a good percentage of their land and were forcing many to work as slaves. The commanding officer, General Lothar von Trotha wrote, "I believe that the [Herero] nation as such should be annihilated, or, if this was not

127

possible by tactical measures, have to be expelled from the country." A guide for the Germans, Jan Cloete, testified as follows.

> I was present when the Herero were defeated in a battle near Waterberg. After the battle all men, women, and children who fell into German hands, wounded or otherwise, were mercilessly put to death. Then the Germans set off in pursuit of the rest, and all those found by the wayside and in the sandveld were shot down and bayoneted to death. The mass of the Herero men were unarmed and thus unable to offer resistance. They were just trying to get away with their cattle.

Survivors were pushed into the desert where the Germans poisoned the wells. Subsequently the remaining Herero and Nama, who were mainly women and children and a few old men, were put into concentration camps under horrible conditions where 50% to 80% were estimated to have died. Since most of the male Herero had died, many Herero women were forced into prostitution with the German soldiers and many German-Herero children were born.

Was the Herero genocide a precursor to the Holocaust? There are many similarities including race ideology, the development of concentration camps, and working people to death. As in the Nazi concentration camps, the Germans in Southwest Africa gave each captive a number and carefully recorded the deaths. More directly, the German geneticist, Eugene Fischer, performed medical experiments on the Herero and mixed-race people. He later returned to Berlin to teach. One of his students, Josef Mengele, was noted for his bizarre experiments at Auschwitz during the Holocaust.

General H. H. Kitchener was dispatched to the Sudan with an Anglo-Egyptian army in 1888 to conquer the independent Madhi state which had arisen in 1881 under the leadership of el-Madhi, an Islamic spiritual and military leader of great ability. Kitchener accomplished this subjugation in 1896. He had the body of el-Madhi (who had died in 1885) dug up, his head cut off, his body thrown in the Nile River, and his head fashioned into an inkpot for Kitchener's writing table.

When I think of that story and the story above about paying cannibals to roast a girl, I think, "Who is the savage?" Western culture tends to dismiss Africans, both historically and contemporaneously, as "savages." To me this is projection and individuals are projecting their own shortcomings or evil onto the other.

I learned more about this concept from Laura Shipler Chico. Laura volunteered for AGLI in Rwanda for twenty months and wrote a number of excellent reports on the healing from the genocide that is occurring there. In a report on Nyamata, one of the areas with the highest Tutsi death rate during the genocide, she wrote:

> Some see genocide as an extreme result of psychological projection: when one group projects all that is hated about itself onto another group, the target group comes to represent all that is bad and shameful and evil about ourselves. Then it becomes not only possible but necessary to exterminate.

I have found this to be extremely thought provoking and wonder if this is not what the United States is doing with "radical Islamic fundamentalists." i.e., when we are talking about them we are really talking about ourselves. When I asked her to elaborate, she replied:

> To put it simply, someone once told me that every time I criticize someone, I should just add three little words to the end of my sentence: "just like me." It is eerie how consistently it works! This is psychodynamic theory — beginning with Sigmund Freud, continuing with Anna Freud (his daughter) and others. The theory talks about the defense mechanisms the mind or psyche sets up to protect the ego — or sense of self. Among these defense mechanisms are things we have all heard of — denial, acting out, intellectualization, etc. One of the most basic ones is "projection" — projecting that which we do not like about ourselves onto someone else or a group of people, in order to preserve our own positive self-image. Absolutely, when folks in the US talk about radical Islamic fundamentalists, we are really talking about ourselves — I absolutely agree that this is part of the complex swirl of why it has been possible to sucker the American public into this war between civilizations. When we listen to how the government characterizes the "enemy" and we add the three little words, "just like us" to the end, frighteningly, it almost always works.

Genocide, called "extermination" in the late nineteenth century, was not just a racial construct. The Boers, now called Afrikaners, were the descendants of Dutch settlers who moved to South

Africa beginning in the 1600's. Baron H. H. Kitchener after his "success" in the Sudan, was appointed to conduct the Boer War in South Africa from 1899 to 1902. He implemented "scorched earth" policies against Boers in South Africa. He cleaned the countryside of all animals, houses, and crops, forced the women, children, and old men into concentration camps and then hunted down the starved men who were resisting. He also built concentration camps for black South Africans. There was insufficient food and almost no medical treatment and the people died in droves — over 26,000 Boers and perhaps 20,000 black South Africans.

The Boer War with its cruelty and bloodshed traumatized this Afrikaner population. They chafed during continued British rule until 1948 when they won the whites-only election because their numbers in South Africa were increasing much faster than the whites of British origin. They immediately began introducing apartheid, the segregation of races — White, African, Colored, and Indian — into their separate communities. As I indicated in Chapter 1, I submit that this extreme policy was a result of the trauma that they had experienced fifty years earlier.

A number of additional points need to be made.

Baron Kitchener was rewarded for his work in the Boer War by becoming Lord Kitchener.

The British opposition in Parliament criticized the brutality of the concentration camps. This was one of the first human rights campaigns and the first small step towards the dismantling of the British Empire that had been built on so much violence.

The only other country in the world that was implementing concentration camps at the turn of the twentieth century was the United States during its conquest of the Philippines. Americans should be under no illusions — Americans behaved as badly as the British and other colonialists of the era using the same rationalizations for destruction of the Filipino people.

The French did similar campaigns in West Africa and the Belgians were noted for their extreme brutality in the Congo.

These days we are used to annual increases in population. From the beginning of the Scramble for Africa in the mid 1880's until the end of the pacification of the various rebellions by 1910, the population in the area of the Congo, Uganda, Rwanda, Tanzania, Rwanda, and Burundi is estimated to have been cut in half. When King Leopold took over the Congo in 1886, there were an estimated ten million people but by the time his personal fiefdom was taken from him in 1908, the population had declined to an estimated five million.

In Kenya, there was considerable resistance to British rule. The British responded to any attempts to oppose them with extreme violence. They not only killed the African men with their better rifles and maxim machine guns, but they also killed the elderly, women, and children, destroyed crops, killed livestock and burned homes and villages. The British used the same "a scorched earth" policy that they used in South Africa. This was standard operating procedure for the British conquerors. Groups such as the Nandi in the Rift Valley, near where I live, resisted for years and were almost annihilated. They comprise a relatively low percentage of the population in Kenya now due to the small numbers that survived the British military onslaught.

The continuous wars for over four hundred years of African history due to the slave trade are frequently mentioned as a major destabilizing factor in African history. The destructiveness of the conquest of Africa by the new self-appointed rulers as they "pacified" the areas under their control is often overlooked. As was learned from the plagues in Europe, when large numbers of people in a society die, there are profound negative consequences to the society. When war includes the destruction of homes, villages, and community, when people are dying of war-induced starvation and disruption increases the number of deaths due to exposure and disease, a society becomes traumatized and loses its cohesiveness. There is a "glue" that holds society together, and when too many people die in a relatively short period of time that society's "glue" disintegrates and the culture collapses. This is one of the reasons that at the beginning of the twentieth century Christianity and Islam were able to make such major inroads into Africa. They were stepping into a vacuum.

Were these various genocides just random acts? Sven Lindqvist's *'Exterminate All the Brutes': One Man's Odyssey into the Heart of Darkness and the Origins of European Genocide* examines this. Lindqvist, a Swede, explores the connection between these genocides in Africa and the Holocaust in Europe.

In addition to the historical examples, Lindqvist gives the intellectual history that made genocide "respectable." Charles Darwin's *Descent of Man* and the concept of the survival of the fittest made genocide seem inevitable. The white rulers of all the European countries believed in a hierarchy of race. The superior race — the white race — would overwhelm the inferior races. The European conquest of the United States and Canada was a prime example of this. The extermination of the Tasmanians in Australia, it was argued, might be regrettable, but was seen as an evolutionary necessity. Darwin himself was in Argentina and saw the European settlers go out into the pampas and murder any Native American that was found so that the pampas could be opened up for European settlement. According to late nineteenth century race theory, the white race was destined to expand throughout the world, even, for example, obliterating the Chinese "race." The point was that the superior race needed land in order to expand and would seize this from the inferior races. Consequently, since it was a natural phenomenon, genocides were considered normal

After Germany's defeat in World War I, it lost its overseas colonies, but Germany retained its racial theories. Germany's expansion would not be overseas, but in Europe itself. Nazis thought that Slavs like Poles and Ukrainians would be useful as laborers, but would eventually die out to the superior Germans. It was believed that Gypsies and Jews were an inferior people because they did not have any territory of their own which they controlled and this was seen as a clear sign of an inferior race. So like the Heroro in German Southwest Africa, like the Native Americans in Argentina and the United States, the Germans surmised that the Jewish and Gypsy population would be exterminated. In time, the other ethnic groups in Central Europe would also decline as the master German race dominated from the Atlantic Ocean to the Ural Mountains.

In Sven Lindqvist's opinion, to see the World War II Holocaust as an isolated, unique event is to ignore and re-write European history. While the defeat of Germany in World War II discredited this hierarchical racial theory, if you listen closely you can still hear echoes in today's discourse, particularly where Africa is concerned.

The Tribalization of Kenya

In 1970, I was in the Mua Hills, part of Machakos District in eastern Kenya. One day I saw a group of Masai, whose home district had to be more than twenty-five miles away, near our home in the Mua Hills. I asked why the Masai were there and was told that the house they were visiting was the original home of the Masai wife who, as a young woman, was married to a Masai man. The Masai are nomadic cattle ranchers and have large herds of cows to pay as bride price for an appropriate wife.

When the Kamba young woman becomes the bride of a Masai, she changes everything. She is going from a sedentary group that survives by growing crops to a nomadic group well know for living on the milk and blood of cattle. She needs to learn a completely different language since the Masai language is not a Bantu language like that of the Kamba. It will be difficult for her to learn this new language, but she is young and by necessity must do so. She will wear new clothes, as she will change from the usual Western style dress to one with colorful wrap around cloths and many brightly colored beads. The tourist will love to take a picture of her — that traditional Masai. Nevertheless, she is a Kamba.

What does "tribe" mean if it can be changed? It cannot be due to heredity if it can be changed. Then it must be cultural. If so, anyone can become a Masai if they want. One of the major "Masai" politicians is in fact of Kikuyu origins.

A person must marry outside his or her extended family. In most tribes, a groom is sometimes encouraged to marry someone outside his group. The woman always moves to the husband's area and adopts his tribe, learns his language and customs, and the children are members of the father's tribe. This has been going on for generations, even long before the British conquered the country. So all Kenyans are a mixture of the various tribal groups in Kenya.

One of our friends is a Kikuyu married to a Luhya and lives in Kipkarren River. She is now retired after being an education officer in Luhya parts of Kenya. She speaks the Luhya language well. She also has an adopted daughter from Rwanda. During the 2008 post-election violence, her Kikuyu neighbor's house was burned down. She did not leave her house once during the two months of violence because she was afraid that she was going to be attacked as a Kikuyu even though she had assimilated into the Luhya group.

So how did the ethnic tribal basis of Kenya and other countries become so important? We need first to return to the British whose culture is replete with kings, queens, lords, ladies, dukes, duchesses, barons, knights, and on and on. For an American like me, I find this elaborate hierarchical system tedious and uninteresting, but this is how the British view the world. It is not only royalty, but also class structure and racial structure. The entire world is a gigantic hierarchical structure with everyone in his or her secure place knowing those whom they must obey and those who must obey them.

When the sun never set on the British Empire, the British imperialists found many societies easily fit into this model. In West Africa, in particular, they found various royal rulers and decided that the easiest and cheapest method of ruling was through "indirect rule." The existing traditional structures would remain in place, but the "ruler" would be subject to the British and the British would make the "rules" they had to enforce. Whatever checks and balances traditional rulers had were now superseded by the authority of the British. One aspect of this ruling hierarchy, again brought from European ideas of kingdom and state, is that kingdoms and principalities were land based with specific boundaries. If there were people outside these boundaries, they were incorporated into existing boundaries or in a few cases, new entities were created.

When the British subdued Kenya, there was only one "tribe" based on the preferred British model with a chief. This was the Wanga tribe in western Kenya whose chief was Mumia. The Wanga were one of the fourteen Luhya "sub-tribes" that spoke a Bantu language. The British were so delighted that they decided that the Wanga should rule all the other Luhya speaking tribes. The other sub-tribes, not surprisingly, did not see it this way, and in time the British were forced to abandon Chief Mumia's claim to most of what is now Western Province.

The British colonialists decided that there was something "unnatural" about this lack of chiefs so they started the process of appointing their own sub-chiefs, chiefs, and paramount chiefs. However, chiefs need to have territory so the British divided up the land so that each tribe had its set area with boundaries. Take the area between the Kamba and Masai near where I lived. Traditionally there were no set boundaries. Groups settled and migrated as they needed. Pastoral groups, in particular, were prone to great movements due to drought or disease. Agricultural groups would move to new areas when their old lands became infertile or unproductive due to drought. The British could not understand this disorder so they drew a line in the sand, I think literally, and said that those on one side were Kamba and those on the other were Masai. People either moved to their side of the line or became part of the group on the side where they were living.

This history has relevancy today. When I was visiting the area of the Kamba in 1999, five Kamba farmers living on the Kamba side of that line were killed by Masai who claimed that the land these farmers were cultivating were Masai lands. Realistically, as in most parts of the world, any number of groups can claim prior rights to any particular piece of land. The connection between a particular group and that a certain land belongs to them became codified as a part of indirect rule. Then, of course, the British used these divisions which they themselves had promoted and given significance in the usual colonial method of "divide and rule."

This identification of an area of land for a specific group had another implication when one remembers that over half of the then sparse population had died in the previous two or three decades. There were large areas of "vacant" land. The British colonial government grabbed these lands and assigned them as enormous estates to British settlers. If there were pockets of Africans on these lands, they were removed and forced to return to their "homeland," allocated to them in the division of the country. Pastoral groups such as the Masai and Kalinjin, who resisted the conquest of their territory and consequently were the ones with the largest decrease in population, were also easiest to move to more marginal areas in the northern and southern parts of the Rift Valley. The central, fertile, well-watered lands were allocated to the British settlers.

Kenya is a large country, but only 20% is arable enough for growing crops. This arable area is less than thirty million acres. Ten million of these acres, over one third of the arable land, were reserved for the few tens of thousand settlers, mostly British. Some had estates of over one hundred thousand acres each, equivalent to a square area twelve and a half miles on each side.

When independence came to Kenya in 1963, the Masai and Kalenjin groups thought that their lost territory would be returned to them. The elders in these groups could well remember being displaced in their youth. The British and new Kenyan government developed a million acre scheme where the British bought out their settlers, the land was divided into plots of twenty to thirty acres, and sold at a subsidized price to African farmers. This scheme worked quite well for farming groups like the Kikuyu, Luhya, or Kisii, but the pastoral groups felt that the land that had been stolen from them by the British should have been returned to them by the Kenyan government. This is one of the main causes of the tension and conflict in the Rift Valley of Kenya today.

Almost nine million arable acres still remained mostly in the hands of large-scale farmers. The British settlers frequently sold out to the new African elite, the loyalists that the British had nurtured and bequeathed the new Kenyan government. Lord Delemare, a British aristocrat, who controlled almost one hundred thousand acres near Naivasha, gave half of this estate to the new Kenyan President, Jomo Kenyatta, as a private gift with the quid pro quo that the Delemare family could keep the remaining half. They are still in Kenya. Some of these estates were bought up by land companies which divided up the farms into smaller lots and sold them to willing buyers. Unfortunately, the people with sufficient funds to buy into these estates were mostly Kikuyu. The Nandi, Masai, and other groups again felt that they were being frozen out in their home area.

People with a racist mentality felt that changing ownership of large estates from white British control to black Kenyan control was progress. They failed to realize that this was just perpetuating the original injustice, that the society was still divided between the many poor and the few very wealthy and that this inequality would lead to an unstable society. It is now harder to dislodge the large landowners because they are Kenyans.

While I am describing Kenya here, this same issue is occurring in other parts of Africa — Zimbabwe, South Africa, Namibia, Angola, even Zambia and Mozambique. European property owners were given extensive estates. Changing the ownership from Europeans to the new African elite did not solve the land issues in these countries, but is the tender for future violence.

A Non-tribal Country is Possible in Africa

I was in Tanganyika in 1964 when it united with Zanzibar and became the new country of Tanzania. Julius Nyerere was president of Tanzania during this time. Tanganyika had originally been part of German East Africa along with Rwanda and Burundi. At the end of World War I, Tanganyika was given to the British as a League of Nations trust territory (later a United Nations trust territory). Partly because of this status and partly because Tanganyika had no major resources that could be exploited, Britain preferred to give preference to its full colonies of Kenya and Uganda. Consequently, at independence in 1961, Tanganyika lagged behind Kenya and Uganda in economic development.

There are one hundred and twenty ethnic groups or tribes in Tanzania. The largest one, the Sukuma, who comprise 16% of the population, do not dominate the country. They live south of Lake Victoria in an area that is not particularly fertile for agriculture and with great variations in yearly rainfall. They did not pursue business or education. President Nyerere himself was from the Zanaki group of about one hundred thousand people, far too small to dominate the country.

President Nyerere made a great effort to promote Swahili as the national language. This was not very easy because textbooks were not written in Swahili and teachers were not trained in Swahili. In Kenya and Uganda, schooling started in the vernacular and then into English so that by secondary school all subjects, except foreign languages, were taught in English. But because of this emphasis on Swahili in Tanzania, almost everyone in the country speaks Swahili, meaning that everyone can communicate with everyone else. This is one of the main reasons that Tanzania never has had any ethnic strife as is so common in the surrounding countries. The other significant reason that Tanzania has not had violent conflict is that President Nyerere retired after twenty-five years as President without ripping off the country and government as politicians were doing elsewhere.

While Nyerere started out with an economically disastrous policy of "African socialism," which seemed to me to be really just state capitalism, by the 1980's this was dropped and Tanzania started the long climb up from being one of the poorest countries in the world until now it has almost caught up with Kenya, the wealthiest country in the region. In other words, Tanzania adopted policies that united people rather than dividing them along ethnic lines. I am certain that a multi-ethnic society in Africa can be developed into a viable, peaceful country. When tribalism or ethnicity is cited as a cause of conflict, it is an excuse for the real issue that a small self-selected group wants to seize control of the reigns of government for their own benefit.

Ethnicity and Statehood

Before World War I, nations were not considered to be connected with ethnicity. Empires, from the Roman Empire to the

Russian Empire to the British Empire to the United States, were not thought of as ethnically homogenous societies. One particular ethnic group usually controlled the handles of power, but they did this in the context of a multicultural nation state or empire. Then Woodrow Wilson, as president of the United States, promoted the concept of self-determination of nations or, more bluntly, that the state be based on ethnicity. He proposed that Europe would be much less prone to violence if each ethnic group were given their own country, even if it were small. Poland, which had ceased to exist as a country for one hundred and twenty-three years, reappeared. The Austro-Hungarian Empire was broken up into Austria, Hungry, Czechoslovakia, and boundaries of other nations were adjusted so that they were contained in their "homeland."

He perhaps did not realize what a can of worms he was opening up. With the United States on the winning side of World War I, he was able to implement this idea during the peace treaty after the war. The number of nations in the world began a long increase until now there are two hundred and three, some no larger than a postage stamp. How many civil wars and rebel movements, such at the Kurds in Iraq, Iran, and Turkey, have been based on the attempt to form ethnic states? Adolph Hitler used this concept as a reason for bringing all ethnic German-speaking people into the Third Reich. The other powers of the world at that time, having accepted the concept of the ethnic state, had no philosophic rationale to oppose the incorporation of all Germans into the German state.

While the late nineteenth and early twentieth century empires were conglomerates of diverse people sometimes in far-flung parts of the world, the empire builders ruled by developing myriads of mini-sub-states. The well-known adage of "divide and rule" was based on the premise of dividing any conquered people into small sub-groups that would have no possibility of confronting the Empire. This was the beginning of the ethnic state in modern times.

Before the introduction of the mini-sub-state, neighboring people were usually quite mixed. People seem to forget that before World War II, much of Europe was filled with various different peoples with no clear boundaries between ethnic groups. With the rise of ethnic countries after World War I and then the shock of World War II, there was a massive displacement of people returning to their ethnic countries. The whole country of Poland, for example, moved substantially west and Poles who were not within the boundaries of the new Poland were forced to move there. Germans who lived in the area now considered part of Poland had to move farther west into Germany. In some cases, the returning people had been out of their "homeland" for generations and did not even know their homeland's language. Europe is now uniting again and the Europeans are again becoming more ethnically mixed as they had been a century before. The European Union is a movement away from the ethnic country towards a multi-ethnic super state.

In North America, there are three countries. In Africa there are fifty-five. Clearly, it is easier to rule a small country with a dense population or a large country without a dense population. Smallness means domination by the stronger. The colonial powers clearly made their colonies in Africa small in size or population so that they would be easy to control. Even the most prosperous or the most populous countries in Africa are still at a major disadvantage when competing with the United States, the European Union, China, or India.

Most of the most populous countries of the world — the United States, China, India, Russia, Brazil, Indonesia, the Philippines, and Nigeria — are multi-ethnic. On the whole, they have worked out systems for dealing with the diversity within their borders that keep each of these large countries from breaking into myriads of ethnic enclaves.

In Africa, this tension between nation state and ethnic state has never been resolved. There are four states in Africa based on ethnicity — Rwanda, Burundi, Lesotho, and Swaziland — all extremely small countries. The divisions in Rwanda and Burundi are not really ethnic since everyone speaks the same common language, live intermingled, and frequently intermarry. The languages of the people of Rwanda and Burundi are very similar. In addition, there are other groups close by that also speak a similar language. These are the Buha, Bushubi, Buhangaza and other groups in northwestern Tanzania, the area around Goma and Rutshuru in North Kivu, Kisoro in Uganda (that was once part of Rwanda) plus Kiyarwandan (the language of Rwanda) groups that have migrated to Malenge in South Kivu, Masisi in North Kivu, and elsewhere. Why do not all these groups come together and form a single ethnic country of over thirty million people? There is a conspiracy theory afloat in the region that this is exactly what the Tutsi rulers of Rwanda are attempting to do.

On the other hand, the other countries in sub-Saharan Africa are clearly multi-ethnic, but in many cases have not resolved the tension between ethnicity and nationhood. As mentioned above, one country that has successfully replaced ethnicity with nationhood is Tanzania where no one group dominates and Swahili has become the lingua franca of the nation.

Kenya, an extremely diverse country, is an example of a country still engulfed in the ethnicity/nationhood dilemma. Even leaving out the various Europeans and people from the Indian subcontinent, there are still five major language groups in the country. Each of these language groups is farther apart than English is from Hindi both of which are Indo-European languages. All Indo-European languages, for example, have the division between masculine, feminine, and usually neuter (he, she, and it). Swahili is not constructed this way. There are seven classes of nouns with the first class being people, the second class being animals, and the third to six classes being things, and the last class concepts. Consequently, the word "*anakwenda sokoni*" can be translated either as "he is going to the market" or "she is going to the market." Unfortunately, this emphasis on uniting everyone as people regardless of gender does not seem to have translated into more egalitarian society with regard to gender.

I speak Swahili decently well. It is a Bantu language. Bantu languages are spoken in most of sub-Saharan Africa south of Kenya and west to the Cameroon. If I hear South Africans who live more than a thousand miles away from Kenya speaking their Bantu languages, I can understand some of their words and the sound of the language is familiar. If I hear a Nandi speaking his language – I live only two miles from the Nandi boundary – it sounds very strange. Except for names of places, I cannot pick out any words at all.

In the old days before the colonials arrived and people were thin on the ground, these various ethnic groups cooperated in matters of trade (food, livestock, fish, items produced in one area and traded in another) and in finding wives from other ethnic groups.

As explained above, the British divided the country into ethnic areas with fixed boundaries. Kikuyu were in Central Province, Luhya in Western Province, Luo in Nyanza Province — these three groups comprise over 50% of the population of the country, but are in the three smallest provinces. In other areas with smaller groups, districts were drawn up along ethnic lines.

This concept is still alive today with the concept of *majimbo*, regionalism. There is a strong political movement, usually by those of the smaller tribes, to designate certain areas of the country for the "original" ethnic group. Much of the most violent conflict during the 1992, 1997, and 2007 elections was due to this concept — people in their ethnic ancestral homeland wished to expel people who came from other areas of Kenya. It is interesting how the group that claims the land is the aggressor, while any settlers from another area, even if they have been there for generations, become the victims. Therefore, in the Nandi area near me the Kikuyu were the victims, but in Central Province, the home area of the Kikuyu, Nandi and other groups became the victims.

"Tribalism" in the United States

When my father moved from Poland to the United States in 1921 at eight years of age, he moved into the Polish speaking section of St. Louis. All his neighbors were Polish. There was a school that taught in Polish. St. Stanislaus Church conducted its services and everything else in Polish. The local stores were owned by Poles. Even in the 1950's when I went to visit my grandparents, it was still a mostly Polish section of town. It is not surprising that my grandmother never learned English because she did not need to. My father lived through, and I think was scarred by, the push for Americanization in the 1920's and 30's. It was an attempt to force immigrants to acculturate, to conform to the culture of America, particularly speaking English.

After one year in America, my father decided to move from the Polish speaking school to the English-speaking public school. His parents did not care and he always signed his report cards himself. This did not make him a slacker, but turned him into an excellent student. He did have a slight accent when he spoke English, but, after he married my mother who was not of Polish background, he only spoke Polish when he visited his parents. Soon his Polish, even to us children, was clearly inadequate because he was always throwing in English words which we could, of course, understand. My father refused to admit to people that he had been born in Poland. It was only shortly before his death in 1999 at eight-six years of age that he agreed that we could put that he had been born in Poland in his obituary.

When I grew up in the 1950's, Polish jokes were still quite common. The "white race" was then quite small since it only included people of English, German, and Scandinavian background. Poles, Italians, Irish, Greeks, and Jews were clearly not really white. I was surprised when I went to Boston in 1961 that Portuguese were not considered "white" because they had North African blood in them. Middle Easterners and North Africans were definitely excluded. Over my lifetime who is considered "white" has expanded significantly to include all the above. Recently it seems that people from the Indian sub-continent are beginning to be considered "white."

In those days, ethnic (tribal) voting was the norm in the United States. In 1960, there was considerable comment on whether John F. Kennedy could be elected president because he was of Irish Catholic background. When he won, Irish Catholics began to be included in the dominant race.

If we turn to 1988, George H. W. Bush won the election because of his blatant use of "tribalism" when he depicted his opponent, Michael Dukakis, as coddling African-Americans by extensively citing the case of Willie Horton, an African-American man, who had assaulted, raped, and committed armed robbery while on furlough in Massachusetts where Dukakis was governor. His picture was in all the news, a menacing looking black man with a big beard, as were the victims, a nice-looking white couple. The Bush campaigners saw that this attack on Dukakis was extremely effective and it cost Dukakis the election. I mention this incident because it shows how ethnicity, race, or tribe is used by a politician for electoral gain. Politicians all over the world use this kind of technique to rally people to vote for them.

This practice continues to the present day. The "birther" movement that proclaims that Barack Obama was born in Kenya, even though it is clear that his mother never even visited Africa, is a present-day manifestation. Polls indicate that 18% of Americans believe this obvious falsehood. Xenophobia against people who are Spanish-speaking is another manifestation. This includes many people in the Southwest whose ancestors have lived in the United States before the United Sates was founded in 1776. We do not call this "tribalism," but it is exactly the same phenomenon. As the old labels lose their potency, there is a need to develop new ones — "Islamic terrorist" is the current new one.

What Does "Tribe" Mean?

Shortly after the post-election violence in 2008 in Kenya, I was giving a talk in St. Louis at Washington University. A young student from Kenya came up to me to say that she had lived in Nairobi through the violence. Before the violence, she had considered herself a "Kenyan." Only with the outbreak of the violence, she, all of a sudden, found that her "identity" was Kikuyu. Something that had before been meaningless in her life became of critical importance. This was not her choice, but a fact thrust upon her.

In another case, I heard about a prisoner in Mombasa who was half Luo and half Kamba, but he had grown up in Mombasa and did not know either the Luo or Kamba language. He then was discriminated against as a person without a tribe.

Many Kenya tribes are divided further into clans. Clans are supposed to have a direct common ancestor, but how much is fact and how much is fiction is difficult to determine. Again, a person inherits his or her clan from his or her father. Between 2006 and 2008 among the Kalenjin group called Sabaot on Mt. Elgon, two clans, Soy and Dorobo, fought over land with over four hundred killed and one hundred thousand displaced. The fighting became so intense that it included people from all other ethnic groups who lived in the area or nearby. As is so often the case, this conflict began with one Soy elder who turned against the Dorobo and he blessed his son to begin armed action against the Dorobo. Although the leader of the armed group and some of his supporters have been killed by the Kenyan army, it is not clear if this conflict has ended, as there are still revenge killings in the area. AGLI conducts healing and reconciliation work between the various groups there.

On the other hand I have met many, usually older people, who do not know English or Swahili and therefore can only communicate in their local language. My first mother-in-law was like this — I spoke to her in Swahili and she replied in the language of the Kamba. We communicated well enough this way, but naturally could not discuss philosophy. For people who only know their local language, they are as confined to their ethnic group as my grandmother was to the Polish community in St. Louis. It is rare these days, though, to find anyone who cannot communicate in either Swahili or English. Children who are being raised in Nairobi frequently are not even learning their "native tongue," particularly if their parents are from different groups.

In the end, we have this ambiguous state in Kenya. Most of the time tribe or ethnicity is not of very much importance. As time goes on and more and more people are moving to both the cities and towns, but even in rural areas, its importance is going to continue to diminish. Nevertheless, when politicians stir up animosities against a particular group and one's tribal identity becomes of prime importance there is still a strong tug of war between those whose first identity is "Kenyan" and that of their ethnic group.

A "Tutsi" Warlord

During the colonial period in the North Kivu province of the Democratic Republic of the Congo, seven Italian families settled in the Masisi area, high in the mountains. They developed extensive dairy farms with European grade cows. It looked like Switzerland. Since the Tutsi from Rwanda were known to be cattle-keepers, they employed many Tutsi to take care of their extensive herds. With the chaos in the Congo that came after independence and the forty-year misrule of Mobutu, the Italian families sold out their estates. One of these farms was bought by Laurent Nkunda, later a Tutsi warlord.

During the conflicts in the Masisi area beginning in 1992, Nkunda developed his own militia. In time, his militia became the most powerful group in the mountains and he ruled the area as a warlord. He claimed that he was protecting the Tutsi from the both the Hutu *genocidaires* who had fled Rwanda after the Rwandan genocide in 1994 and the local Congolese groups called Mai-Mai.

In 2007 when Nkunda was at the height of his powers, I visited both the area around Goma where the internally displaced camps were and the territory in the mountains controlled by his troops. There were many Tutsi inhabitants of the internally displaced camps. If he was the protector of the "Tutsi" as he claimed, why did not these Tutsi move back to Masisi? Moreover, I learned that his troops were of all ethnic groups as he was paying a $100 bonus to any young man who would join his forces. So it was not an "ethnic" force.

All "rebel" forces that are trying to overthrow the government of their country must have grievances, a cause to rally around, an excuse they can give to their supporters and the international community for their violence. This is a façade. The real purpose, obvious in the case of Nkunda, was the desire to control the mineral, agricultural, and human wealth of Masisi for the enrichment of himself and his supporters. His use of "tribe" was only a method for him to excuse to a gullible world his actual power motives.

It was remarkable how easy it was for the African National Congress to tour African countries in the early 1960's and receive all the weapons, training, and funding that they wanted for violent resistance in South Africa. The problem is that hundreds of other Africans — claiming discrimination and exploitation of their group by the ruling elite — have done the exact same thing. This behavior by both "rebels" and those who support them has been one of the necessary conditions for the continued armed insurrections and violence on the continent.

Those elite guerrilla fighters in South Africa now control the South African government themselves. These elite felt that they "sacrificed" during the freedom struggle. Now they feel that they are due just rewards. The result has been a focus on enriching this small segment of the black population as they enter the wealthy, privileged society of formerly white-only South Africa. Those at the bottom have been mostly ignored except for the rhetoric occurring during elections. While racial inequality has diminished to a certain extent, wealth inequality continues as before.

The international community must become more astute in its analysis. The excuse that one must resort to armed conflict because of tribal injustices is just a smokescreen. If a "rebel" were interested in reform, he would not destroy his own country and people, but would develop a campaign to correct the perceived problems. The real reason is power. Rebels, who loot, destroy and kill in their own homeland gain power in the government and then go about looting the whole country. Who thinks that leading a group of guerilla fighters in the bush could be appropriate training for governing a country? In the 1970's and 1980's there were numerous military coups in Africa. After decades of misrule by the military, people learned that governing is not ordering people around like in the military, but convincing them to act appropriately through law .

Any appeal to tribe, ethnicity, race, or other construct should be looked upon with suspicion and in no case can this be a justification for destroying, looting, and killing in one's country.

Do Not Buy Into Tribalism

Even in Rwanda where the two groups of Hutu and Tutsi were so institutionalized, the concept was used as a deception. The pre-genocide government called itself a "Hutu" government, but in reality most of these Hutu came from a small clique from the northwest of the country where the president was born. During the genocide itself, the Hutu Power government had to bring in *intera-hamwe* from outside Butare Province in the south of the country because the Hutu there, who were excluded from the government, did not support the Hutu Power takeover. The three "Tutsi' presidents of Burundi before 2005 all came from the same area of southern Burundi and were related — they were from a group that was not even called "Tutsi" before they used this to gain support of the other Tutsi in Burundi. Similarly, during the post-election violence, people in Kenya attacked Kikuyu even though it was a very tiny elite of Kikuyu who ran the country.

Almost all rebel groups claim that they are supporting their "tribe" against the discrimination of those in power. This is a charade to fool the gullible international community. The real goal is seizing the power of government and enriching themselves. Daniel arap Moi was President of Kenya for twenty-four years. Yet, his constituency in Baringo is not one wit more developed than other districts. "Tribalism" does not explain anything. One must always look for more hidden agendas whenever tribalism is being used as an excuse.

This is not to say that the concept of "tribalism" has no power. During the genocide half a million Tutsi in Rwanda were killed because of their "tribe" and "Tutsi" are not even a tribe by any kind of definition. The point is that if the international community stops kowtowing to the concept, then rebels will be unable to use it to further their own goals. Nowadays all countries in the world are multi-ethnic. If divisions do not exist, they can always be manufactured. It was two clans of one "tribe" who fought each other on Mt. Elgon near my home. If people want to fight, they will always find divisions. Our work is not to give credence to those divisions.

Calls to implement ethnic homelands in Africa, even if they are made by Africans, are a throwback to a time that has long passed and a recipe for continued conflict. When the European powers divided up Africa, they paid little attention to ethnic considerations. As a result most countries have diverse populations and many ethnic groups inhabit more than one country. Somali can be found in Somalia, Ethiopia, and Kenya; Masai in Kenya and Tanzania. Even Rwandans were and are the majority population of Goma and Rutshuru in North Kivu.

In these multi-ethnic countries, one group — sometimes a "tribe," sometimes a clan, sometimes just an extended family — gains control of the levers of government and exploits the situation to their own advantage. Sooner or later the marginalized out-groups contend for their share. Frequently this means a rebel, guerilla force is formed and, when successful, turn the tables on the former ruling group which then may form its own rebel force. Conflict will continue in perpetual cycles.

The answer to this problem is not supporting the group with the latest grievances, but to develop mores and institutions that promote equitable sharing of a countries resources and strong protection of minority rights. This is how multi-ethnic countries survive and prosper.

Chapter 8
Perceiving Other Customs

Family Life

When I grew up in the 1950s, the ideal was the nuclear family with a father, mother, and children all living happily in a nice neighborhood. However, with the increase in divorce and unwed parents, the ideal was becoming more often the exception than the rule. In this traditional ideal, if the breadwinning husband is promoted to a job in a distant place, the family follows along.

This is not the situation in Kenya. As noted before, the British conquered the various ethnic groups and then gave ten million acres to British settlers. These settlers needed many laborers to farm their immense farms. The Kenyans were not interested in working for the European farmers. To force this labor onto the British farms, the colonial government passed a hut tax on every house in the colony. This tax was so high that a person had to work at least six months out of the year in order to pay the tax.

The British settlers needed many laborers and had no interest in the effect on their wives and children. Consequently, they developed rudimentary housing for their male laborers, supplied them with food and minimal wages, usually just enough for the men to pay their taxes. This forced the men to leave their families behind and live frequently in single-sex hostels or houses. As time went on this became institutionalized and the worker was expected to live away from his family.

Today, when a person is employed in Kenya, the employer either provides housing on site or a housing allowance, usually 15% of the salary. The wife and children remain behind on the land inherited from the husband's ancestors.

The woman who lives next door is a nurse at Lumakanda Hospital, but her husband works for an NGO in Juba, Southern Sudan so I only see him when he is home on leave. Much of the town housing in Lumakanda is blocks of small one-room "pads" available for government workers to rent using their housing allowance. The workers live in their rented rooms and go home usually once a month when they are paid. So many people are taking public transportation on the first weekend after payday that Gladys and I try to

Row of single rooms rented to employees at $15 to $25 per month.

avoid public transportation at that time. *Matatus* and buses are over crowded and the fares are increased substantially. Moreover, the expense of the trip home can take a significant amount of the low wages that people do receive so that many are unable to go home even once a month. This is great economic inefficiency.

The real hardship, though, has to do with the breakup of the family. When couples are separated, it is unlikely that they will remain celibate. Perhaps some are saints, but many are not. This leads to the situation where the worker leaves his wife in the countryside with the children and finds another "wife" where he works. Sometimes the country wife does not know the second wife exists until the man dies and the unknown wife and children appear. I know of many cases where the husband, living apart from his wife, takes on another wife. Frequently, the husband stops supporting the country wife and his children because he is now spending his income to support his other "wife" and any children he may have with her. When the wives and their children learn about these arrangements, there is tremendous bitterness and hostility between the first wife and her children and the second wife and her children. This animosity can carry down through generations. I know a case where the grandchildren of a man with multiple wives are still extremely hostile to each other so that it has become a family feud.

In some cases, over time, a husband will try to be posted in his home area. This is particularly easy for teachers since there are schools everywhere, but almost impossible for policemen since they are not allowed to be posted in their home area. As the Kenyan economy improves and there are more wage earning jobs, this trend is increasing. This practice, I think, is the root cause for many of the social problems in Kenya including polygamy, female poverty, child neglect, and unwanted pregnancies.

Bride Price

One of the cultural issues in this region is the custom of "bride price." When a couple is engaged, part of the tradition is a pre-marriage ceremony where the groom's family promises to pay the bride's family a "bride price." This can be a considerable amount of goods — many cows and goats or sheep, honey, beer for the celebration, and other items. The concept is that the bride has been raised in her birth family but the benefits are now going to the groom's family because her husband's family will be using her labor and services. Notice that this transaction is between the two families and not between the bride and groom themselves. I have attended a number of these pre-weddings and they tend to be the same. There must be someone who will compare the bride to a nice cow that they are receiving as bride price from the groom. They will extol her virtues and say that no amount of bride price is worth her value. The groom's family will say how they will take good care of their "new cow" and extol the virtues of the betrothed as a good husband.

In former days, in Gladys' area, a typical bride price might have been eight cows plus other goods. Now people are not as interested in cows so money has been substituted for all but one or two cows. This financial contribution can be modest or quite expensive.

I see two problems with this custom. First, many husbands claim that they have bought their wife and she and the children are his property. He, therefore, believes she must obey him. This plays into the patriarchal nature of the society and can lead to domestic abuse.

The bigger problem is that there are families who will "sell" off their daughters for material gain. This also only works when the girl is young, fifteen or sixteen years old. If the girl is older, she will have developed a will of her own and will not agree to be married to someone she does not want to marry. Traditionally, this has encouraged women to become brides at a very young age.

Our niece, Jacqueline Mideva, on her wedding day.

Fortunately, in Kenya, many girls are unwilling to be married off as child brides as they wish to pick their own husbands. Yet many couples circumvent this whole process. My observation is that there are, in fact, few weddings. Since a marriage ceremony including the bride price is elaborate and expensive, they are mostly done by families that are fairly well off. Many couples just live together and never have a wedding. These common law marriages may or may not last. In most Protestant churches if a person wants to be a leader in the church, they must be officially married in the church. Recently Gladys went to a wedding of her aunt. So did her aunt's children and grandchildren. She had never been officially married and wanted to assume a leadership position in her church. In order to do this, she had to have the official wedding decades after she began her common law marriage.

In the later 1930's my first mother-in-law, Priscilla Mateta, had to deal with the effects of bride price. When she was about fifteen her father gave her to a neighbor, who was perhaps in his mid-forties, as a third wife. She had become a Christian which meant that she was against polygamy. Her father had already received the bride price and the day of the wedding came. She refused to be married. Her new husband's family carried her to her new husband's home, put her into a hut, and guarded the door. She cried and screamed but this was considered normal behavior for a young bride. Her elder brother, Joshua Kioko, who was studying at a bible school near Machakos heard about this forced marriage and the opposition of his sister. On the wedding day, he walked thirty miles from Machakos to Kilungu, the site of the wedding, and went to her new home. He demanded his sister not be married. He forced his way into the hut and took his sister back home. This destroyed the marriage and the father had to give back the bride price — including what had been consumed at the wedding.

The disappointed groom had Kioko arrested for attacking him when he forced his way into the hut. This, though, was the colonial days and the American missionaries spoke with the British administrators and had him released. Clearly, for the missionaries to have one of their young converts resist polygamy was an important witness. My future father-in-law, Wilson Malinda, was studying at the same bible school as Kioko and some time thereafter married my mother-in-law in a very Christian fashion.

Polygamy

Sometimes in Africa, an English word can have a different meaning than it has in the United States. In the Great Lakes region the word, "orphan" means someone who has lost one parent, not both as in the United States. Since the larger society and the government do very little for the child in Africa, and since basic needs are sometimes insufficient, a child with only one parent is at a great disadvantage in the task of growing up. If the father dies, there is likely to be little money for clothes, schooling, medicine, and even food. If the mother is the one who has died, frequently the father marries a new wife, has other children, and the children of the first wife are neglected and abused as in the story of Cinderella. These orphans are frequently helped by other family members, the church, or other well-wishers including the many orphan programs that Westerners help support. If both parents have died, then the child is called a "double orphan." These children, of course, are the ones in dire straits. Some are taken care of by grandparents, but this frequently is not a good solution because the grandparents are old, usually not economically active, and have already done their maternal and paternal duty.

Likewise, the word "polygamy" has a different meaning in Africa than elsewhere. Except for the affluent, who can afford court costs, there is no divorce. If a man leaves his first wife and acquires a second one, he is still considered a polygamist. In this sense, I and many other Americans would be considered "polygamist" because, while I married and divorced my first wife, I now have a second wife.

Another issue here is the definition of "wife." In the United States, this would mean that the couple is legally married. If a couple cohabits for seven years as married, then they are considered "married" even if there has been no legal tying of the bond. In Africa, though, it means that the couple is living together as "husband and wife." When a man takes a second woman, she becomes a second "wife." If the wives live together in the same compound, they are referred to as "co-wives."

Polygamy is legal in this region of Africa. Muslims are allowed to marry up to four wives. Christian churches, on the other hand, will marry only a man and his first wife. What happens if a polygamist is "saved" and wishes to join the church? Can he become a member? To do so, does he have to get rid of one of his wives? This is an issue of controversy in the Quaker church in Kenya and various denominations have resolved the issue differently.

There are numerous arrangements for polygamist marriages. One of my favorite Africans books, Carmera Laye's *The African Child*, describes, very warmly, the benefits of growing up in a polygamist household where all the wives live together and share. In one case in Tanzania in the 1960's, I knew a chief who had eight wives who lived together. In this case, some of the wives were political marriages to seal relationship with neighboring groups. Children of the wives considered themselves brothers and sisters.

One of our relatives has this kind of arrangement, as she is the second of three wives who all live together in the same compound. One day when I was visiting Kenya during the time I lived in St.. Louis, I ran into this relative on the road and she invited me to her nearby house. On her homestead, there were three separate houses in the compound, lots of children, and young grandchildren. I was received very warmly by a woman who I later learned was the third wife. The compound was quite large and well kept. The wives, now with children and grandchildren, worked together as a team and clearly supported each other in the ways I mentioned in Chapter 4. In this case, as Gladys later told me, everyone seemed to be happy with the arrangement.

In some cases, the older wife encourages her husband to take a younger second wife so that the new wife will take the burden off her of caring for the husband. In two cases I know, the younger wife was the much younger sister of the first wife. Another common reason for the first wife to want a "co-wife" is if the first wife is barren. If the second wife then has children, the first wife will consider them as her own and help raise them. If the first wife is barren and she does not agree to a second wife, there is a great likelihood of her being kicked out of the family so that the husband can marry a "fertile" wife. I do know one couple with good education and jobs who did not have any children. Because they were a very Quaker Christian couple, the husband could not take a second wife. This couple dealt with the situation by taking in numerous children of their siblings, including a number of orphans.

The more common arrangement is where the husband has his wives in separate homesteads. In the late 1960's I knew a sub-chief in Kenya who had four wives and each lived on a different plot. A chief and sub-chief are the lowest rungs of government service, but the position does give the sub-chief status and a certain amount of income and wealth. As he toured through Mua Hills, he would spend the night with the wife who lived closest to where he happened to be in the evening. He had eleven children by each of his first three wives and eight by his last for a total of forty-one children. As the father of all these children, he was still expected and required to provide for all of them. Considering this extreme burden, I thought he did quite well because he was relatively wealthy.

Usually the polygamist is a man of wealth and prestige. When he dies, there is often a great tussle between the various wives and the half-siblings over his estate. For the wealthy, the lawyers end up with a nice share. For the less wealthy, this can lead to tremendous family disruptions, particularly, for the second common law wife and her children.

Polygamy is a controversial issue. Recently there was a proposal in the Kenyan Parliament that the first wife had to agree for the husband to take a second wife but the bill went nowhere. Then there was a proposal that at the time of the first marriage the husband and wife had to agree if there would be a second wife. This bill also went nowhere. Kenya is a patriarchal society and it is the men who are the greatest supporters of polygamy.

Change Agents for Peace, Inc., a Quaker organization based in Nairobi, conducted focus groups in northwest Rwanda. The groups agreed that the most pressing issue in the area was polygamy. In this area, a man takes a very young wife and has children with her. Then he takes a second and even third wife and has more children. However, he does not have the resources to take care of these wives and children so they are left destitute. In Kenya, polygamy is decreasing because women are marrying much later in life. Moreover, as women get more education and have more employment opportunities, their dependency on a male provider lessens.

The United States has serial monogamy — marrying the first wife, divorcing, and marrying a second wife — while Africa has polygamy. Average Africans do not understand America's serial monogamy any more than Americans understand polygamy. Except in the case where wives live in the same compound, the facts on the ground are not too dissimilar, particularly when you add in the common law marriages and extra-martial affairs in the US context. The difference is that a politician like John Edwards can be destroyed by an extra-martial affair, while in Kenya this would just be taken as the normal behavior of an influential, wealthy male.

This illustrates one of my main points. Basic human nature in the world is the same. There is a need to regulate marriages, husbands and wives, and sexual relations, and the customs regulating these aspects can be quite divergent.

Circumcision

When I was growing up, I did not understand why the issue of circumcision, as discussed in the Bible, would have any significance. Now when I live in a society where some ethnic groups are circumcised and some are not, I understand why it is a major issue.

I paid the high school fees for a former student from Rwanda where men are not circumcised. He went to school in Thika, Kenya, a Kikuyu area where men are circumcised. He told me that, in four years of school, he never went to the bathroom when another student was present so that they would not learn he was uncircumcised. In Kenya, the only group that does not traditionally perform male circumcision is the Luo. Raila Odinga, the current Prime Minister, is from this group and one of the campaign slogans against him in the 2007 campaign was that one should not vote for an uncircumcised man. I doubt that anyone who is claiming this actually knows if he is uncircumcised. During the ethnic clashes in early 2008, some circumcised groups forcibly circumcised Luo men.

There is also female circumcision. Traditionally the Luo and Luhya did not practice female circumcision. All the other tribes did, although there are various methods of doing female circumcision. The early Christian missionaries to Kenya were appalled by the custom and convinced the colonial government to outlaw the practice. A recent survey found that 49% of Kenyan women in the 40 to 49 age group had been circumcised, but only 15% of Kenyan women in the 20 to 29 age group. As I mentioned in Chapter 3, there is a very active campaign against the practice.

Reproductive Issues

When I was in Kenya in the 1960's, it was supposed to have the highest birthrate in the world with 4% population increase each year and an average of eight children per woman at the end of their child bearing years. It was true at that time that almost every woman from about sixteen to forty was either pregnant or had a baby at her breast or both. The child mortality rate and the maternal death rate were also high. Family planning was almost non-existent in the late 1960's.

By the 1970's Kenyans were becoming concerned about this rapid increase in population. By the 1990's the birthrate had dropped to 4.6 children per woman in one of the fastest declines in fertility ever recorded. After that initial dramatic decline, there has been no subsequent decline in the last twenty years. Why? One of the significant reasons is that resources went to HIV/AIDS at the expense of birth control. Family planning has been neglected so that the current demand is not even being met. It is estimated that 25% of the women in Kenya who want contraceptives are unable to access them. The prohibition on giving US funds to family planning groups by the Reagan administration and both Bush administrations badly hurt the availability of resources for family planning.

I have little idea how population statistics are collected in a country such as Kenya. Most children are born at home. If they die in infancy, they are quietly buried and, as is the custom here, rarely mentioned. Recently the Kenyan government declared that a child needed a birth certificate in order to enter school. Since many parents did not have birth certificates for their children, each weekday there is a long line in front of the office in Lumakanda that registers births and produces the birth certificates.

This is a greater concern in the case of abortion. Abortion is illegal in Kenya except in the rare case of saving the life of the mother. Abortion in situations of rape, incest, or child abuse is not allowed. There are an estimated one and a half million babies born each year in Kenya. The number of abortions commonly reported is three hundred thousand. I have no idea regarding the veracity of this number of abortions since almost all of them are illegal and, therefore, secret. Using these approximate figures means that 17% of the pregnancies are aborted. Since abortions are illegal, they are induced by all kinds of unhealthy methods. This results in almost twenty-five thousand annual admittances of women to Kenyan hospitals as the result of botched abortions. Using these figures again means that 8% of the abortions are injurious to the health of the mother. Of these, more than two thousand die, one of the leading causes of maternal deaths in Kenya. One out of every one hundred and fifty abortions leads to the death of the mother. The result is an unhealthy situation where, because of the scarcity of birth control methods, large numbers of women have unsafe, illegal abortions that result in a high rate of maternal death.

This also leads to another surprisingly negative consequence. According to the Western Province health department, there were eighteen thousand cases of infanticide in that province over a two-year period. I have no idea how they obtained this figure or how accurate it is. If correct, this would mean that approximately 5% of the births in Western Province during those two years ended in infanticide. Every once in awhile I read about such incidents in the newspaper. When Gladys was a child, she knew a family where a brother got his sister pregnant. When the baby was born, it was put on goatskin on a rock and left to die.

Unlike the situation in North Kivu which I described in Chapter 1, in Kenya, rape is dealt with in a professional, non-judgmental manner. I know of a nineteen-year-old woman who was raped during a robbery. The next morning she was taken to the local government hospital and she was given a medical examination, treated with the morning-after pill to block pregnancy, and the appropriate medicines to inhibit STDs and HIV. More importantly, there were no psychological issues with her family and those around her because they did not blame her or stigmatize her for a rape over which she had no control.

Homosexuality

I have had more than one Kenyan say to me that homosexuality does not exist in Kenya. The interpretation is that this is a degenerate life-style brought in by godless Westerners. The claim is that it is wholly against African tradition. Remember my comment in Chapter 4 that "tradition" is frequently used by the speaker to justify his or her position.

We have a niece who attends a secondary girl's boarding school. One of the rules of the school is that "lesbianism will not be tolerated." Another is that "chronic lesbians will be expelled from the school." This clearly implies that it exists in the school. If it did not, there would be no reason for the rule. Homosexuality definitely exists in Kenya as everywhere else in the world.

In some tribal traditions, there is a custom where a woman can marry another woman. If a woman is barren or her husband dies before she has children, she can become a "husband" and marry another woman. In such cases, she must follow all the customs of the groom such as paying bride price. She then marries the chosen "wife" in a traditional marriage ceremony. The "husband" then secretly picks a male — usually a close relative — with whom the wife sleeps in order to become pregnant. The male father has no rights over the child. The two women raise the children as their own. While it is not necessary that the two women be in a lesbian relationship, it is clear that this custom would be an excellent, accepted arrangement for a lesbian couple.

Without doubt, though, homosexuality is a hidden, taboo subject and most gays, lesbians, and bi-sexuals are in the closet. Homosexual acts are illegal in all African countries except South Africa. These laws were enacted during the colonial period and even when such countries as England abolished the sodomy laws in England in the 1950's, they did not change them in their colonies. There is a tabloid newspaper in Uganda called "Red Pepper" that "outs" gays by revealing their names and challenging the government to prosecute them. Clearly accusing someone of being gay or lesbian could be an excellent way of discrediting a person. This is a tactic I have seen used a number of times in Africa.

In October 2009, a Member of Parliament in Uganda, David Bahati, tabled a bill in Parliament entitled "The Anti-Homosexuality Bill." This was a most drastic, homophobic bill. A homosexual could be put in prison for life and under certain circumstances could be given the death penalty. A parent or a teacher who did not report a gay or lesbian to the authorities could be fined $2,500 or put in jail for three years. A landlord could be sentenced to seven years in prison for renting to someone gay. Medical personnel or those working on AIDS prevention could also be severely punished. A reporter named Jeff Sharlet revealed that it was a secretive association of Christian evangelicals in the United States called "The Family" which was behind this bill. This bill aroused a lot of opposition in Uganda and even more from the international community including the United States government. At the time of this writing, the bill has not been passed and has been considerably watered down, but is not yet dead.

There is an historical reason why Uganda is as homophobic as the modern country began with this as an important issue. Catholic and Protestant missionaries arrived in the Kingdom of Buganda in 1875. Buganda, just north of Lake Victoria, was and is the largest, most prosperous area of the current Uganda. The Buganda Kingdom was ruled by a king, called the Kabaka. The missionaries attempted to convert members of his court. Within ten years, they had converted some of the pages and other members of the royal court. One of the "duties" of the male pages — who were teenagers — was to have sex with the Kabaka when he demanded it. Both the Catholic and Protestant missionaries strenuously opposed this practice. For the pages to show that they had become true Christians, they had to oppose the Kabaka's sexual advances. As more and more of the pages and other members of the Kabaka court converted, this became a major issue. Finally between 1885 and 1887 the Kabaka had twenty-two Catholic and more than twenty Protestant converts executed. These are the Ugandan martyrs who the Catholic church has made saints.

Males and females are much more segregated in this region of Africa than they are in the United States and Europe. Due to lack of sleeping space and the custom I mentioned in Chapter 4 of not having a set bed and bedroom, males or females frequently sleep together in the same-gender room. The result is that it is much easier to be a closeted gay, lesbian, or bi-sexual in the Great Lakes region.

In studies of AIDS transmissions, a common ways that married women become HIV+ is through their husbands who have had sex with other men. Since homosexuality is such a taboo subject, little campaigning is done to inform the gay community on AIDS transmission through gay sex. If AIDS transmission is going to be contained, then it will be necessary to overcome this homophobia.

In a cosmopolitan city like Nairobi there are now pro-homosexual civic organizations lobbying for gay rights. Homosexuality, nonetheless, is still illegal and in February 2010, there was a case where people were arrested at an alleged homosexual wedding.

Yet on the other hand, there is a tolerance that would be surprising even in the United States. One of our nieces was studying to be a teacher. At her school, she pointed out to me a transgendered man — a man who dressed as a woman — who was walking down the road with other women from the school, and who associated mostly with other females. Unlike in the United States where such a person might make sex changes through various hormone treatments, this man/woman did not have the funds to induce any kind of biological changes. My point here is that his/her transgender did not seem to be of any great concern to the other Kenyans around him. Oddly enough, I think this can be explained by the fact that Kenyans are much more accepting of diversity in conduct than the media induced conformity in the United States.

Section 3

Understanding Peacebuilding

This picture represents the extent of my modeling career. A woman saw this picture of me and liked the T-shirt so much that she obtained permission to have them made up for sale to peace workers. The T-shirt reads:

Peacemaking is hard work...listening, risk, endurance, forgiveness, service, prayer, courage, faith, perseverance, confronting, hope, empathy, patience, love, repentance

Center for Peace Learning, George Fox College, Newburg, Oregon

On the back side it reads
But consider the alternatives.

Chapter 9
Healing and Rebuilding Our Communities

Origins and Development of Healing and Rebuilding Our Communities (HROC)

When I was in the seventh and eighth grade, boys were given a class called "shop." I enjoyed it because I liked using tools and making things. When I entered the ninth grade, I chose "shop" as an elective. In 1986 when I was out of work, I started helping some friends repair houses. Rather than be "gainfully employed" as my mother called it, I started doing home repair, mostly by myself, but with the help of my children when they were on school vacation. I would stand up in Quaker meeting after worship and say, "Who needs to have their house fixed?" From then on, I would have enough work to fill my availability.

I had learned to live frugally and home repair gave a modest income. More important for me was that it gave me a lot of flexibility to pursue peace and justice issues that I had always been involved in. During the next twelve years, I did such things as organize an American speaking tour for a South African anti-apartheid activist, taught beginning college English in prisons, and spent a month in Alabama on a work camp rebuilding African-American churches destroyed by arson. In 1995 when my daughter, Joy, was doing her research on the her book, *The Pigment of Your Imagination,* I spent a month with her in adventures as we traveled overland from Nairobi, Kenya to Harare, Zimbabwe. As Joy predicted, this renewed my interest in getting re-involved with African issues. In 1996, I became a representative to Coordinating Council of the Friends Peace Teams. In March 1998, after I suggested that Friends Peace Teams send a delegation to East and Central Africa, the African Great Lakes Initiative was born.

When I first wrote to the East and Central African Yearly Meetings about having a delegation from the United States visit, one of the first responses was from David Niyonzima, then General Secretary of Burundi Yearly Meeting. His belief was that Burundians needed trauma healing work because everyone in the country was traumatized by the events of the on-going civil war which had begun in 1993. I was prepared to teach non-violent direct action and conflict resolution skills such as are proscribed in Alternative to Violence Project (AVP). I even was prepared for peacemaking based on the Bible as preferred by evangelical Christians, but I had no knowledge or experience in trauma healing. As part of the delegation to Rwanda and Burundi, I was accompanied by two individuals who had worked on trauma healing — Carl Stauffer, an American Mennonite working on peacemaking in South Africa and Ute Caspers, a German Quaker who had worked with the secondary trauma of children of Germans who had experienced the horrors of World War II.

In both Rwanda and Burundi, I was a participant as Carl and Ute led one and two day workshops on trauma healing. What I realized then was that the trauma we were dealing with was both the individual's traumatic experiences and the community's traumatic experiences. It is fortunate that we had someone there who had been working in South Africa, where the trauma included the violence of the apartheid regime so that the trauma healing included both the individual and societal aspects of recovery. This was different from the trauma healing work that was being done in the United States with its strong emphasis on the individual. The American approach assumes that all trauma is an individual experience so that it is the person only who needs treatment and not the society as a whole.

I also realized another major different from the American setting. Social work in the United States had become professionalized, regulated, and bureaucratized so that only highly trained, accredited people could intervene in situations of trauma and recovery. Whatever common wisdom people have that could help is discounted. When a traumatic situation occurs, such as the Columbine massacre, professionals rush in to help, as they should. The trouble with this approach is that the professionals are there for a short time, but trauma is not healed in a few days or weeks. It is a gradual and pervasive process that plays out over a long period of time with many vicissitudes. Where are the professionals then? Wealthy people, of course, can continue with private counseling, but the poor and even middle-income people are left to their own devices.

As a result of the delegation and the interest in trauma healing, AGLI's first major program was to start trauma healing work in Burundi. Carolyn Keys and Brad Allen from the United States and

Adrien Niyongabo and Charles Berahino from Burundi were the first team that trained for three months at the Quaker Peace Centre in Cape Town, South Africa. We chose the Quaker Peace Centre, first because it was a Quaker institution in sync with our ideas on trauma and healing. Plus it had been involved in the anti-apartheid struggle and the truth and reconciliation that occurred in South Africa after the end of apartheid in 1994. We thought that this would be a much more pertinent to the situation in Burundi than any training the people could get in the United States. When the group returned to Burundi, they developed and experimented with a one-day seminar called "What Is Trauma?" We found that people in Burundi were like people in the United States before the return of soldiers from the Vietnam War. Burundians did not have a concept of psychological trauma. When people were abnormal, it was considered to be due to "demons" or "craziness." Thus, everyone avoided those people who were showing signs of post traumatic stress disorder — as Americans learned to call it when they began to work with the Vietnam veterans.

Another American AGLI volunteer, Peter Yeomans, who had helped introduce AVP to Rwanda and Burundi, later studied at Drexel University for a PhD. As part of his graduate work, he did two academic studies of the HROC program in Burundi.

In one of Peter's surveys, he ask seventy-eight HROC participants in Cagura, Burundi, to endorse items from a list of nineteen traumatic events listed in the Harvard Traumatic Questionnaire. Participants were half Hutu living in the community and half Tutsi living in an internally displaced people's camp. The frequencies with which participants endorsed each item as an event they had experienced or witnessed are listed in the table on the next page.

What is amazing about these figures is that I have never experienced any of these traumatic events and the average person among these Burundian respondents had experienced 9.5 of these 19 traumatic events — half of them.

David Bucura, then General Secretary of Rwanda Yearly Meeting, asked me numerous times to bring some kind of trauma healing to Rwanda. Finally, in January 2003 with financial support from the American Friends Service Committee, AGLI held a one-month seminar in Kigali. We brought Adrien Niyongabo from Burundi and Carolyn Keys, now back in the United States, to spearhead the training. From this training, the twenty participants developed the initial version of the three-day Healing and Rebuilding Our Com-

Harvard Traumatic Questionnaire

	Experienced	Witnessed
Lack of shelter	97.4%	-
Lack of food and water	96.2%	2.6%
Ill health and no medical care	96.2%	2.6%
Loss of personal property	91.0%	0.3%
Combat situation	100%	-
Narrowly escaping death	78.2%	16.7%
Rape	11.5&	20.5%
Sexual abuse/humiliation	7.7%	7.9%
Serious physical injury from combat	17.9%	9.0%
Forced to hide	100%	-
Forced to hide among the dead	12.8%	15.4%
Betrayed and placed at risk of death	33.3%	14.1%
Confined to indoors because of danger	82.1%	2.6%
Forced to harm or kill a family member or friend	11.5%	16.7%
Forced to harm or kill a stranger	16.9%	14.1%
Disappearance/kidnapping of spouse	12.9%	25.7%
Disappearance/kidnapping of son or daughter	5.1%	23.1%
Unnatural death of family member	71.8%	5.1%
Imprisonment	19.2%	33.3%

munities (HROC) workshop. Then, over the next four months, the participants conducted twenty-five experimental workshops in Rwanda and the program was born.

This is the original group in Rwanda that, in 2003 after a month long trauma healing training, developed the Healing and Rebuilding Our Community program. They then conducted the first twenty-five workshops in order to test them out.

Adrien Niyongabo returned to Burundi to duplicate the new HROC program he had helped develop in Rwanda. Nevertheless, there were still gaps in the program. We needed to develop the methodology to train HROC facilitators who could continue the work in their local communities. We soon began calling these individuals "healing companions." In the AVP program, on which HROC is modeled, there is a three-tier process for a person to become a facilitator. First, the person takes a basic three-day workshop, followed by an advanced three-day workshop, and lastly a three-day training for facilitators' workshop. They then serve as apprentice facilitators for up to five workshops as they gained sufficient experience to be an AVP facilitator. We realized that to become a HROC facilitator was much more difficult than becoming an AVP facilitator because the deep emotions caused by trauma is much more complex than teaching the simpler conflict resolution skills of AVP. As a result, the HROC training got facilitators is two weeks long, following by apprentice workshops, and then an additional one-week follow-up training where the new facilitators can discuss their experiences.

HROC is firmly based in a basic tenet of Quakerism, that there is that of God in every individual. Below is the set of six principles that were developed for HROC:

Principle #1: In every person, there is something that is good.

Principle #2: Each person and society has the inner capacity to heal, and an inherent intuition of how to recover from trauma. Sometimes the wounds are so profound that people or communities need support to reencounter that inner capacity.

Principle #3: Both victims and perpetrators of violence can experience trauma and its after-effects.

Principle #4: Healing from trauma requires that a person's inner good and wisdom is sought and shared with others. It is through this effort that trust can begin to be restored.

Principle #5: When violence has been experienced at both a personal level, and a community level, efforts to heal and rebuild the country must also happen at both the individual and community level.

Principle #6: Individuals healing from trauma and building peace between groups is deeply connected. It is not possible to do one without the other. Therefore, trauma recovery and peace building efforts must happen simultaneously.

HROC's approach to learning grows directly from these six underlying principles. HROC workshops rely on participants' own experiences of violence, trauma, and healing to provide the backbone of curriculum content. Rather than provide multiple didactic lectures, HROC trainers invite participants to discover their own existing knowledge and their own inner wisdom about how to heal and how to help others. This approach builds a strong sense of community among group members, instills a new confidence in a wounded self, and ensures that the lessons learned are steeped in the context of the particular conflict and the post-conflict recovery process. The fact that the program relies on eliciting actual experiences enhances its adaptability to varying contexts and cultures.

The Basic HROC Workshop

In the Rwandan HROC workshops, ten of the participants are Tutsi survivors of the genocide and ten are Hutu from the families of the perpetrators or "released prisoners" who confessed to participating in the genocide. In the Burundian workshops, the Hutu and Tutsi from the two sides of the civil war are brought together. We have done a few workshops in Uganda and later we expanded the program to Kenya and North Kivu province of the Democratic Republic of the Congo. Although most of the people in a workshop are from the same community and in most cases know each other, they have not communicated with each other on a personal level for a decade or more. When they gather the first day each group sits apart, does not make eye contact with the others, and exhibit other signs of nervousness such as remaining silent or, when speaking, talking in a hushed tone of voice. I am astounded when I think of how the three HROC facilitators are going to deal with such hostility.

Let me describe the three days of the workshop with quotes from the participants to show the effect of each session.

The most important aspect of the first day is to develop a secure environment where everyone feels free to talk and respected by the others. This may be the first time since the genocide or other traumatic event that this has happened.

In this workshop, I have discovered that there are many kinds of trauma. Before I was thinking that only having lost family members is traumatizing. Now I have seen that the wrongdoer can be traumatized by the horrible things she/he did.

The agenda on the first day includes understanding psychosocial trauma — a new concept for most participants, causes and symptoms of trauma, small group discussion on "the effects of trauma on you." The concept of post traumatic stress disorder

HROC Participants in a small group discussion.

(PTSD) postulates that people who experience traumatic events can have considerable psychology damage even if physically they have not been harmed. Tutsi and Hutu participants are randomly combined in small groups. Later the small groups share their insights. The day ends with a relaxation exercise to calm people before they return to their homes and families for the night.

> We were blind. Learning about trauma healing skills has allowed us to shed light on our past, present, and future. Personally, I realize that the fact that we have been bearing all the bad events in us has brought back the violence again.

The second day begins with learning good listening skills, followed by learning the stages of grief and loss. The grief session, what we would call a guided meditation, is one of the most difficult sessions of the workshop. Many participants end up crying for their lost loved ones and their previous life. Constructive and destructive ways of dealing with anger are presented in the afternoon.

> Myself, as well as my neighbors, have lost many relatives and the situation we are in is unbearable. But I discovered that the main issue is that we have been keeping all inside us. We did not want to tell God, neither our friends about them. Grief can destroy one's life and body. We now find new skills. God and friends can comfort me.

> Having participated in this workshop, it has lifted me to another stage of understanding. I have a neighbor with whom I am in conflict. I discovered how I have been acting under my anger. Now I am ready to meet with him and tell him that I have acted wrongly. I will ask for forgiveness. Yes, I have been an evildoer.

On the third day, the trees of mistrust and trust are introduced. This is an apt analogy for the African rural setting. The participants list the roots, branches, and fruits (with fruits such as retaliation, revenge, and capital punishment) of mistrust on a drawing of a tree. They conclude by cutting down that tree. Next, they discuss the roots and fruits of trust, eventually concluding that the bad roots need to be replaced with good roots which then yield good fruits (rehabilitation, resurrection).

169

Symptoms of trauma: tug of war between avoidance and remembrance. This exercise indicates the fight between wanting to forget everything that happened and the human need to remember. As a participate suggests a trauma symptom , he or she is assigned to pull on the side — if a person says, "drinking," he or she is put on the avoidance and, if he or she says, "flashbacks," he or she is put on the remembrance side. This illustrates the pulling that occurs in the brain of the traumatized person.

When we talked about the mistrust trees, participants expressed how the mistrust tree is real in their hearts and the consequences of such evil. They openly manifested their willingness to uproot that mistrust tree because it is the origin of all horrible times they passed through for generations.

We have to plant the trust tree in our hearts so that every Rwandan can eat its delicious fruits.

The afternoon of the third day is a "trust walk" where each participant is blindfolded and led around by another participant and then the roles are reversed.

The agenda was composed of role-plays, trust walk, tree of mistrust/suspicion, tree of trust and group discussion. What a good day! It was very touching, inspiring, full of love to see how survivors and ex-prisoners were holding each other [in the trust walk] and carefully they walked together.

170

By the end of these workshops, people, who only three days before would have stayed out in the downpours of Central Africa rather than seek shelter with their opponents, who would have refused to ask for water if they were thirsty because they were afraid they would be poisoned, are leave talking and laughing and inviting each other over for dinner.

I am very happy to see that the person who had the courage to hide my husband and myself when the killers were looking and following us is now with me in this room. We need to accept that there are trustworthy persons within each ethnic group although we passed through horrible periods.

At the end of a workshop, a number of things should happen. Participants should have a good understanding of psycho-social trauma, ability in identifying it in themselves and others, and some basic skills to work with traumatized individuals. The participants should have reconnected with members of the "enemy" side and re-asserted their common humanity. This should then bring about changes in their behavior as they reconnect with family, neighbors, and "the other" with a positive, empathetic, loving attitude.

My Observations of a HROC Workshop

In November 2006, I was a participant in a HROC workshop in Byumba, in northern Rwanda. This was the first apprentice workshop for three recently trained healing companions — a Tutsi man, a Hutu man, and a Tutsi woman who was the wife of a Hutu who was still in prison. Theoneste Bizimana, the HROC coordinator in Rwanda, was the lead facilitator who would mentor the apprentices. The participants were three Hutu wives of prisoners, six recently released Hutu prisoners, and ten Tutsi females. All three Hutu women were illiterate and dressed in the style of poorer women — a blouse with two cloths, one wrapped around as a skirt and the other as a shawl, which could have many uses from carrying a baby to protection from the cold. One of the Tutsi participants, a woman, was also married to a Hutu man who was still in prison. During the genocide if a Hutu man was married to a Tutsi woman, he could "save" her by being extra diligent in the campaign

Agnes Ndayishimiye, standing on left, at end of a HROC workshop said,
"I am happy that I leave this workshop with a new dream that there
will be a special day. That day, I see myself going to the Gitega prison
where our former administrator [Hutu chief of the commune who is accused of organizing the killing of Tutsi in the Mutaho area] is kept. I will
ask to see him. I will be bringing him food. I will hug him. He will not,
maybe, recognize me. I will tell him that I come from Mutaho [Tutsi] IDP
camp. I will show him that love has replaced hatred. I will be happy that
day."

Agnes' wish took almost a year to arrange. This group from Mutaho
visited those arrested and imprisoned for leading the killing of Tutsi in
Mutaho. The prison was in Gitega about thirty miles away. The group
brought gifts of food and money. At first, the prisoners were very suspicious of the group because they had been in jail for over ten years and no
one had ever come to visit them. This visit was so unique — survivors of
massacres visiting those in prison accused of killing their loved ones —
that it was covered on a Burundian radio station.

to kill Tutsi — a real Faustian bargain. Afterwards these women
were ostracized by both their own Tutsi family, because their husband had been so active in the genocide, and their Hutu in-laws
who blamed her, that is, her ethnicity, for bringing so many difficulties to the family. One of the Tutsi women was a person who had
not experienced the genocide because she and her family had lived
for generations in the Democratic Republic of the Congo. Yet since
they spoke Kiyarwandan, the language of Rwanda, when the Congolese civic war broke out in 1998, they were forced back to
Rwanda.

Byumba is in the north of Rwanda on top of a high hill so the weather was cold even during the sunny middle of the day. The Friends Peace House, our partner organization in Rwanda, had organized the workshop and had rented a small one-story house with three bedrooms and a large living room that could comfortably fit twenty-five people. It was along the main road into town and built in the usual style of brick walls and corrugated iron roof.

The first day I went in early, before the workshop began. The participants all came from the local community and so knew each other. Nonetheless, the Hutu women sat together, the Hutu men together, and the Tutsi women on the other side. There was no talking and no one greeted each other. This included me, which is unusual since an *mzungu* is normally greeted and acknowledged. Only when a beggar came into the room and tried to ask me for money, did one of the participants shoo him out of the room. The tension was intense.

The workshop began, as always in this region, with a song, prayer, and short bible message. After opening introductions and a review of group guidelines, the first exercise that the facilitators led is called "A Big Wind Blows." This involves having one less chair than the number of participants, much like "Musical Chairs." The person standing calls out a trait — "a big wind blows for everyone wearing glasses," or "everyone with green clothing," etc — and people with that trait got up and found a new chair. The one left standing called out the next trait. This enlivening activity made people laugh. After the exercise was over, the facilitators asked what happened. People quickly responded that everyone was now "mixed" since they were no longer sitting only next to those who were like them. Later someone commented that the various characteristics were held by different people in the group, regardless of their ethnicity. Some of the tension was thus broken and the first step towards building a secure environment had begun.

The most difficult exercise was on the second day. This was the grieving session when people would remember those they had lost and the traumas they had gone through. None of the apprentice facilitators was willing to handle this exercise so Theoneste facilitated this session. He brought up a chair and sat in front of the group. This was very important because it put the facilitator on the same level as the participants in both a physical sense and a metaphorical sense. For hierarchical people in Rwanda, accustomed for the leader to be standing in front, it is very difficult to sit down in front of a group. Theoneste, speaking in a slow, low, reassuring tone of voice with a lot of silent pauses, then led the group through a guided mediation. He held those nineteen people in the palm of his hands and he asked them to remember those they had lost, happy scenes they had experienced with those people, and then, after about thirty minutes he returned them to the present.

I was sitting next to a woman named Fidele. She was about fifty years old and, unlike the Hutu women, had a fashionably cut brown dress with bright flowers on it. While this showed that she was better off economically than the Hutu women were, she also wore that same dress all three days of the workshop. Fidele was the first person to begin to cry — a facilitator gave her a tissue to blow her nose. Others cried. Theoneste then brought the participants out of the mediation into the here and now of the group in the room. The mood was somber and the tea break at the time allowed people to privately assess the experience they had just gone through.

It was after lunch on the second day that Theoneste informed me that Fidele told one of the facilitators that one of the released prisoners in the workshop was one of the men who had killed her eldest son. This was the first time she had seen him since the genocide as he had just been released from prison. Behind the scenes, the facilitators talked with Fidele and the man who had killed her son. He could only have been released if he had admitted to what he had done. Fidele's husband and all five of her children had been killed during the genocide — her eldest son had been beaten to death only about a block down the road from where we were holding the workshop.

Near the end of the third day, there is a time for testimony. The facilitators had arranged that this perpetrator would speak first, acknowledge what he had done, express remorse, and ask to be forgiven. He was the second to speak. He admitted that he had "killed the son of someone in this room." He indicated that he had been in jail for a decade for this, had admitted to his participation in the genocide, and was returning to the community where he was doing community service. He asked for forgiveness.

Rwandans are stoic people who do not publicly show their emotions. By the third day of the workshop, a secure environment had been developed where people felt safe enough to show their emotions. It is difficult to determine how this is developed, but it is partly the silly games called "light and livelies" that get people to have fun and relax, partly the listening environment and the respect that everyone is given when they say anything. Fidele did not hide her emotions. She talked for almost twenty minutes about her dead son. He has just finished high school and had received a scholarship to go to the university because he was good at "traditional arts." Her son and the perpetrator had grown up together and played with each other as children. In the end, she turned to him directly and said in a very stern and controlled voice, "I forgive you for what you have done, but you must never do anything like this again and you must make sure that none of your friends do anything like this every again."

After this exercise and the wrap up of the three-day workshop, something extraordinary happened, which was not part of the agenda. Someone decided to play a game. Two tall men took a blanket and people were put on two sides. One person from each side was put on a spot at the middle of the blanket and then the blanket was dropped. The winner was the person who could name the other person fastest. The loser was then "captured" and put on the winning side. I cannot believe how this simple game brought such laughter to this group of people — they were acting like a bunch of kids at a birthday party. I remembered the tension at the beginning of the workshop. It was as if these people had rediscovered the joy of living together again.

After the Basic Workshop

We soon realized that one three-day workshop was not sufficient for the healing of a person, let alone a society. The facilitators could not conduct an emotional, liberating workshop and then just walk away never to be heard from again. Our first strategy was to have a follow-up day one or more months after the original workshop. In the follow up day, there is time for sharing about how the original workshop affected their everyday existence.

When we introduced AVP in Rwanda in 2001, we made the mistake of having a few workshops all over the country. This resulted in having no discernable community effect. Rather than hold one workshop in a community, we needed to offer five workshops to include about one hundred or more people. With HROC, we have continued to focus on the communities where we began and then sometimes expanding to neighboring communities. This would create a large enough group of trained persons in the community so that they could provide on-going support for each other.

We also found that, after we had done these workshops and the follow-up days, that a public presentation was effective. The participants from all the workshops plus invited guests such as the local administrators, religious leaders, and other notables would gather for a day of celebration. This would include singing and dancing, poetry reading, testimonies from participants, and the usual speech making by the notables. In Burundi, where drumming corps are the national "sport," there is a drumming group to perform vigorously including not only drumming, but also dancing and singing. The day ends with a simple lunch together. The common meal is an important aspect of the peacebuilding. For some reason, Africans have a great fear of being poisoned. If a person gets an intestinal disease, some one is suspected of having poisoned the person. Consequently people are unwilling to eat with those they consider their "enemy." Therefore, the sharing of a meal together becomes a visible sign of reconciliation. Surprisingly, we have found that this tactic does not work in Kenya because the Kenyans are not satisfied with anything less than a major feast including the slaughter of a bull. Since this is not an efficient use of our scarce resources, we do not have community celebrations in Kenya.

Our next step was to encourage the trainees to form a group, which they frequently call an "association." These groups usually select one Tutsi and one Hutu as chairperson and vice chairperson. Some groups still meet regularly, while others naturally fall by the wayside. Their purpose is to continue the healing that has occurred in the workshop, follow-up day, and community celebration and become a force for reconciliation in the community. Some of the "graduates" of the workshops use their newfound insights to help others recover from trauma. This is usually their children, spouse, and close family members and neighbors.

I remember at one of the first community celebrations we held in Ruyigi in Burundi, one of the participants gave this testimony. In his community, there was a "crazy man" who would do things like take his clothes off and put them on top of his head, wailing. With such strange behavior, he was ignored and avoided by the community. After the HROC workshops, this participant decided that he would talk to the man to see what he could find out. He found him one day and sat with him on a log. He learned that during the fighting in 1993, this man had watched his wife and nine children be killed. He said that whenever he saw this man, he would stop and talk to him. While he did not become "normal," his behavior did improve. Another female participant commented on how there was a mother in her community who was continually beating her ten year old daughter because she was acting "strange." The participants worked with this mother and made her realize that the daughter was showing the signs of trauma and that beating her would only make her worse. As she counseled this woman, she changed her behavior towards her daughter.

As the years have passed by, HROC did not want to neglect those with whom we began the program. As a result, an advanced HROC workshop was developed and is offered a year or more after the first cycle of basic workshop, follow-up, and community celebration has been completed.

There are also two special groups that have experienced the trauma like everyone else but also have additional traumas. The first are HIV+ women. Usually they have had terrible experiences during the conflicts, but also have to deal with the stigma of being HIV+. Until recently these women would die quickly, but with the introduction of anti-retro viral drugs, many are living much longer. But they face extreme discrimination and, when they show visible signs of the disease, they are ostracized by the community — from their family, from their housing, from their occupation if they have one, and shunned by the society. Therefore their trauma is not in the past, but in process. An additional part of the workshop is living successfully while HIV+. After taking part in these workshops the women have frequently developed support groups.

The second group is the Twa who are the third "ethnic" group in Rwanda and Burundi, making up less than 1% of the population and severally discriminated against. As people who lived in the forest and hunted wild animals, buried the dead, made clay pots and being the jesters, they became a marginalized group shunned by both the Hutu and Tutsi, they have additional traumas.

We start with all Twa participants in the HROC workshops since they do not feel free to talk if Hutu or Tutsi are present. In Rwanda, after the initial all-Twa basic workshops, HROC plans to follow up with an advanced HROC workshops including half Twa and half Tutsi/Hutu participants. We have found that not all of our Rwandan facilitators can conduct the Twa workshops because some cannot hide their disdain for the Twa. We do have one excellent Twa facilitator who helps considerably in these workshops.

Under normal circumstances, Twa will not even come to a workshop when invited, or to a meeting when called by the government. Our success in getting them to attend is a great accomplishment for which we have been commended by local government officials.

Lessons Learned from the HROC Workshops

As soon as we began doing HROC workshops, we received many testimonies like the following:

> I would have been the big loser if death had taken me away before attending this HROC workshop. I had seen how happy are those who came from these workshops you are organizing and I wondered what they were given. I was overloaded with my bad feelings and this workshop has been an opportunity for me to put down some of them. More, I had been quarreling with my wife and many times I used violence over her. Thank God that I have learned how I can manage my anger. I am ready to change and bring peace in my family.

Perhaps he said what he was expected to say and that he actually is still "using violence" over his wife. Here is a testimony from the wife of another man:

> After the workshop that I attended, I wished that my husband would get this extraordinary chance too. Fortunately, God answered my prayers! He participated in the last one you conducted. My home has become a paradise! Before we attended these workshops, my husband was always furious. He was treating us as slaves. My home was a hell. Since he had participated in the HROC workshop, he has now time for the children and me. When he comes from work, he greets us, tells us how things have been for him and asks us how we have been doing too — what he never did before. Now he consults me before making any decision. You understand that there is reason for me to be this joyful woman.

This is the first lesson I learned from the workshops. Frequently, the first step made by a participant is to stop beating/

screaming at their spouse, children, family, and neighbors. I did not realize that one of the major effects of the workshop would be dealing with domestic violence. I had thought the workshops were focusing on relationships between hostile neighbors. When I gave this some thought, though, I realized that traumatized people take out their anger and frustrations on those closest to them, their family. I think we have things backwards when we say that peace must start in the family, then the community, the nation, and the world. Family violence is the result of societal trauma. Trauma frequently originates from conflicts in the larger world bringing violence into the family as wounded people take their anger and bitterness out on those near them. There is too much domestic violence in the United States which we attribute to personal problems. We must realize that this domestic violence is the result of societal issues. We need to look at the conditions in American society which lead to so much domestic violence and address the roots of this violence.

One question I am frequently asked is how much of what participants learn in the workshop carries over to their everyday life. Here is one example:

> The skills that I got in the workshop that I attended have enabled me to be compassionate in helping others. A few days ago, on the queue at the hospital waiting for our turn, I saw a woman sitting under a banana tree, crying and saying things like a crazy person. I immediately went to her, sat beside her and holding her in my arms. She kept on crying! After a while, she stopped crying and looked at me very surprised. I told her that I felt pity to see her alone. I asked her what happened and she revealed that her child had passed away. I listened to her and we finally sent somebody to go and call her husband. This was a great experience for me. I could not accept that I would have been empowered to that level.

We also learned that the workshops helped even traditional institutions. In Rwanda, Burundi, and elsewhere in the region there are local traditional courts where people can take minor cases if they wish. The judges are termed "wise men." Due to bribing of the judges, these courts have fallen out of favor among many of the local population. Therefore the story of this judge is significant:

I am a "wise man" who helps adjudicate local cases. I used to ask for a bribe from one of the two parties in conflict so that I may give him or her favor. Just after the last day of the workshop I attended, one woman came to me with money in hand. Trying to hand it to me, she said that she wanted me to help her to win the case opposing her to her neighbor. I listened to her and when she was done, I quietly told her that I could not touch her money. Instead, I suggested that she could go and meet the one with whom she was in conflict and try to talk about the issue. Two days later, she came back happy for they were able to resolve the issue by themselves. Another man came with the same intention but still I refused the bribe. I told him that I am no longer the same person they used to see. HROC has changed me! I am happy that people in my community know that I have abandoned that worthless habit and that they can unify by themselves. Thanks for the HROC workshop because I have got light and courage. I have become conscious that bribe is one of the roots of the mistrust tree. And I have up-rooted it!

Workshops sometimes have concrete results as the following testimony from a Rwandan genocide survivor indicates. As I mention in Chapter 3, proper burial of the physical body is an extremely important cultural value in this region:

Before we [survivors and released prisoners] could not even talk to each other or sit next to each other, but after the workshop we could talk. The one who killed my family asked for forgiveness, explained what he did and accepted it. It was not easy for me to forgive him, but I did and little by little he became close to me. And then, the killers told us where the bodies of our lost family members were, and then we could go find the remains and bury them properly. After HROC, I found out where my sisters were and buried them, and many others were found.

The same can be said for those who were released from prison:

[Before HROC] when somebody was knocking, I was thinking that they were coming to beat me. If somebody said 'Oh, I need you,' I thought 'He's coming to beat me.' I could sleep during the day, the night I could not sleep. I would stay home because I feared being beaten. I had no appetite. I was thinking they would come back to take me again to prison. I had fear to see a soldier.

Before the workshop, no one could come to my home, even for salt. I hated them [Tutsi survivors] so much. I had fear to meet those people. I could not talk to them and thought they might put me again in prison. And even for the first day of the workshop, it was like a dream, it was beyond my understanding. I was angry at them, and as the workshop moved on I understood them, because they taught us to live with others. And I saw, yes, it was possible, and I changed my heart. I would not have changed without the workshop; I would have stayed angry.

As mentioned in the workshop that I observed in Byumba, some of the most difficult cases involve Tutsi women who are married to Hutu men. This means that the family was torn apart during the conflict and many times the in-laws wish or actively promoted the death of the Tutsi wife. This is the testimony of Margaritte, a fifty-two year old Tutsi who lives with her nine children. Although she is a Tutsi, her children are Hutu because their father is a Hutu.

I am deeply thankful to the person who started these workshops. Things were going from bad to worse if it were not for the HROC workshop I attended. I had begun to see images and hear voices like what I lived through during the war. It was like a movie! Then I even started to consider my husband as an animal. It was hard for me to live with him. HROC gave me a relief! It was hard for my husband to believe it. He is now convinced that it is real.

When the war took place, I was pregnant. One month later, I went to hospital for delivery but my child died just after birth. There was no need for me to stay in the hospital for nobody from home could come and visit me. I chose to return home though I had not started feeling well. When Hutu begun lynching Tutsi in our community, all my in-laws left me and some of them would have been happy seeing me dead. We were in very difficult relationship, my husband and me. He gave himself pleasure to beat me so often. My children and one of my brothers-in-law were the only ones who understood my sorrows and comforted me. One time I was going to be killed. A group of Hutu came to my home with traditional weapons. While they were going to beat me on my head, the chief of the sector, a Hutu man, showed up and all of them disappeared immediately. He then recommended that my son would never leave me alone at home until the situation was back to normal. Listen, I remained alone in my community as a Tutsi; all the others were killed! Being able to share with those I met in HROC workshop tremendously helped me. I have been able to let it go. I have no more flashbacks; neither nightmares. Helped by my children, we worked on issues with my in-laws. My mother-in-law is now my mum. We got reconciled. May HROC last forever ever!

Agathe

I am frequently asked if participants use and convey what they learn in a HROC workshop with others. Here is a testimony of a woman named Agathe, who lives in North Kivu in eastern Congo and was greatly affected by the fighting there:

When I was fifteen, I was in love with a young man and I got pregnant. When I told him, he told me to go away. After two weeks, he married someone else. When my parents later asked who was responsible, I told them. They had heard that he was married and they chased me away. My brothers said that if they ever met me again, they would kill me.

I walked for ten miles, and where I went, I suffered. After birth, my family looked for me. They said we could live together but that they would not provide for me. I must take my child to the father. But the father said "No," as he would have nothing to do with the child. So I did not know what to do with my child. I sold cassava flour trying to sell enough to at least get a little bit of soap. I got no help from my family. They said I just brought them shame. Whenever my child got sick, I had no money. I would go out into the bush and find herbs and try to help my child.

I thought of joining the army so that I could come back and kill my family. But God came through for me. I had already registered and enlisted to join the army. But then I thought that I should not go without saying goodbye. I went to ask advice from my sister, but I asked her not to tell me not to go. Instead, she told me she had just come from a [HROC] workshop. Then she said she would accompany me to the military office if I wanted her to. When she told me this, I cried. Then she called the office and it turned out there were no flights that day for the army. So I stayed the night with my sister.

I kept thinking about what I was doing. Even if I went into the army, I was going with my child, my baby. Through the night my sister read to me what she had learned at the workshop. I was not satisfied. After awhile, she sent me an invitation [to a HROC workshop]. She said it might be helpful for me in the army. I went to the teachings and felt the facilitators were like my brothers. Then my heart started to loosen up and I chose not to join the army.

Conclusion

I frequently am challenged about the HROC program because it can affect only a small group of participants and is not the "magic bullet" that will solve the problems in the region. But "magic bullets" are top-down answers where people think that some possible resolution to the problems can come from the government, the United Nations, NGOs, or the international community.

I, on the contrary, am a grassroots person. For me what is important is what happens between two individuals or small groups of people. If a man attends a HROC workshop and stops beating his wife and children, that is huge! If two neighbors who are at loggerheads can solve the issues between them, that is important. If "enemies" can stop avoiding each other because of mutual suspicion and can learn to re-engage, that also is of utmost significance. If Agathe with her little child in the story above does not join the army, I feel that the value of the workshop has been justified.

It is also very difficult to quantify the results of these workshops. If you asked the question, "Have you stopped beating your wife or child?" what validity is there to the answer? As a result the major NGOs and funding organizations have been reluctant to finance programs like the HROC workshop. This leads to a more basic questions, "How do you change people's attitudes?" Our response in the HROC workshops is to tap that inner good that everyone has, to have confidence in people that they can, on their own volition, change for the better, and to not expect a predetermined result from the workshop.

Lastly, there is a lesson that can apply to all of us as this participant from North Kivu noted:

There is one exercise we did of remembering someone who did something good to you and thank that person. Through others' sharing I realized how many times I have been ungrateful, how many times I take things for granted, thinking they are minor, therefore no need to say, "Thank you." From now on, I have decided to be grateful. Sometimes I feel that whatever was done is minor but I have to be grateful.

Chapter 10
My Theology of Peacemaking

Revenge or Reconciliation?

D
o you believe that reconciliation is possible between enemies? Is revenge and retaliation a basic human trait that makes true reconciliation remarkably unlikely?

Western literature considers the discussion of "revenge" as a serious issue. Homer and the Greek classics are filled with stories of revenge. Once when driving from Washington, DC to St. Louis, I happened to turn on the radio just as the female protagonist in an obscure Italian grand opera was exuberantly praising her bother for killing their mother in revenge for her participation in helping to kill their father. Shakespeare's *Hamlet* is based on whether Hamlet should revenge the death of his father by killing his uncle. In *Moby Dick*, Captain Ahab is seeking revenge against the white whale because he bit off his leg — this is a rather absurd reaction and the story "works" only if one considers Captain Ahab to be obsessed. Then the United States has the late nineteenth century example of the Hatfield and the McCoy families who killed each other in revenge for thirteen years until the Kentucky and West Virginia state militias were called in to restore order.

When I was a boy in Sunday school, I was told the story of Joshua and the Battle of Jericho where his army walked around the city for seven days and then blew their trumpets and the walls fell down. I remember drawing a picture of Joshua, his soldiers with trumpets, and the falling walls. As I grew up, I thought this might be a nice example of a non-violent method of warfare. It was only when I was an adult that I read the following verse of Joshua 6:21.

> They devoted the city to the LORD and destroyed with the sword every living thing in it — men and women, young and old, cattle, sheep and donkeys.

In other words Joshua committed genocide. If it happened today, he would be in front of the International Criminal Court for crimes against humanity.

Sadly, there are many current stories of revenge and retaliation, including the 1998 Clinton administration bombing of a factory in

Sudan in retaliation for the bombing of the US embassies in Kenya and Tanzania. This was later confirmed as a mistake. This, I do not think, is the way to a more peaceful world.

When Laura Shipler Chico finished her tour in Rwanda as a volunteer with the African Great Lakes Initiative, she wrote the following passage in a report:

> Is it the Quaker notion that there is that of God in each of us that gives the Friends here such gall? Is it that unwavering hope that even a man who has butchered and hated and thieved can be redeemed? Or is it simply a thirst that comes out of raw hurt, to find each other again? Whatever it is, Rwandan Evangelical Friends, through Friends Peace House, are doing something that very few other groups in Rwanda have tried. They are bringing killers and survivors together. They are inviting them to sit down and look each other in the eye.

Venancie is a Tutsi survivor of the 1994 Rwanda genocide. In 2007, she attended a HROC workshop. Before the workshop she said that she did not think she could ever forgive the killers. The workshop was also attended by the Hutu man whom she witnessed killing her two brothers and younger sister. He had just been re-leased from prison. On the third day of the workshop, there is a trust walk done in pairs. One person is blindfolded and the other leads the "blind" person around. Then they switch places. Here is what Venancie said when she was paired up:

> During the trust walk, the person who killed my family was my partner. I was shaking because my partner was a known killer and strong. I thought he might throw me down. But he also had fear and he took me gently, kindly. I asked, "Will you lead me in peace?" After the trust walk with him, I felt it was not good to stay in my grief and had no fear against him.

Bethany Mahler, a American master's student from the School for International Training, attended this workshop and wrote:

> When you come from a place of comfort and security, where there was always someone to tuck you in at night, trust is easily built because there is no reason not to trust.

In 2008, Gladys and I met with elderly people at the Igunga II internally displaced camp in the Congo. Here is one of the elderly women telling of the hardships they were having in the camp. This included the fact that they received only a small part of the rations that were supposed to be given to them by the international relief agencies. Much of it was stolen before it got to them and could be bought for the going price in Goma, still intact in the bags labeled as relief food. Since they were elderly, they did not have the energy and ability to go to town to look for a day laboring job to supplement their rations. This theft was particularly hard on them.

In Rwanda, there is every reason not to trust. To behold a shy, widowed woman close her eyes and offer her hand to the man that destroyed her once-happy life was singularly beautiful. This small movement, this slight touch was everything. You imagine there is that kind of strength and benevolence in the world, but you rarely get to witness it. That day in September, I saw a world transformed through the eyes of every Rwandan in that room, a transformation in the richest, most profound sense of the word.

Here is an example from a Hutu prisoner after he confessed and was released:

I have accepted what I did in the genocide and I have been released. Through this workshop I see that I caused trauma to many people, especially those whose relatives I killed. I traumatized myself because I had an animal heart. I had done that, but I ask pardon. Forgive me. I did bad to you, to all

Rwandans, even to myself. I believe since now we become brothers and sisters, we can all say together, "Never again."

When people, usually mothers, see their children fighting each other because of ethnicity, they think, "When these children grow up, will there be another cycle of violence worse than the last one?" "Worse than the genocide" is hard for me to imagine. The next round will not be genocide, but a mutual slaughter, so perhaps it will be much worse. People who have survived this kind of experience realize that reconciliation and return to normal interactions with the enemy is essential for long term peace. As Salvator from Burundi said, "We adults ought to find ways to get along together as different ethnicities so that our children can start from there."

Sylvain , a Hutu from Burundi, makes another point:

Before the workshop, I liked to be alone most of the time. My heart was exhausted from carrying all the bad stuff I had. After the workshop, I remember that is when I slept more deeply than any other single night since 1993 [when the Burundi civil war began].

What strikes me most about the peacemaking theology in the New Testament is that it goes beyond the usual responses of flight or fight. Jesus' time was one full of repression and resistance. Some of the common people passively endured the oppression by the Roman Empire and the Jewish high priests. This included the Essene who migrated to the caves near the Dead Sea awaiting a more propitious time. Others resisted by banditry or in religious revivals such as were led by John the Baptist. Jesus indicated that there was a third way as in this passage written by the apostle Paul:

Do not repay anyone evil for evil, but take thought for what is noble in the sight of all. If it is possible, so far as it depends on you, live peaceably with all. Beloved, never avenge yourselves, but leave room for the wrath of God; for it is written, "Vengeance is mine, I will repay, says the Lord." No, if your enemies are hungry, feed them; if they are thirsty, give them something to drink; for by doing this you will heap burning coals on their heads." Do not be overcome by evil, but overcome evil with good. Romans 12: 17-21.

The Healing and Rebuilding Our Communities program is no more than an attempt to implement, in a concrete, personal way, this third method of resolving violent conflicts. Mahatma Gandhi and the Rev. Dr. Martin Luther King, Jr., were well known in the last century for using the concepts of non-violent direct action in specific campaigns to end oppression. There are hundreds, even thousands, of other less well-known examples. This, I feel, is the path the world needs to pursue if it wishes to have lasting peace rather than continuous cycles of revenge and retaliation.

Forgiveness

My understanding of forgiveness has been transformed through my work in the African Great Lakes region. Prior to this work, I had assumed that someone who had wronged a person had to ask for forgiveness. Then the victim needed to assess the sincerity of the perpetrator's remorse and decide to forgive or not to forgive. My concept of forgiveness was challenged when I read the following testimony of a Tutsi survivor from Burundi who attended one of the early HROC workshops.

I am a Tutsi living in the internally displaced person's camp. I was around ten when the war reached our area. I remember that day when a Hutu badly beat my young brother. My mum asked our Hutu neighbor to escort her so that she could take my brother to the hospital. Pitilessly, he told her "Do not you know where you have buried your husband? Take him there too!" Hopelessly, my mum and I went to the hospital but my brother died in mum's arms before we could reach the hospital. We turned back and took the trail to the cemetery. Only two of us, two females, buried my brother. This would never have happened before the war. After we were done, we went home crying. Since that time, I considered the Hutu man as a monster as well as his wife and children.

After the HROC workshop I attended, I used to sit and meditate. One day, I decided to rebuild the destroyed relationship with that family. Unfortunately, the man had died. Still, I went to his daughter, who is almost my age, and told her my sad story. I openly told her that this was the only reason that I hated them. She was very sorry to hear what her father did to us. In tears, she humbly asked if I would be eager to forgive her father though he had died, her family and her too! I responded to her that that was my aim for coming and talking to her. We are now friends, real friends. I have forgiven! Without HROC workshop skills, especially the tree of trust, I am not sure if I would have come to that decision.

Through this and other stories, I have realized that my assumption that the offending person needed to ask for forgiveness was invalid. In another case, a rape survivor from the North Kivu Province of the Democratic Republic of the Congo indicated that she did not even know who her attackers had been and would not want to meet them. She forgave them nonetheless. This made me realize that forgiveness is an internal action on the part of the victim.

Often times, victims report how they were filled with grief, anger, hostility and thoughts of revenge. When a victim releases these ideas by seeking forgiveness in his or her heart, we frequently hear about how that person feels like a heavy load had been lifted off his or her shoulders. One man commented, "Now, I feel human again." In another case, a woman who had been badly treated by her relatives realized that her anger and bitterness towards her relatives was not hurting her relatives, but herself. She went to forgive and reconcile with those relatives who had mistreated her.

The first half of this verse is one of my favorite Biblical passages:

And Jesus said, "Father, forgive them, for they know not what they do." And they cast lots to divide his garments. Luke 23:34.

The question, though, is "Who are the 'them' that should be forgiven?" I think that it is referring to the Roman soldiers who were executing Jesus, the Roman administrators of justice including Pontius Pilate, and the Jewish religious elite that wanted him out of the way. I think it also includes Judas Iscariot.

In 2001, I attended an inter-denominational prayer breakfast in Bujumbura, Burundi at Novahotel. It was supposed to be the finest hotel in Bujumbura, but was rather run down at that time because of the civil war in Burundi. More than fifty people, mostly pastors of various Protestant denominations, were in attendance. The pastor leading the discussion used verses in the Bible about Judas Iscariot as his text. He gave the usual explanation that Judas was an evil person because he was the one who betrayed Jesus. Judas has come to mean "one who betrays another under the guise of friendship." When the pastor had finished his ten minute presentation, he encouraged the audience to give their opinions. Other speakers were not so hostile to Judas. One pastor said that Judas did not think he was doing anything particularly important when all he had to do was to identify, with a kiss on the cheek, the person who was Jesus. For this he was paid the small sum of thirty pieces of silver. "Did not everyone at one time or another do some simple, seemingly minor transgression like this?" Another participant commented, "Did not Judas, when he realized the implications for what he had done, throw the money on the ground and commit suicide and thus atone for his betrayal?" I have wondered why I have remembered this discussion so vividly. I think it is because, through their interpretations, I was seeing Judas, the betrayer, from a completely different, much more sympathetic angle.

In the healing from the violence in Rwanda, Burundi, and the eastern Congo, the survivors many times forgive the perpetrators as they realize that they did not know what they were doing. In Rwanda for instance, genocide survivors say that the perpetrators were under "bad government" because it was the then Rwandan government that asked, even forced, people to kill their neighbors. Many of those in Rwanda who refused to participate in the killings were killed themselves. Rather than focusing solely on the transgression, the survivors were looking at the conditions that made the acts of violence possible.

Forgiveness is how a person can recover from anger and bitterness and again become a loving person. The following testimony from a person pushed out of his house during the 2008 post-election violence in Kenya illustrates this point:

> HROC has really changed my living style with my neighbors. During skirmishes, my house was burnt down by people I knew. I had promised never to forgive, talk, or even greet them. But in the workshop where I learned that when you want to heal, you start with yourself then others, I cooled my temper down, took action of forgiveness, and now my ene-

mies are my great friends. Some came last month to help me boma [build] my house.

This testimony from a HROC participant from North Kivu, also shows the benefits of forgiving:

[Before the workshop], forgiveness was not in my vocabulary. If you offend me I will keep it and sometimes I used to write it in a certain book for reference. I never thought of others when I do offend them. When we did the mistrust tree, I realized how I am filled with hatred, anger and pride. I realized what kind of fruits I am producing especially in my family.

There are people who offended me when I was not yet married. Now I have three children and I keep on talking about it. Maybe my children have heard me talk evil about those people and they will also hate them because of me. My first step is to burn the record book. If someone offends me, it's better to talk to the person. And she may, after realizing her fault, ask for forgiveness. Even if she does not ask for forgiveness, it's ok because I will have done my part.

Forgiveness is often the first step in resolving a conflict, a restoring of the wounded relationship. It looks forward towards the future rather than dwelling on the past injustices.

I cringe when I hear people ask, "Do you forgive the person who harmed you?" Forgiveness is something internal, the Inner Light, as Quakers like to say. It must be completely voluntary, a self-realization on the part of the forgiver. It cannot be induced by a question. For this reason the HROC program does not push or ask for forgiveness, but allows it to develop naturally. As people go through the process of recovery from trauma — feeling safe, remembering and grieving, reconnecting, and realizing their commonality with others in the group — they begin to reassess their inner wounds. As they listen to people who have similar or even different stories to tell, they realize that they are not alone. I remember the testimony of one woman who said that others had worse stories than she did — she survived by being at the bottom of forty-eight people who were killed around her. I myself can not imagine what could be worse. This, then, can lead to real, restorative forgiveness.

Conflicts are not resolved when they are suppressed by violence. They only fester and later explode. Resolving conflicts, including those large, seemingly intractable international ones, can only happen when the various sides are given opportunities to both speak and listen. This can lead to true, internal forgiveness, as one HROC participant commented, "Hatred is replaced by love."

The soldiers, the Roman judges, and the Jewish elite crucifying Jesus did not ask for forgiveness, but Jesus, in his wisdom, forgave them anyway.

Transforming Power

In January 1999, I visited Rwanda for the first time after the genocide, Rwandans had a good understanding of the mechanics of the genocide. They understood how the Hutu Power *genocidaires* used the downing of the plane carrying the Rwandan president as an excuse to seize power and eliminate the Tutsi and those moderate Hutu who opposed them. They also understood how the *genocidaires* had organized the *interhamwe* youth militias who — with the support of the army, police, and government apparatus — had perpetrated the genocide. They knew how the Tutsi-led Rwandan Patriotic Front had militarily defeated the interim Hutu Power government and took control of the country. What they could not comprehend was "How could we have killed each other like this?" This is a religious question.

The trappings of Christianity had been brought to Rwanda early in the twentieth century — churches, priests and ministers, songs, prayers, holy days — but the essence of the religion had been missed. Killing one's neighbor was clearly not part of the ethics of the Christian Bible. Before the genocide, Catholics were estimated to be more than 80% of the Rwandan population. The Catholic church was heavily involved in the genocide. The Catholic Archbishop of Rwanda, Vincent Nsengiyumva, had been part of the Hutu Power inner circle until he was told by the Pope that he had to withdraw from such a politicized position. He was later assassinated by Tutsi soldiers. Many priests encouraged their Tutsi parishioners to congregate in their church compound and then brought in the *interahamwe* to slaughter the Tutsi members of their congregation. One of my former Tutsi students told me that none of his children would now walk into a Catholic church because of what the church did during the genocide.

This existential question of "How could we have done this to each other?" is one of the main reasons that the AGLI programs of Alternatives to Violence Project (AVP) and its offshoot, Healing and Rebuilding Our Communities (HROC), have resonated so well with Rwandans.

AVP is based on the Bible verse Romans 12:2, which says:

Do not conform yourselves to the standards of this world, but let God transform you inwardly by a complete change of your mind. Then you will be able to know the will of God — what is good and is pleasing to him and is perfect.

The AVP program was developed in 1975 as a non-sectarian program to attract people of all faiths or no faith to develop non-violent methods of conflict resolution — particularly for long term prisoners in US prisons. The program emphasizes the transforming power to do good that everyone has regardless of what he or she has done in the past. Unlike some other religions that emphasis the evil in people and that people are born in sin, the Quaker theology is based on the idea that there is that of God and that of goodness in everyone. The reason AVP workshops are so effective in Rwanda is that they answer the question posed above: "Perhaps we did terrible things to each other, but we can be transformed." This is a statement of hope, a statement of love, and a statement of the power to change.

Immediately after the genocide over one hundred and twenty thousand suspected perpetrators of the genocide were imprisoned, often for ten or more years. If a prisoner confessed to what he had done, he went before a local *gacaca, a* grassroots court in his community. If the community and court felt the prisoner adequately confessed to what he had done, he was released back into the community, but required to do restitution work.

We must realize that the perpetrators of the genocide are wounded and traumatized like the survivors. Here is the testimony of one Hutu perpetrator:

Prison, it was bad, beyond understanding. You could not sleep lying down, there was only room to sit; many died from disease. Even sometimes there was no water, and once I went four days without food...I realized I had many symptoms along with the others who had been in prison. When I remembered sleeping among the dead in prison, it made me want to be alone and not speak. Even though I was released, I still felt imprisoned and did not trust others...I was only doing my thing, I could not talk to people about my problems. I thought I could only live with prisoners. But after the workshop I felt free in my heart, it let me release my fears and helped me to form relationships with survivors... Even if I have a conflict with someone, it no longer destroys the relationship

The purpose of Quakerism, of Christianity, of all religions, is to make people better. That is to love, support, and interact so that, as the Lord's Prayer says, "thy kingdom come, thy will be done, on earth as it is in heaven." There are no evil people, but only people who have done evil things. Anyone can be changed for the good. In evangelical terms, anyone can be "saved" or "resurrected."

Evangelical Quakers have complained that the AVP and HROC programs are not explicitly "Christian" and sometimes do not support these programs. I think that this is a misjudgment of the programs. The implicit nature of the workshops allows people to decide on their own volition to become "better," to realize that they can leave behind whatever very bad or evil things that they did in the past and become model human beings. The punitive nature that is common in too many American religions and that has made American society a leader in retribution and punishment, is, in my opinion, an unchristian one as it denies that of God in everyone.

I once sat in front of almost one thousand Rwandan genocide perpetrators in a re-education camp before they were going to be released back into the communities where most had done atrocious things. I have met the perpetrators face to face.

The world of hate, bitterness, animosity, and violence can be transformed, if and only if, we try. Only if we open our hearts and minds to allow it.

Chapter 11
The Post Election Violence in Kenya

Our Situation in Lumakanda

As I mentioned earlier, in 2000, Gladys and I moved to St. Louis to help with my declining mother who had a slowly progressing case of Alzheimer. We decided that after being with my mother, we would move to Kenya to be near Gladys' elderly parents. Gladys bought a plot in Lumakanda and we began building a small two-bedroom house. In April 2005, my mother passed away. In September 2006, we learned that Gladys' mother had cancer of the esophagus and she died three months later with Gladys at her side. In March 2007 after my mother's affairs were settled, we moved to Kenya to help take care of her father, who was healthy, but in his mid-eighties.

My life in Kenya was routine. Most days I would spend the morning on my computer, communicating with my co-workers in Africa and, due to the seven or eight hour time difference, in the late afternoon with people in America. About once per week we would go to Eldoret, a town about thirty miles away, or Kakamega, a town in the other direction about fifty miles away, for shopping, banking, and other needed tasks. We would frequently go to Kakamega because we could stop by the Friends Peace Centre-Lubao and discuss peacemaking matters with the staff there.

This was not a lonely life since Gladys' relatives, friends and acquaintances continually dropped in to see us. Those living within walking distance would drop in for tea or lunch, while those from farther away, would spend a night or two with us. Most Sundays we would attend Lumakanda Friends Church which was only a block and a half from the house. While I returned to the United States in the fall to sell our house in St. Louis, Gladys added two more bedrooms, a dining room, and a full bath onto our two-bedroom house in order to accommodate the many visitors,.

Ten months later, by the time of the Kenyan election, Gladys and I were pleased at how easily this major transformation had been achieved. We sold the house in St. Louis, moved from an urban setting to a rural one, and from a place where we were probably below average in income to one where we were one of the wealthiest in the area. Gladys was happy to be among her family and friends as we both became quickly involved with the local community. In retrospect, I marvel at how oblivious I was to the impending political violence as danger signs were popping up which I just ignored. I was happy to be in Kenya as I worked with the staff at the Friends Peace Centre in Lubao and enthusiastically signed up to be an election observer.

Context of the Election

Kenya gained independence in 1963 and has had elections for president, members of parliament (MP), and county counselors every five years since that time. Jomo Kenyatta was elected continuously until he died in 1978 when his Vice-President Daniel arap Moi succeeded him. While other Kenyan politicians thought Moi was just a figure-head, he was a wily politicians who outfoxed his opponents and continued as president. By 1978 Kenya was already a de facto one-party state and in 1982 Moi made it legally a one party state. It is really hard to lose when there is only one party. Regime change by a democratic vote became impossible.

The system of government in Kenya is a mixture of the parliamentarian system from England and the strong presidential system of the United States. This hybrid leads to an extremely strong central government where the president of Kenya controls not only the executive branch, but also the judiciary and legislative branches. He also appoints all the members of the election commission and the leaders of the security forces.

With the end of the Cold War in 1991, the international community realized that one-party democracy was not democracy, but the perpetuation of corrupt regimes. In Kenya itself, opposition to one-party rule was also building so that in 1992, Moi was forced into a multi-party election. Wily as always, he was able to divide the opposition and won the election with 36.4% of the votes to 26% for his nearest rival. At the next election in 1997, he also won against a divided opposition. Moi had 40.6% of the vote, Mwai Kibaki had 31%, and Raila Odinga had 10.8%. But there was concern that Moi's vote was padded by fraud. Moreover, in both 1992 and 1997 there was considerable violence in the Rift Valley where an estimated one thousand people were killed and hundreds of thousands displaced. Since this was the days before the Internet and cell phones in Kenya, Moi was able to close of the areas of violence to the media so that little information was available to either the Kenyan public or the international community.

In 2002, Moi was barred by the constitution from running for another five-year term. Everyone united against Uhuru Kenyatta, the son of Jomo Kenyatta, and Moi's handpicked successor. He was defeated by a coalition leaded by Mwai Kibaki, former Vice-President and Minister of Finance, who received 62.25% of the votes. Kibaki ran on a platform of reform to abolish the imperial presidency and decentralize local decision making. I visited Kenya shortly after the election and the mood in Kenya was euphoric. I myself considered this as revolutionary because it was the first time an African dictatorship was removed by a democratic election.

At this point President Kibaki, had the opportunity, the mandate, and the support to make those changes that Kenyans had been calling for. Alas, as soon as Kibaki got into power, he forgot those campaign pledges to de-centralized the government. The all powerful imperial president was too good to dismantle. He reneged on his pledges to those who had supported him in the election and government reverted to a mostly Kikuyu controlled oligarchy.

A constitutional commission was appointed to develop a new constitution. Our good friend, Florence Machayo, was appointed to be one of the delegates because she had run for parliament and lost, but her political party appointed her to the commission. The major issue in the new constitution was to dismantle the imperial presidency and institute a more decentralized system of government. When the draft was handed to the government, they changed these provisions and reinstituted the imperial presidency. As a result most of those who had worked on the draft, including Florence Machayo, rejected it and worked for the "No" side. The draft constitution lost resoundingly with 58% rejecting the draft and only 42% supporting it. Most of the No side then coalesced to become the anti-Kibaki coalition for the December 27, 2007 election.

With elections occurring every five years, one major difference from the United States is that elections cycles are rare. In the US, elections are very common, at least one election every two years for the House of Representative, but with primary elections, local elections, and other special elections, in most years there are two or more elections in communities in the US. Because of this five-year election gap in Kenya, each election cycle begins the process all over again starting with registering of the voters. Many voters would have died since the previous election and many more new voters need to be enrolled. There is no League of Women Voters as in the United States that handles the mechanics of each election. Consequently, most election officials, except for the chief election officer in each polling station, are recent unemployed high school graduates hired as temporary workers. The result is that the polling staff is not experienced, leading to mistakes and the possibility of candidates seeking election by fraudulent means.

In 2007, Mwai Kibaki was a seventy-six years old incumbent President running for a second and last term on the Party of National Unity (PNU) ticket. This party was formed only a few months previously as his election vehicle. His main challenger was Raila Odinga, a sprightly sixty-two year old, the son of Oginga Odinga, one of the major early figures in Kenyan post-independence period. President Moi had put Raila in jail for eight years for opposing his rule. Raila's party was the Orange Democratic Movement, (ODM) which was formed in 2005 to successfully defeat the proposed constitution promoted by the government. The last major candidate was Musyoka Kalonzo, of the Orange Democratic Movement-Kenya (ODM-K) party, who had also been involved in the defeat of the 2005 Constitution. Kibaki's ethnic group is Kikuyu, the largest, most dominate group in the country based around Mount Kenya; Raila is Luo, the third largest group from around Kisumu; and Musyoka is a Kamba from Eastern Province, the fifth largest tribe. There were five other minor candidates. On the plus side, one had to say that this was a competitive election unlike those from 1963 to 1992 where the ruling party dominated so much that the election for president was really only pro forma.

National elections in Kenya are based on ethnicity or tribe. A candidate from a certain tribe, by expounding ethnic solidarity, is able to get 90% or more of the votes from his home area. For the Kikuyu, the largest tribe in Kenya, this translates into about 20% of the vote. The candidate then makes alliances with other tribal leaders — the office of vice-president is one of the plums dangled in front of leaders from other tribes. The winning candidate assembles a coalition that brings him into power. Odinga's tribe, the Luo, are the third largest tribe at only 13% so he is at a disadvantage as he has to bring in more of the other tribes into his coalition in order to overcome the numerical advantage of the Kikuyu.

This is how tribalism is used by politicians for their own benefit. First, the politician proclaims that he or she is the leader of his or her tribe. In order to get their fair share of government resources, the tribe must support their leader. If it does not, then other tribes that do support their leader will get the resources and the tribe that does not will be left destitute. If the leader is convincing enough and get 90% or more of this tribal vote, he will be indisputable leader of the tribe. With this, he or she will negotiate a position in the government. In the end, the "tribal" leader has hoodwinked his tribe because the benefits will accrue to him or her and his or her families and closest supporters. The average citizen will see little benefit. When that leader is accused of corruption or misuse of office, he or she will wave the tribal flag so that his or her tribesmen will unite behind him or her, stating that this is a political ploy to destroy the tribe. For reasons that I can not understand, this works. Regardless of the fact that few benefits trickle down to the average tribal citizen; that the tribal leaders' family and cronies become exceedingly wealthy; that this tribal politics destroys the unity of the country; and that conflict rather than a working together to improve the whole nation results, this unjust system continues.

The 2007 elections for members of parliament (MP) were also highly competitive as there were over two thousand candidates for the two hundred and twelve seats. This means that a candidate could win with a small percentage of the votes. The reason there were so many candidates is that MPs are paid $190,000 per year in salary and benefits, one of the highest in the world. The only qualification outside of being a Kenyan citizen is to be fluent in Swahili and English. Unlike the US where incumbency almost guarantees re-election, incumbency in Kenya is a great liability as the electorate frequently votes even powerful people out of office.

Pre-election Violence

During the three month campaign period prior to the December 27 vote, about twenty-five people had been killed. An assistant minister's government vehicle was found filled with traditional weapons — bows and arrows, machetes, clubs, spears, etc. He denied any knowledge of or involvement with this shipment. Although the election law stated that anyone using violence would be disbarred, nothing happened. Three candidates were fined a little over $1,500 for inciting violence, but they remained in the election and never paid their fines. There were very few women candidates, around 10%. Women, in addition to men, had been beaten up by rivals including one female MP candidate who was hospitalized. Every candidate visited the beaten candidate in the hospital to condemn violence against women. William Ruto, one of the top Orange Democratic Movement officials, slated to be the prime minister when a new constitution was developed, was attacked in the Kisii area as he got out of his helicopter and had to be hospitalized. Two minutes before this attack, a senior Minister, Simeon Nyachae, the Minister of Roads in the Kibaki government, had been shown on TV talking to the leader of the attackers who had a bow and arrow. He was not reprimanded.

Locally in Lumakanda, we heard of a few cases of violence. In this area of Africa, all candidates form youth groups that "help" out with the election, but frequently are the source of violence. These youth attend candidate's rallies, put up posters, conduct parades with their candidate, holding and shaking branches to indicate support, and, most unfortunately, are used to intimidate voters and at the worst form militias with traditional weapons that attack opponents. Two women in Lumakanda, who were given funds to bribe other women, were attacked by the youth supporters of an opposing candidate. Their money was taken and their dresses were ripped apart. Our electrician was the youth leader for one of the MP candidates. When he and four others were putting up signs for his candidate, his group was attached by over ten members of a rival candidate. He told me that he ran as fast as he could in order to keep from being beaten. Two of his co-campaign workers were not so fortunate and ended up in the hospital.

Bribing

There are many methods of rigging elections. In Kenya, one of the preferred methods is bribing of voters. The election culture has degenerated so much that, while a voter may take bribes from a number of candidates, he or she will not vote for a candidate who has not given a bribe. Therefore, a "clean" candidate cannot win. On the national level, when Lucy Kibaki, the wife of the president, gave a speech to women in the Coast Province, each woman who attended was given a $15 note in reward for listening to her. This was reported in the *Daily Nation,* but was considered nothing out of the ordinary. Where we lived, $15 was considered the appropriate bribe amount for a vote for a Member of Parliament. Once, as Gladys and I were walking in town, we saw a group of women crowding around a certain shop. A candidate for county council was giving out sugar as a present to the women so that they would vote for him. Later in Gladys' father's area, Gladys saw women going to a certain house to get a pound of sugar, worth about a dollar, as a bribe from one of the candidates.

It costs a lot to win an election as a member of parliament, at least $100,000 I would estimate. Consequently, candidates ally themselves to particular political parties in order to receive adequate funding for their bribing. This means that the political parties have to gather huge sums in order for their candidates to win. There was a major set of scandals early in the Kibaki administration called Anglo Leasing, named after one of the fraudulent companies involved. In this case, dummy companies were given fake contracts by the Kenyan government and the beneficiaries pocketed the proceeds. The total amount of these fraudulent schemes was half a billion dollars. Unfortunately, one of the politicians in defense of the fraud — in a rare moment of honesty — let slip that this scheme was necessary so that the ruling party would have sufficient funds to win the next election.

Of course, with such blatant bribing, no one considers any election to be fair, but rather the winning candidate has bought his position and therefore, the winner owes nothing in return. This works two ways — the citizens do not expect anything from their representatives and the representatives feel that they have no further obligation to their constituents. In the end, though, this is the main reason so many of the current officer holders lose the next election. Their election has been a business proposition rather than a commitment to represent the needs and concerns of their constituents.

Election Observing

The Quaker organizations in Africa in 2002 developed an organization called Quaker Peace Network-Africa (QPN-Africa). This group of forty to fifty representatives meets about once every two years so that Quaker peacemakers from all over the continent can discuss the history of the conflicts and peace programs, their approaches to peace, and plans for the future peacemaking activities.

At the second conference in 2003 in Rwanda, James Mageria from Kenya explained to the gathering how, during the 2002 election in Kenya, the Kenyan electorate was able to successful bring regime change to Kenya. This was done peacefully and democratically through highly organized work by the churches and civil society in Kenya. This made the members of QPN realize that it should address elections, which were one of the main causes of unrest and violence in the East and Central African countries. QPN-Africa decided to develop a program of election observing, beginning with the 2005 Burundi elections. Since that time, it has observed elections in the Democratic Republic of the Congo (2006), Rwanda (2006 and 2010), Kenya (2005, 2007 and 2010), southern Sudan (2010 and 2011), and again in Burundi (2010). In addition to local observers, QPN's policy is to bring some international observers from the other countries including surrounding African countries and others from Western countries. This gives added creditability to the observations and allows the foreign observers to see how elections are conducted in other countries. The observers are given one day of training and a questionnaire to complete. After each election, the questionnaires are compiled into a report.

I signed up to be an election observer in Lumakanda at the local Lumakanda Primary School. I was one of the forty-nine Kenyan and twenty-nine international QPN observers. These observers were concentrated to observe in polling stations in Nairobi and western Kenya. At the one-day training conducted by QPN, I was given an identification badge and an election bag with a lot of material on the election prepared by the Electoral Commission of Kenya. The procedure and rules were laid out in the booklets. Our job was to watch for and notice any one of a number of infractions such as unregistered voters, voters missing on the voter role, election officials conducting their jobs properly and not influencing voters, and so on. If we saw an infraction, we were allowed to report this to the polling officer in charge; if the problem was with the polling officer in charge, we were to report infractions to the Quaker Peace Network.

Shortly after 5:00 AM on Thursday, December 27, I went to the school to begin my observations. Since this was the first time I was an election observer, I was tense because I did not know what to expect or how I would be treated by the election officials. This was a large voting station with more than two thousand voters. Since there were so many voters, they were divided into four "streams" according to alphabet, each in a different classroom. This brought me my first dilemma as an election observer — should I watch all four streams or concentrate on one of them? I decided that I would stay mostly in one of the streams. I chose the J to K stream because many Kenyans in the Lumakanda area have names which begin with J or K. The voting officials welcomed me as my role in the voting process was well defined. I relaxed and by noon the routine had become rather boring as I watched the same thing happening over and over again. The voters were lined up outside the door, and came in one by one, showed their identity and voting cards, their name found on the voting register, they were given ballots, they filled them out, dropped them into the voting box, and had their index finger on their left hand dipped in indelible ink.

It was a long, uneventful day as I reached home well after 9:00 PM. The biggest issue that arose was what to do with illiterate voters. If they came in with a relative to help them, there was a booklet, which explained this and a form for the helper to fill out and sign. On the other hand, nothing was said about the illiterate voter who came in without a family member. In my polling station, there were about twenty-five of these, mostly elderly women, but including one young man. For the first three illiterate voters, the head of the polling station called me and one other neutral observer over to witness that she was writing down correctly what the illiterate person wished. Neutral observers such as me are people who are not representing a political party but only observing the voting process. The partisan observers were ones sent by each political party to watch the voting. There were twelve of these at my station. I had not thought about this, but this was contrary to my position as a neutral observer since I was now a part of the electoral process rather than just an observer. Yet on the other hand, how could I refuse? Then after the first three times, the election officer in charge called all the election observers to witness the vote. Now when they all gathered around the voter, it was clearly no longer a secret ballot. I had a lot of time to think about this during the day and in the end, I could not come up with a satisfactory method of dealing with this problem.

I stayed for the counting of the votes after the polls closed at 5:00 PM. This was accomplished quickly and without much controversy. Any vote, which was considered invalid for any reason, was shown to everyone who could object if he or she wished. In every case, the invalidity of the vote — such as marking two candidates — was clear and there were no objections. As expected, Raila Odinga of the Orange Democratic Movement overwhelming won this polling station. Odinga had 349 votes to Kibaki's 58; other candidates had 12, and 8 were invalid ballots.

Early Friday morning I wrote up my report on my election observing. My conclusion was as follows:

> While the voting was satisfactory, I do not think this can be said about the election process as a whole. The primaries were not fair and free, there was too much violence and intimidation, bribery, use of government resources, and other election irregularities to consider the whole election process to be considered fair and free. I would hope that the Electoral Commission of Kenya can close many of these loopholes for the next election in 2012.

I emailed my report to the organizer of the QPN observers and then took a *matatu* the seventy-five miles to Viyalo where my father-in-law lives. Gladys had gone early in the morning because she was arranging the one-year memorial service for her mother, a major gathering in Luhya tradition. The service was to take place the next day. Totally unaware of what would soon happen, I took three changes of clothes, my laptop and modem, and a small amount of time on my cell phone. I felt that I had properly played my small part in the election and that the voting had gone well. My thoughts quickly changed from the election to the up-coming memorial service for my mother-in-law.

The Announcement of the Election Results

On Saturday, the three-hour memorial service for my mother-in-law went well with over five hundred people in attendance, including Gladys' father and his seven daughters. This was similar to the funeral service, without the burial itself. The church choirs sang many songs, friends and close relatives made a short comment, and the preacher gave a long sermon, all in remembrance of Gladys' mother. There was no mention about the tallying of the votes.

In the meantime, the Electoral Commission of Kenya was beginning to announce the results. On Friday evening, Raila Odinga, the challenger, was ahead by over one million votes. Early Saturday before the service began, we heard on the radio that his lead was cut to around 300,000 votes and then in the evening by only 30,000 votes. Then all day Sunday there was no announcement of further results for president. This made people suspicious as they were speculating on the delay. By this time, I too worried that something fraudulent might be taking place. It upset me that this might happen after I had observed such peaceful voting in Lumakanda.

On Sunday evening, the final results were announced. My stepson, Douglas, who, like many young Kenyans, is very interested in politics, and I were sitting outside my father-in-laws house, listening to the radio, while Gladys and her sisters were dividing up her mother's clothes and belonging. Finally, about 6:30 PM, the radio announced that Mwai Kibaki was declared the winner by about 300,000 votes. Supposedly by chance, the Chief Justice of Kenya was at the State House and, rather than waiting for a few days so that there would be a large swearing in ceremony with many visiting foreign dignitaries, Mwai Kibaki was sworn in as President quickly at a private ceremony.

I was shocked. I concluded that the election had been stolen. I could not believe that the Kibaki government could be so blatant and obvious in how it stole the election. On Friday evening when Odinga was ahead by more than one million votes, I noted to Douglas that it was almost mathematically impossible for Kibaki to catch up as he would need to capture the vast majority of the remaining votes. I felt like a foolish pawn as I had played my minor part as a local election observer and then blindsided by such an obvious manipulation of the results.

From my father-in-law's house, I could see the town of Mbale, about two or three miles away. Within fifteen minutes of the announcement, I could see six plumes of smoke as *matatus* owned by Kikuyu were being sent on fire. Kikuyu and Kikuyu owned businesses and building were being targeted because Mwai Kibaki was a Kikuyu. Shortly thereafter, I could hear gunshots or perhaps the firing of tear gas canisters.

I received a number of text messages but I had no idea of how accurate they were. I wrote at that time, "We have little information. There are no papers, no calling cards and the radio is uninformative. The only thing being broadcast is that 'everything is under control' and 'remain calm.'" What was clear is that we were not returning home on Monday as we had planned.

Return Home to Lumakanda

Our stay at my father-in-law's house was "a surreal quiet" as the country erupted into violence. I realized, though, that we were in a good place to stay. We were in the countryside in the home area of the Luhya, the group my wife belonged to. Violence in my fathering-law's house was unlikely because it was not in an area with Kikuyu who were suddenly being targeted. Yet as the "rich *mzungu*," I was not certain that the violence would not spill over to me. Therefore, I decided to be as inconspicuous as possible by not leaving my father-in-law's compound.

I had not taken any extra calling cards to put more airtime on my cell phone. Since calling people was much more expensive than text messaging, I only text messaged. Nonetheless, both Gladys and I had to husband our messages since no more calling cards for cell

A destroyed building in Kipkarren River.

phone time could be obtained. I quickly ran down the battery on my laptop and, since my father-in-law had no electricity, my communication with the wider world of the Internet quickly ended. My father-in-law's radio could only pick up local Kenyan stations, which continued to give almost no information on the situation. There were no newspapers available. I felt isolated, cut off from that world that I usually corresponded with every day. I was worried that those who were close to me would hear nothing from me and conclude that something "bad" had happened to me.

Those two days of Monday and Tuesday were the longest "vacation" I ever had since there was absolutely nothing to do. Once I heard some drumming and wondered if this was a sign from the youth to come out of their houses with traditional weapons to attack Kikuyu. A few minutes later, two boys passed by with plastic five-gallon drums on their way to the river to draw water — they were beating on them with sticks so this was the ominous drumming I had been hearing. Another time, a woman came up the path wailing that her only son was killed in Nakuru, a Kikuyu area. She wailed, "They should have killed Kibaki instead."

Wednesday morning, I learned one thing. It is cold at five thousand feet above sea level on the equator at 5:00 AM on the back of an open truck. Samson, Gladys' brother-in-law, obtained a truck to carry us back home. He was a policeman so there was an armed guard sitting in the front of the truck. Besides Gladys and me, there were Samson's wife, Josephine, one of his daughters, another of Gladys' sisters, an aunt, and a cousin. These relatives lived in Lugari District with us or, in the case of Gladys' aunt and cousin, on the way to Lugari District. The seventy-five mile ride was cold and bumpy. There were almost no vehicles on the usually busy road — in two hours, we passed less than ten and most of these were near the major town of Kakamega. We crossed four roadblocks where youth had put stones to stop vehicles — one was right by the Friends Peace Center-Lubao sign. Since it was so early in the morning, we did not see any of the youth involved. When it was dark, it was difficult to tell what damage had been done, but at dawn when we reached Kipkarren River near our home, I noticed at least ten destroyed shops.

Lumakanda

Shortly after I returned, I walked through Lumakanda. Since the town is the district seat and has the district police headquarters in addition to the local police station, there had been no violence. I understand the police had patrolled the town right after the election announcement. The police, armed with automatic weapons, were very evident, talking with townspeople about the situation, but this was not that unusual in Lumakanda. Most shops were closed — those that were open were selling out of goods. All the private vehicles in the region — from *matatus*, to tractors, to pick-ups, to a couple of big transit tractor-trainers were parked at the police stations. Right outside the town center, homes of Kikuyu had been looted and burned. Kikuyu and other who had fled the violence were at the field next to the local police station, many with only what they had been able to carry. I had no way to determine the number.

We did not worry about food as we had fourteen and a half two hundred pound bags of corn in our house so we could have eaten *ugali* for years if necessary. I do not like the local bread, called "Supa Loaf" and equivalent to Wonder Bread in the US. However, after not having any bread at all for almost a week, I looked forward to this poor excuse for bread. Under the circumstances, we ate what we had.

The next day directly to the north, I noticed a large plume of black smoke. What did it mean? Had another building been burned in the countryside? Or was it just some normal burning of trash? Considering the tension, everything was under suspicion.

A report I wrote on Friday, sums up our situation that first week back in Lumakanda:

Gladys and I are doing fine, staying at home like newly-weds. I walk around town for exercise and observation twice a day, once in the morning and once in the late afternoon. It is dry season now and the sun is very hot during the middle of the day... By the way anyone can call or text message us and we are not charged to receive calls or text messages. Yesterday Eden Grace sent 500/- of airtime to me. Then someone sent me a long article with many pictures and over 100/- was wasted in trying to download it. It was like a person dying of thirst dropping his bottle of water. Somehow, Malesi at Uzima Foundation sent 300/- to me today so I am wired for another day or two. Dawn Amos figured out a way to forward airtime to my phone from the US which she has done. Unfortunately, it has not arrived — we speculate that the people in Nairobi that have to send it on to me are not at work. Here in Lumakanda, we have a better radio and we are able to get BBC so we listen to it on the hour to see if there is any update.

While this may sound picayune, that is how a person responds. What may seem like trivial matters, in this case, connections to the outside world, is of prime importance. I can well understand those people I visited at Musama Church in Burundi in 1999 when they felt so grateful that someone from the outside had cared enough to visit them.

Response to the Internally Displaced People in Lumakanda

Those who were being pushed out were mostly Kikuyu whose ancestors came from Central Province, over two hundred and fifty miles away. The conflict was based on the concept that the local Nandi group considered the Kikuyu unwelcome immigrants to their territory, the Nandi "ancestral homeland." The Nandi wished to push the Kikuyu out of their homes in the area so that they would return to Central Province. Since most of the Kikuyu had been born in Lugari District and had lived there their whole lives, they had nowhere to go back to in Central Province. This concept, though, did lead to "pushing them out" rather than killing them as had happened in other conflicts in the African Great Lakes region. I consider this the primary reason that, even though six hundred and fifty thousand people were displaced, so few, only one thousand three hundred people, were killed during this violence.

There is a glue that holds a society together. It consists of many things — customs, culture, respect for others and their property, laws and their enforcement by the police and courts. The glue in Kenyan society was always weak. There was much on-going non-election violence before the voting. For example, the clashes on Mt. Elgon that AGLI had begun working on, others clashes in Molo and Rondai, continued deadly conflicts in the pastoral areas, and many acts of violence including the common practice of lynching suspected thieves. The police and the courts are noted for being corrupt. Within the culture, there exists great jealousy of any one or any group which seems to be doing better than others are. That little glue that Kenyan society had was disintegrating and chaos was overtaking normalcy.

On Thursday, January 3, during my morning walk, I saw that the internally displaced people (IDP) were being moved from the police station to the Lumakanda Primary School where I had been an election observer. This was because the field next to the police station had only two latrines, clearly insufficient for the hundreds of people living there. Moreover, people were sleeping under trucks and the like. While the classrooms had vacant windows and doors, at least there was a roof and there were more than twenty latrines at the school. I watched as people were moving their goods to the school — clothes, mattresses, firewood, pots and pans, a car battery, etc. It is difficult to know how many people there were, but I guessed it was in the hundreds. While much is made of the wealth of the Kikuyu, these people moving into the school looked no more prosperous than the average Kenyan. Many, particularly children, were without shoes or wore only flip-flops. At first a cow and a calf were driven in, then a herd of fifteen cows, a few calves, and about twenty goats, then another of six cows and a calf. A pick-up truck was pushed in — the driver did not have gas or perhaps he did not want to use gas when going downhill. It was full of food — mostly corn or corn meal for *ugali*. I was told that there would be police protection at night.

In the afternoon, Gladys and I went on our usual walk around town. Naturally, we stopped by the school where the displaced people had moved. When we went in, we noticed that there were eight Red Cross personnel. Fortunately, we had met Herman, the Red Cross leader, previously in better times. He was willing to communicate with us about the condition of the IDPs and consequently the other Red Cross workers, one who was a member of Lumakanda Friends Church, were as well.

Here is what we learned. I really was a bad estimator. I thought there might be a few hundred displaced persons but no, there were two thousand five hundred and six at the school. There were a total of seven camps in Lugari District. The one in nearby Turbo had fifteen thousand at the police station. Another camp had five thousand, another four thousand, another two thousand, and then a few with only hundreds. This totals over thirty thousand displaced people, which would be over ten percent of the people in the area

After we talked with the Red Cross staff, we walked around the school compound to see how people were situating themselves. As usually happens, the young children under five were excited to see an *mzungu*. As is my custom, I would then shake hands with those who were not too afraid of me. I greeted the women, most of whom were cooking the evening meal. I did see Silas Njoroge, the leader of the camp, stopped to shake hands with him, and discuss the situation a bit.

People from the same village or place where they were evicted stayed together at the school. One section was for the men and another for the women and children. There were about twenty-five classrooms in the school so this meant that each classroom would have about a hundred people in it. At night, mattresses were spread all over the floor with many children sleeping on one mattress. I was also told that people were still coming in and that there were many people still in the countryside who had not yet reached the IDP camps. I also learned that some were not Kikuyu. If a person were married to a Kikuyu, he or she would also have been targeted. Gladys and the Red Cross workers pointed out to me some of the Luhya in the camp.

The Red Cross had not sent any assistance yet and there was a shortage of food in the camp. Since most of the people had run away with just what they were wearing, there was a shortage of clothing, cooking and eating utensils. A large truck drove up while we were there with many bags of corn. We were told that someone had gotten these from his storehouse before it had been burned down. Some children had been separated from their parents and the Red Cross was trying to reunite the children with their parents — in the meantime, the children were being assigned to a new "family" to look after them.

One of the problems for the Red Cross workers was that they did not know how long the IDP camp would last. Would the situation be resolved in a day or two, a week or more, a month or even longer? It was therefore difficult for them to plan. I wondered, even after the situation calmed down, how long it would take people to return to their homes. Herman said that they would return home because a home can be rebuilt. However, how long will that take and will people have the resources to rebuild?

On our way home, we met Festus, the medical officer in charge of Lumakanda Hospital. He was working day and night. He was clearly weary, doing as best he could in the circumstances, and as befuddled as everyone else as to how this could happen. There was no blood supply at the hospital so he was sending wounded patients in need of blood to the hospital in Webuye, a town twenty miles away. The hospital ambulance, he said, was going back and forth day and night, but he worried what would happen when the tank of gas was finished. This implied that people who needed a transfusion would then not survive. On Sunday night there had been many wounded at the hospital — some died, but he said, "There were many wounded people last night also," clearly indicating that the fighting was still going on in the countryside. He pointed in a northeast direction to illustrate where many of the wounded came from. The hospital had about fifty beds and I expect all were filled with patients including perhaps two to a bed if needed..

On Saturday, Florence and Alfred Machayo, our Quaker neighbors dropped by to see us. They had gotten a little fuel for their car and decided to use it to see what was happening in the area. They went to Turbo, the next town east on the highway. They told us that almost nothing in Turbo was open. They also said that on the night of the election a Kikuyu had parked a truck in their compound. Area youth informed them that they were sympathizers and if they continued with this, the youth would burn the Kikuyu truck and as "punishment" their own car. A Kalenjin neighbor had agreed to take care of a few Kikuyu cows, but these were stolen along with his own as "punishment." Due to this possibility of retaliation, Florence and Alfred suggested that any relief work should be done through the Friends church so as not to put people into jeopardy.

The next day, Sunday, concerned by the plight of the internally displaced people, I stood up in Lumakanda Church and said that we needed to do something to assist them at the primary school. This was immediately well received and, much to my surprise, an additional offering was made. More in line with what I had expected, the church appointed a committee of seven to develop a plan for helping the IDPs.

The next afternoon, the committee members appointed by Lumakanda Friends Church met at our house to discern the way forward. They decided to go the next morning as a delegation to Lumakanda School to meet with the leaders of the camp and the Red Cross staff. They would find out what would be the most suitable needs that could be fulfilled given our resources. We had received a donation of $472 from Quakers in Bristol, England, and the Sunday collection at the church. This translated to only eighteen cents per person at the camp so we would have to focus on something do-able. The committee would figure out what was best and then Gladys and I would go to town on Wednesday and buy what was suggested. The church members would then go to the camp, have a prayer meeting with the people in the camp, and give the donation to the Red Cross to distribute. In Kenya, every meeting, every distribution of support, begins with a song, prayer, and short message from the Bible. If possible, we planned to make similar delivery the following week.

The AGLI work campers from the previous summer had brought some children's clothes, toothbrushes, and medicines, which had not yet been distributed. Alfred Machayo picked them up at the Friends Peace Center-Lubao and dropped them at our house to be part of the donation. Malesi Kinaro from the Peace Center sent a letter of introduction from Friends for Peace and Community Development and T-shirts, saying on the front, "Friends in" and "Peace" on the back. Folks on the delegation would wear them during the distribution in order to identify themselves.

I could no longer get BBC on my radio and I wondered if it had been jammed. I worried that the Kenyan government might want to keep information from Kenyan citizens. BBC was the best source of information on what was happening in Kenya and twice people in the United States heard reports from BBC before I did (because I was asleep) and asked me about them. Later BBC came back on the air so it must have been just a temporary broadcasting problem.

Other issues developed from the conflict. Prices in town for food went up 25% to 50%, except for meat. The town used to slaughter a cow every day, but when the same cow was being sold on the fourth day, people stopped purchasing meat for fear that it might be spoiled. Since people were worried about their finances, they did not buy meat so the price had not gone up.

The following Tuesday, January 8, Kibaki named his cabinet, mostly filled with appointees from his inner circle. Shortly thereafter, we got a text message from Eden Grace, who lived in Kisumu, a town a hundred miles to the south on Lake Victoria. She reported she was seeing fires and hearing gunshots. We had planned to go to Kakamega on Wednesday, but this made the trip doubtful. When morning came, we called Malesi and Getry who were in Kakamega and both said that Kakamega was calm. We went to Kakamega and back. *Matatus* were few and crowded. The fare was double what we usually paid. The drivers and conductors, who were formerly mostly Kikuyu, were all Luhya or Kalenjins. People were much more subdued than before as there was not much hassling even with the high fares. Later after the violence subsided, fares went down, but as usual not to where they had been before the election.

We saw a dozen or more burned houses and shops on the main road to Kakamega and a very large store next to the bus station in Kakamega which had been completely burned out. The lines at Kenya Commercial Bank were long so it took me over an hour to access the ATM. Moreover, the ATM had a lower limit than usual on the funds we could withdraw. But we got enough to last for a week or two for our immediate needs. We were also able to buy $75 of cell phone calling cards at the regular price. This would last us for more than two weeks if we were careful with our calling.

I bought my first newspaper since Dec 28 and we bought two loaves of bread. I reported, "Bread, calling cards, and a newspaper

From left, Josephat Ukiru, Gladys Kamonya, Daniel Ahinda, and Jotham Siva, members of the committee from Lumakanda Church. They are holding a box of soap distributed later that day.

— what a wonderful life!" It is interesting how important simple things can be when you cannot get them. We bought rice, sugar, flour, salt, and the other items for the Lumakanda Church committee to take to the school the following day.

The Lumakanda church committee met at the church, got a local police vehicle to carry the goods — two one hundred and ten pound bags of rice, two forty-four pound bags of salt, five twenty quart containers of cooking oil, and ten boxes of soap — to Lumakanda School. The committee was very warmly received and the Red Cross gave them a receipt for the goods delivered. Gladys requested that the rice be used for the small children because it was difficult from them to eat the corn because it had insecticide in it which gave them diarrhea .

The Move to the Turbo Police Station

At this point the big question was what would happen to the IDP camp when school opened the following Monday. The IDPs were going to be transferred to the IDP camp at the Turbo Police Station eight miles away. This was against their wishes as Turbo would be much farther from their homes than Lumakanda. There were already around twenty thousand people at the Turbo Police Station. I would be able to visit them in Turbo, but this would be more difficult as I had to walk to the junction at the main road and take a *matatu* to Turbo, climb the hill to the police station, and return back home. There would be no more two times a day visits as a round-trip would take five or six hours.

My step son-in-law, Job, was a motorcycle taxi driver. He told me that during the days of no transportation he would sometimes drive people to Webuye twenty miles to the west of Lumakanda. He would be stopped at Kipkarren River and elsewhere along the road and asked to show his identity card and say something in his native language to indicate that he was not a Kikuyu. Since this was ODM territory and orange was the color of the Orange Democratic Movement, he started wearing his orange ODM hat to show where his loyalties lay.

When we went to church on Sunday, January 14, we found about one hundred 200-pound bags of corn in the back. After church, I asked George, the owner, why they were there. He replied that he had a big farm on the other side of the road where the Nandi were the dominate ethnic group. He felt he would be the next target. "When they finish with the Kikuyu, they will then come for us," meaning the Luhya as they had in previous times of conflict. He had moved all of his furniture out of his house and taken it to the homes of his relatives nearby. This is another small indication that the violence is not essentially political, but a chance to plunder and loot. That day, I heard two reports of cows being stolen. In the past, this rarely happened in Lumakanda but it had now happened to one of the men who helped build our house. His cow was pregnant and people do not kill pregnant cows because the meat is not good to eat. Six months later, to the amazement of us all, this cow returned on its own to its owner.

On Monday, Gladys and I went to Turbo where the Lumakanda IDPs had been transferred. Turbo town was about four blocks long with three gas stations, a post office, a section of small wooden shops, and a block of substantial concrete shops. I had heard that Turbo had experienced a rough time during the violence, but it was another thing to see an entire block of large shops burned out. Most of the wooden shops and one of the gas stations, because it was managed by a Kikuyu, had also been burned. I was horrified at this destruction since it made no rational sense.

After we viewed this destruction, we climbed the hill to the police station and found our "refugees." It was heartbreaking to compare their situation before the violence to that in the Turbo IDP camp.

They were happy to see us. "You have followed us here," was a common comment. The women, in particular, were very pleased and welcoming to Gladys who had been part of the contingent that had brought them the first allotment of food. The refugees had been placed in a just harvested cornfield so there was not even any grass. For the previous two nights, they had slept on the ground in the open. Now, men were building eucalyptus pole houses with plastic tarp tops and sides. A few had found iron sheets, perhaps salvaged from their burnt shops or houses, which made a more solid wall. The wind was blowing very hard, almost constantly, forcing me to hold my hat on my head, so the plastic tarps were flapping loudly. I thought this din would make it hard to sleep at night.

The people in the camp told us that they had not received any food since they arrived from Lumakanda two days before. Blankets were their first request. Predictably, the delivered rice had run out since there had been only two one hundred and ten pound bags, enough to feed the children for only two or three days at best.

On Tuesday, we traveled to Kakamega. Gladys went to the supermarket to buy food for our household. While she was in the store, the supermarket closed its doors and blocked everyone inside because the police were chasing hundreds of youth through the town. I doubt anyone would have wanted to venture out.

The next day, Gladys and I went to Eldoret with Malesi, Getry, and Shamala, our partners in Friends for Peace and Community Development. We went for a listening session with the staff of the Eldoret Prison where we had done some AVP workshops with the staff and inmates. The group of about twenty-five people was very diverse but had no Kikuyu because they had all left town. My favorite image was of one of the guards, who was an AVP facilitator, indicating how good AVP was with his automatic rifle planted on the floor with the end pointing directly at his face. I have become so used to seeing police, and guards, with guns, I did not even notice this until he spoke about AVP.

They described the situation in Eldoret as bad as everyone was affected. One Luhya woman, whose husband was a Kisii, was threatened after she was seen helping some of her in-laws. What a dilemma to be attacked for helping out family members just because they happened to belong to another group. Others described how most of their neighbors were burned out. A Kalenjin said that most of the destruction in Eldoret was done by villagers from the countryside. Everyone who was over twenty-five years old was required to join in a "warrior" group and these were the ones who did the attacking, such as at the church which had been burned down outside of Eldoret. These "warriors" can only be stopped by their elders if the elders refuse to bless their attacks. This was what happened to calm down the town. The same person told us that on December 30 the violence was spontaneous, but now the violence was being planned and therefore could be much worse

On Thursday, we went to Kakamega. I helped interview new candidates for an additional AVP position because we were having so many requests for AVP workshops. Gladys went to town with Getry to buy relief supplies. The funds for this were supplied by the American Friends Service Committee (AFSC). When we delivered the goods at the IDP camp in Turbo, the police gave us a rough time. The head officer said that the food had to be inspected by the Health Department to make sure it was fit for human consumption to prove that we were not bringing poisoned food. Two police officers at the entrance asked Gladys why we were helping the Kikuyu when they were the cause of all the problems. As Gladys talked with the police, I found the camp leaders who knew us well. One of the leaders and the camp clerk came and talked with the police, letting them know that we were their friends. We unloaded the goods and the clerk wrote down a list of what we delivered. It was late in the afternoon and they were pondering whether they could distribute the goods before nightfall. I suggested that they at least give out the blankets since it would help keep people warm in the cold night due to the cloudiness and rain two days previous.

The few *matatus* and trucks had green branches on the front and back. According to ODM, which had planned demonstrations for that day throughout the country, those supporting them should be carrying branches and not participate in any kind of violence. Those branches were a sign of support for ODM so that the *matatu* or trucks would not be stopped by youth. When the *matatu*, which we had hired to carry the goods, pulled into the IDP camp, questions came quickly about why the owners had put branches on their *matatu*. The folks in the IDP camp clearly did not support ODM. The driver and conductor replied that they had to do this in order to move safely down the roads. Such is the ambiguity of the situation — even though the IDPs we were helping did not like it, they had to keep the branches on their vehicle in order to travel.

On Saturday, January 19, Gladys and I went for a walk to her sister's house about two miles down the hill. We passed the house of Silas Njoroge who was the Kikuyu leader at the IDP camp. His house was looted, but not burned, probably because it was close to town. Further, down the road his brother's house was looted and burned including all the corn he had in storage. They are considered the "richest" Kikuyu in the area, but neither one had a particularly fancy house, much like many of the people around here.

On Sunday, at Lumakanda Friends Church, the preacher for the day was Jemimah Mujete, the wife of the pastor, James Mujete. She lived in Eldoret and was having to move because she rented a house owned by Kikuyu. She had been warned by the youth that they were going to burn down the house she was renting. Many of the houses around her had already been burned down. She took as her text, Mathew 5:20 which reads, "I tell you, then, that you will be able to enter the Kingdom of Heaven only if you are more faithful than the teachers of the Law and the Pharisees in doing what God requires." The main part of her sermon was that Christians do not take up weapons to use on their neighbors. She gave the example of a pastor who took a spear to join in on the violence in Eldoret. This man, she clearly indicated, was not a Christian.

This was the sermon in a small church in an out-of-the-way place. I think that this is a common feeling among Kenyans who go to church. While this is a Friends church, this message could be heard in many Christian churches here. In essence, the God-fearing Christians were against the violence. There is a division between the "God-fearing Christians" and the nominal Christians. The church-going Christians shun those who do not attend church and make little outreach to them. This is particularly true of the youth. Consequently, when violence came, the God-fearing Christians had no points of contact with the looters. They were cowed down by fear, many expecting to be the next target of the wrathful crowds.

At this point in time, we were being lulled into feeling that the worse was over and the situation might be improving. The following weekend, though, Kikuyu youth began "revenge" attacks, in Nakuru and Naivasha, towns on the road between Nairobi and western Kenya. The paper said ninety additional people were killed. The police were reported to be just standing by as they were unable to control the events. Later, the army was brought in to Nakuru to control the town. At this point I wondered if Kenya would not erupt into a full-scale civil war. While Nakuru was one hundred and fifty miles from Lumakanda, I feared that the violence there would spark additional violence near our home.

The Quaker Reaction to the Violence

During this renewed violence, Friends United Meeting (FUM)-Africa Office spearheaded a consultation for Quaker leaders in Kenya in Kakamega to consider the Quaker response to the violence and crisis. The consultation started on Thursday evening and went on through Sunday. This was an opportunity for the Quaker leadership in Kenya to really assert themselves as a peace church. I hoped that they would grab the opportunity. They did.

The Quaker members traveling from Nairobi on their way to Kakamaga saw the beginning of the renewed violence in Nakuru as they witnessed a burning gas station from the bus they were traveling in. The road was closed by the end of the consultation so they had to take an airplane from Kisumu back to Nairobi. The consultation was well attended with fifty-seven Quaker leaders. Fifteen yearly meetings plus all the major Quaker organizations were present. People were very serious and concerned. By the end of the consultation, they had decided to form what was later named the "Friends Church Peace Teams." They appointed a coordinating committee of thirteen at large representatives plus the head of the six major Quaker organizations. At the time, I was somewhat surprised that I was one of the thirteen nominees as I had played a quiet role during the conference.

The next day we had planned to go to Kisumu because AGLI was conducting forty-two one-day listening sessions with the staff of the US Center for Disease Control (CDC). Yet, the situation was deteriorating. At 8:00 AM Monday morning, Eden Grace from FUM who lived in Kisumu, texted me, "I'm hearing that they are already burning and slashing [destroying] near the stage [bus station] in Kisumu." Five minutes later she texted, "Hearing gun shots now." By 10:00 AM she wrote, "They have closed all the roads and the airport. We are hearing much gun fire."

On that day, only eight people out of the forty people showed up at the CDC listening session in Kisumu as most of the participants were distracted by the events going on around them. We cancelled the workshops for the next day. The Sunset Hotel, where the workshops were taking place and the facilitators were staying, was quite safe and they did not experience any violence. The hotel was in the wealthier, more secured section of Kisumu.

One of the major problems of life in Kenya during the chaos was to know what was true from what was rumor. For instance, we got a call from Janet Ifedha, an AVP facilitator from Kakamega, asking if the bridge over the Kipkarren River was being destroyed by youth. It was not, as we had just gone over it. It was hard to tell truth from fiction with regard to the events of yesterday. We were told that Nandi youth were coming up the road to attack Kikuyu and burn Kikuyu houses up here in Lumakanda. Police were at the small bridge coming up the hill to Lumakanda, fired shots at them, and they fled. I did not think this was very plausible since they would not know where the Kikuyu lived or had lived. Then the next day, when we went out for a short trip to Florence Machayo's house for a meeting of Lugari AVP facilitators, we saw that at the Lumankanda junction with the main road, all the signs, except that

221

of the Jehovah Witnesses, had been destroyed. Two tires had been burned on the road and we could see where the pavement had been burnt and potholes were beginning to form. So what was the truth?

Then about 2:00 PM on the same day, a man was walking by our house and talking on his cell phone. He said in Swahili, "A Luo has been killed in Lumakanda." Wow. Gladys went out to find out. She was told that some Kikuyu had come to shell their dried corn and that it was suspected that they would spend the night and attack the local people. This is not feasible as I think it would be certain suicide on their part to stay. Nevertheless, this is what people might believe. The violence in this region was frequently enhanced by the concept, "You are trying to kill me, so I will kill you first." Of course, the other side thinks the same thing so preemptive violence occurs. We heard that crowd of local youth collected at the house and the police disbursed them, killing one. Later our electrician told me that the person had been killed by the police when he was taking some things from his house and the police mistakenly thought he was a looter. I was not certain if someone was killed.

He also told me that a person had been killed by the police in Kipkarren River the day before. We passed through Kipkarren River the next day and the normally very busy town was almost deserted. Was this evidence that someone had been killed?

Therefore, truth, the reality of what actually is happening around you, is difficult to grasp because all those normal markers you have about your surroundings are suspect. It is so easy to be "sucked in" by rumors. Yet, to understand the dangers around you, you have to listen to others.

I commented in my report for the day, "Enjoy watching the Super Bowl. There you can watch reality on TV and get instant replay from many angles on anything dramatic or controversial. Here we live in a state of unknowing."

Planning for Peace Work

By the end of January, few thought that the situation in Kenya was about politics — that is, who won the election. The election was no more than a "trigger" that unleashed all the hidden, covered-up resentments that had built up over the years and decades.

Here is an example. Moses Musonga, the General Secretary of the Friends World Committee for Consultation-Africa Section, buried his brother-in-law who had been killed with six arrows in his body in a conflict around Kaimosi, the home of the original Quaker mission, between the local Luhya and Nandi groups. Both these groups strongly supported ODM during the election. Someone claimed that a cow had been stolen and in retaliation a house was burned down and tit for tat fighting escalated until three people were killed. This violence had really nothing to do with the election outcome, but resentments among two neighboring groups.

In another instance, our brother-in-law, Wilson Mugalla, an over the road truck driver, carried cement from Mombasa to the Rift Valley and returned with tea for export. In the Rift Valley, he was beaten up and both his two cell phones and money he had just borrowed to expand his house were stolen. Fortunately, they did not burn his truck. Again, both Wilson and the Kalenjin who attacked him were politically on the same side.

On Friday, February 1, we attended the first meeting of the Friends Church Peace Teams (FCPT) and the next day, I chaired a meeting with the AVP facilitators from the region. The media was reporting that things were calming down. There was no one in either of those two meetings who felt that this was true. Perhaps things are calmer in Nairobi but not in Kisumu. Or perhaps the death of ten people was no longer "news." Or the media was tired of saying the same thing over and over every day. Many doubted that a political agreement would calm the escalating violence.

There were seventeen facilitators at the AVP meeting. After we finished the de-briefing mentioned above, we discussed how we could reach the young people responsible for much of the violence. and the programs we would like to do. We decided that our goal for the next six months, pending raising sufficient funds, was to do one hundred AVP workshops with two thousand youth in at least five sites in western Kenya. We hoped that in the next week or two the facilitators would go back to their communities and develop concrete plans for AVP workshops with the youth.

After over a month of discouragement and disbelief concerning the motives for the destruction around me, of the depressing thoughts trying to understand how average people could attack others for such flimsy reasons, and uncertainty of whether things would calm down or turn into greater chaos, I was relived to be involved in peacemaking activities and working to deal with the violent youth. Yet I was still apprehensive that we would be able to accomplish anything if the situation further deteriorated.

FCPT Relief Efforts

At the first meeting of the Friends Church Peace Team (FCPT), the new organization began its work by forming an "Emergency Relief and Reconciliation Program." On Thursday, February 7, FCPT conducted its first major activity. About thirty Friends visited a number of internally displaced people in the Trans Nzoia District next to Mt. Elgon in the Rift Valley. With funds donated from the United States, England, and elsewhere, a truck filled with corn, beans, rice, sugar, salt, cooking oil, blankets, and soap, was delivered to those displaced during the violence.

A Quaker pastor working for the National Council of Churches of Kenya, through his work, knew of about ten places where approximately four thousand people had not received any assistance from the Red Cross or the government of Kenya. These people noted that the Red Cross trucks passed them by to deliver food and supplies to the Kikuyu who were in an IDP camp down the road. As non-Kikuyu, they saw this as another example of the government's favoritism to Kikuyu over other people in Kenya.

Gladys and I joined the group going to a small shopping center with a few small shops on the side of the road. This center, called Misemwa, officially had two hundred fifty nine IDP families, totaling one thousand six hundred people, an average of about six people per family. The amount of food we unloaded seemed massive — fourteen two-hundred pound bags of corn, for instance. Yet, each family was given only about ten pounds of corn, two pounds of beans, a blanket, a cup of sugar, a half cup of salt, a few ounces of cooking oil, and the families with children some rice. This would be enough only for two or three days. Of course, the place was packed with people waiting patiently for the distribution. I estimated that two-thirds of the families were headed by women. There were many small children; the older ones, I hoped, were in school.

These people were not Kikuyu, the group usually targeted in the violence in western Kenya, but mostly Luhya with some Sabaot, a Kalenjin group. There was no internally displaced persons' camp like we were visiting in Turbo as the people lived in houses in the

224

area. In the small Seventh Day Adventist church at the center, eight women were living with their children. Others had rented a room in the area and a few were staying with relatives. One woman told me that she had moved with her husband and four children — and a fifth was well on its way — to live with her sister who also has four children and there was not enough food for this suddenly, vastly expanded, family. All the displaced people had come with nothing more than what they could carry.

As usual, when one delves into the details of conflict, the situation is different from the usual simplistic explanation of Kibaki versus Raila, Kikuyu versus Luo. The people here had fled from Mt. Elgon where there has been an active conflict for the last year and a half. A human rights group in nearby Bungoma had tallied four hundred dead and one hundred and fifty thousand displaced people before the election violence began on December 30. This compares to the estimate of thirteen hundred dead and six hundred and fifty thousand displaced from the post election violence. Since the post election violence was political and covered much of the country, it seemed that it was "more important" than the long simmering one on Mt Elgon. In November 2007, Gladys, Getry, and I had visited the area affected by the violence on Mt Elgon. We saw a large group of people, with bundles that they could carry, waiting to board a large truck to take them from their homes. All the houses on the hillside where they came from had been burned down.

This conflict in Mt. Elgon was between two clans of the Sabaot group, the Soy and Ndorobo, over land. The first group, which thinks that they have not been dealt with fairly in the land distribution by the Kenyan government, has formed the Sabaot Land Defense Force (SLBF). They had obtained automatic rifles and retreated into the forests on Mt Elgon to hide. The election results were used by the Sabaot Land Defense Force as a reason to attack anyone in their area from another group. This included Kikuyu who fled to the IDP camp nearby, as well as the Bugusu, a sub-group of the Luhya. Sabaot who did not support the violent wing were also sometimes targeted and had to flee to Misemwa.

I talked at length with Mildred, one of the eight women living in the church. She had six children, the youngest was on her shoulder as we talked. Her husband had left for the day when the SLDF came in red uniforms and told them to leave. She fled with her children and the few things they could carry. She had no idea where her husband was and there was little way for him to find out where his family had fled. She did not want to return to her farm on Mt. Elgon, where she had lived for twelve years, but has little idea what the future would bring for her.

Andrew, his wife and four children were attacked in the middle of the night and had fled down the mountain with nothing but what they wore. He lived in a room in a house nearby. He survived by doing day labor when he could find it. He also told me he did not want to go back to his home on Mt Elgon. When I asked people, they told me that the land on Mt. Elgon was very fertile and well watered and that is why they had bought plots there in the past but it was now too dangerous to return.

I was told also that during the previous night, there had been some unconfirmed killings and hundreds more had fled down the mountain. These newly displaced people were not on the list of two hundred and fifty nine families to receive the aid we had brought.

After three hours distributing the relief supplies at Misemwa and a short sermon and prayer, we left and joined the other people at a small cafe where we all got a snack and discussed the pros and cons of what we had done for the day. The general feeling was that we were pleased with the distribution because we had given food and supplies to people who obviously were in need. We did find it much more difficult than anticipated because people were trying to get more than their share, others were inappropriately being added to the list, and, when others gave out the relief supplies, they gave more to their own family and friends than they did others.

Although the food seemed to be little in relationship to the need, I still felt good knowing that we had helped as we were able. In this kind of work, one cannot get discouraged by the unmet needs, but must focus on what has been accomplished. If people only ate well for a few days, it was still better than having to scrounge around for a little food and going to sleep hungry.

The Situation Remains Unclear

Tuesday, February 5, on our way to Kakamega, we stopped by Florence and Alfred Machayo's house. Alfred was not there because he was accompanying a Luhya friend who was a magistrate in the Nandi area. The magistrate had been told by the area youth that he had to leave Nandi in a week or his house would be burned down.

He was looking at his plot in Lugari District to determine if he could live there with his family. In other words, one family quietly, as far as the media is concerned, displaced.

The paper reported that over one thousand teachers had not reported for work in North Rift Valley and that many students had also not returned. When we visited the Lumakanda people in the Turbo camp, they told us that their numbers have been increasing, though they did not give us an estimate, I guessed in the hundreds. This included two communities in Lugari District, which formerly had not been attacked. While their mood had never been high, more than a month in the camps had sapped whatever hope and energy they had. They felt that they would now be in such a precarious living situation for the foreseeable future. Pessimism ruled.

After more than a month of unrest, houses were still being burned. The violence of the past month compelled people to flee as soon as they felt that they were targeted. The targets were no longer only the Kikuyu in the western provinces where we lived, but anyone who did not live in his or her "home" area.

The following Monday, The *Daily Nation* covered all those affected by the violence including children not in school, children in IDP camps, colleges and other institutions who had lost their staff, manufacturing businesses that were closed, hospitals and other government offices which were understaffed as the employees fled, roads that were not being built, lost employment, and other costs of violence. A Quaker in Nairobi whose wholesale establishment was looted says he would re-open after the situation was restored to normal. A large-scale farmer told me he was cutting back on the acreage of corn he would plant the following month because he did not know if he would get seeds and fertilizer or what price he might have to pay. The cost of travel had doubled and the price increase did not seem like it was going to go down to where it had been before. I saw people wanting to get a ride in a *matatu*, asking the fare and, seeing that it is more than they had, decide not to take the ride.

At this point in the middle of February, I reported that I was very discouraged. There seemed to be no progress towards a political settlement at the top — without this, those in the countryside would continue to do whatever they felt like doing. I was reminded for William Butler Yates' lines:

Things fall apart; the centre cannot hold;
Mere anarchy is loosed upon the world,

This is a picture from our February 25 delivery of food to the IDP camp in Turbo. Pastor James Mujete, the pastor of Lumakanda Friends Church, is saying a prayer for the goods, which are stacked in front of him. Our new vehicle in the background made it much easier to deliver food and carry people. There had not been significant rain in this area for almost four months. The IDP camp was at the top of a hill on fields that grew corn last year. The place was totally dry. The soil was very loose. The wind blew much of the time, sometimes very hard, and the dust blew everywhere. In an hour my hair, like that of everyone else there, was covered with dust. They told me that a cow dies almost every day because there is not sufficient grass to feed them. As I looked at the cows, I could see that many were thin with ribs showing.

> The blood-dimmed tide is loosed, and everywhere
> The ceremony of innocence is drowned;
> The best lack all conviction, while the worst
> Are full of passionate intensity.

As an individual, I felt captive the situation, which was so much larger than I was and those around me. Even as I tried to assist in organizing peacemaking projects, I felt helpless concerning the larger chaos that was engulfing the communities around me.

Who Was Responsible for the Violence?

In a discussion with youth at our house near the end of February, Getry commented that the youth were being blamed for all the violence. A local youth, Anthony, responded that on the evening the violence started, many adults were telling the youth to attack the Kikuyu. If the youth killed someone, they were told they would get a reward. Anthony said, and the others agreed, that there was a lot of peer pressure to join in the attacks. These youth really faulted the older people for promoting the violence.

This made me reflect on the US. It is the elders (Bush, Cheney, and the generals) who sent American youth to war in Afghanistan and Iraq. The Kalenjin elders sent their warriors to attack the Kikuyu. It was the elders in Lumakanda who encouraged the youth to attack the local Kikuyu. Where the elders did not encourage the youth such as Webuye, the youth were not violent. Webuye was an example where the youth did not do any physical damage because the older people in the town told them not to.

On February 29, we had tickets to fly to the United States in order for me to conduct a three week speaking and fundraising tour. Raila Odinga of ODM had called for a general strike to begin on February 27 when we planned to travel to Nairobi to catch our flight. On February 26, US Secretary of State, Condolezza Rice, visited Kenya and met with both Kibaki and Raila. We have no idea what she said to the two, but it was clearly quite drastic because negotiations, after almost two months of stalling, began to proceed quickly. ODM called off the general strike and we traveled to Nairobi with no problems. At the airport as we were waiting to board the plane to the United States, the big screen TV showed Kibaki and Raila signing a power-sharing accord with Kofi Annan, the former UN General Secretary who mediated the agreement, in the background. This ended, at least for the time being, the violence in the country. Now it was time to heal, to return to normal life, and to tackle the many problems that led to the post election violence.

This was a great relief to me and I expect to other Kenyans and people around the world following the conflict. The chaos had made me live on a pinpoint for the previous two months. Every step I made had the possibility of danger. Any slight mistake could have dire consequences to me personally or to others around me. Yet on the other hand, I did not want to be paralyzed into inaction as so many others were. My most important mistake was to be lulled into complacency before the voting. Unlike many Kenyans and expatriates concerned about Kenya, I realized the election process in Kenya was volatile. What I did fail to read properly was that the pre-election violence was a clear indication of the larger post election violence that followed. I remember any other two months of my life as a blur, but these two months from the announcement of the election results on December 30, 2007 to the signing of the accord on February 28, 2008 define a well-remembered sequence of events as any traumatic experience does.

Conclusion

While I had been in insecure situations previously, such as during the civil war in Burundi and visiting Masisi in eastern Congo when it was controlled by rebels, this was the first time for me to live through an extensive period of unrest. On July 5, 1969, I had been in Kenya when the politician, Tom Mboya, was assassinated. Kenya, at that time, seemed to be falling apart, but then for some unknown reason it pulled itself back together.

At no time during those two months did I feel physically threatened. As Getry told me, "You are not one of the targeted people." Moreover both in my father-in-law's house and in Lumakanda, I was living among the Luhya, my wife's ethnic group. Had I lived nearby in Turbo or Kipkarren River where there was a lot of violence, I might have felt differently.

It is strange how calm, but alert I became during these difficult times. I became very cautious and quickly postponed any activity if there was the slightest possibility of violence. While I spent a lot more time "doing nothing" at home, my senses were very alert at every beating of a drum, the amount of traffic I could see on the road, a fire in the distance, and just overhearing talk in the town.

The uncertainty was difficult. Were things going to get better or worse? Frequently I was fearful of another major escalation in violence. Most times this did not happen, but sometimes it did.

Although I was one of those people who did not think that Kenya was a "stable" country, the violence made Gladys and me to assess if we should remain in Lumakanda. As the situation returned to normal, we realized that we had built a nice house in Lumakanda, that we were close to many relatives and people Gladys knew from her original home in Viyalo, that we were comfortable with the people in town, and that moving would probably not guarantee anything because there was no way to predict how the next round of violence, if there were one, would play out

On the more positive side, if there is such a thing, because of my experiences in the region, I knew that the earlier we began peacemaking and reconciliation work, the better. Therefore, within in a week after the violence erupted, we were visiting the local IDP camp at Lumakanda School. As soon as I could move about, I began organizing peacemaking activities. This was helped by the fact that people from overseas were extremely generous in supporting this work so that funding itself was not a stumbling block to action.

I, like most other people, am left with the fear that at the next election in August 2012, there will be renewed violence, perhaps even worse than in early 2008. On the one hand, this fear is a great motivator to do peacemaking work, but on the other, it is an unsettling feeling of potential doom. The optimistic and the pessimistic parts of me — and I think of most people in Kenya — vie with each other about that future.

The Blind Men and the Kenyan Elephant:
Nine Interpretations of the Violence in Kenya in Early 2008

During the post election violence in Kenya I received an email from Hezron Masitsa, the AVP-Coordinator, that a Kenyan, Joran Shijenje, had been shot and killed on his way home from work. This story seemed like more of the same violence. However, the Kenyan had been shot coming home from work in Baltimore, Maryland. During the two months of conflict in Kenya when an estimated one thousand three hundred were killed, there were about three hundred and sixty homicides in the California which has about the same population as Kenya. In normal circumstances Kenya's homicide rate is equivalent to that of the US. So the violence in Kenya is similar to what Americans live with every day.

There is an Asian parable about blind men and the elephant that became popular in the West through a nineteenth century poem by John Godfrey Saxe. The tale involves a group of blind men who touch an elephant with each one touching a specific yet different part. One man feels the side of the elephant while another touches the tusk. When the men come together for discussion, they are in complete disagreement because each one of them know only a part of the elephant. The story is often used to indicate that reality may be viewed differently depending upon one's perspective, suggesting that what seems as a truth to one person may be relative due to the deceptive nature of perception.

This post-election conflict in Kenya can be interpreted in at least nine different ways. You may find that you feel comfortable with one or more of those interpretations and reject others. I have versions of the "elephant" that I prefer more than others.

1. **"Ancient Tribal Hatreds:"** Almost all the international coverage of the crisis in Kenya was based on the interpretation that the conflict was due to "ancient tribal hatreds." In fact 43% of those murdered in Kenya were killed by the police and not in ethnic fighting. Contrary to international and Kenyan law, the police used live bullets against demonstrators, rioters, and looters.

While the international media was focusing on those burnt to death in a church outside of Eldoret, the Kenya media was focusing on those killed and wounded by the police in Kisumu. Of the eight-two people killed in Kisumu, the home city of the Luo, no Kikuyu were killed by the Luo; all were killed by the police.

While the violence was explained in the international media as "ancient tribal hatreds," the two groups – Kikuyu and Luo – do not live next to each other and probably did not have much extensive contact until about the 1940's during World War II. Therefore any problems between the two groups could not be considered "ancient." Moreover, these two groups were allies during the two major changes in Kenyan politics — the campaign for independence from the British in the early 1960's and the overthrow of the Moi regime in 2002.

Here are a number of examples of incidents that contradict the "ancient tribal hatred" concept.

• A Luhya woman from Lumakanda Friends Church hid a Kikuyu woman who gave birth on Dec 30 when the violence started.

• A Luo I know told me his brother hid a Kikuyu in his house.

• Three thousand people in Kibaki home constituency in the center of Kikuyuland voted for Raila. There were seven other candidates to vote for including other Kikuyu if they did not want vote for Kibaki. Raila continually said that many Kikuyu voted for him.

• There was a hit list out for twenty-five Kikuyu who had "betrayed their tribe." They were the human rights advocates and leaders of NGOs who had criticized the government over the election tallying, the use of live bullets, the restrictions on press freedom, and the right to hold demonstrations. In other words, some of the most vocal critics of what happen were Kikuyu.

• Part of the violence in Naivasha was Kikuyu gangs fighting other Kikuyu gangs. Since this does not fit the media stereotype, it was been ignored in the international coverage.

• There are large areas of Western Province, perhaps over half of the area, and possibly also parts of Nyanza and Rift Valley provinces where the Kikuyu were not forced out, their houses and shops were not looted and burned, and they continued living peacefully with their neighbors.

• Many non-Kikuyu have been in the forefront of visiting and bringing relief to those Kikuyu in IDP camps. The Red Cross volunteers who were helping at Lumakanda were mostly local Luhya.

I will discuss this more in the next chapter on the media perceptions of Africa.

2. Stolen election: The second interpretation is that the conflict was a result of the election being stolen by the Kibaki government. Those people who supported Raila Odinga and his Orange Democratic Party (ODM) felt that the election had been stolen from them. They had gone patiently and properly to the polls to vote and then the results were manipulated. ODM planned a rally at Uhuru Park in Nairobi where a million of his supporters were expected to attend. Although freedom of assembly is one of the freedoms people have, the government blocked the park by ringing it with riot police who used tear gas, water cannons, and live bullets to disperse those who were planning to attend. As could be expected, many of the youth, who were tear gassed, rioted and, thus, began the destruction in Nairobi. Other cities which were supposed to have demonstrations had the same result. For some reason the authorities in Kapsabet, in the volatile Rift Valley province, allowed a demonstration there which went on peacefully. The demonstrators blew off steam, went home and there was no violence.

The difficulty with this interpretation is that, in a counterfactual world where Raila Odinga became president, the problem would still be the same — a sharply divided country — with only the faces of power having changed.

3. Class warfare: A third interpretation is class warfare. The election results were no more than a trigger for decades-long tension due to economic inequality. During the five years of the first

Kibaki term as President, after years of stagnation, the economy had grown robustly reaching 7% in 2007. But this growth in income had mostly benefited the wealthy. Kenya is a nation with one of the highest rates of inequality in the world. Kenya is supposed to be a poor country yet the Kenyan elite is extremely wealthy, many whom are Kikuyu. The average person, who has no direct contact with the elite, took out their pent up rage on their Kikuyu neighbors who were economically no better off than they were.

Another aspect of this inequality is that government funds, economic development, and business opportunities were confined to Nairobi and Central Province, the home area of the Kikuyu, while much of rest of the country was starved for funds. All people paid taxes which were disproportionably spent in the center of the country. The violence was a response to these economic injustices.

4. Youth rebellion: Another interpretation is that the violence was a youth rebellion. Many youth felt alienated perceiving that they had no stake in Kenyan society and no hope for a better future. While older people tended to vote for Kibaki, the youth tended to vote for Raila. I was at a meeting where two parents said that they had voted for Kibaki, while their children had voted for Raila and this had created tensions in the family. The youth who voted for Raila were voting for change and a better future. They felt that their vote had been stolen from them, after they had gone naively, as it turned out, to the polls to vote for change.

5. Land issues: In the Rift Valley, but also in other parts of the country, there are issues over ownership and control of land. When the British came to Kenya at the beginning of the twentieth century, the Kalenjin and Masai groups in the Rift valley gave military opposition. As a result the British crushed them, and drove the surviving Masai and Kalenjin north and south into the marginal areas of the Rift Valley. In this fertile, and now ethnically cleansed region, the British created the "white highlands," giving large estates to British settlers. When Kenya gained independence in 1963 the Kalenjin and Masai thought that the lands seized from them would be returned. What actually happened was that many of these large estates were transferred from the departing British settlers to the new ruling Kenyan elite who were mostly the loyalist supporters of the British during the struggle for independence. Other estates were bought up by land companies and sold off as small plots to those who could afford them — in most cases, this meant the Kikuyu from Central Province rather than the original owners of the land.

These land issues have not been resolved, but allowed to fester. In the 1992 elections there was violence in the Rift Valley which Kenyans in Lumakanda tell me that it was even worse than the 2008 round of violence. At the time of the 1997 election there was additional violence in the Rift Valley. On Mount Elgon since June 2006, over four hundred people had been killed over a land dispute among two clans. There had been other deadly disputes in Molo, Rongai, Laikipia, and elsewhere. The election results triggered additional violence in these areas as the original inhabitants wished to push out recent immigrants

6. Violence as usual: Although Kenya, unlike many of its neighbors, had the reputation of being a peaceful, calm country, I had always considered it otherwise. On May 5, 1969, I was in Kenya when the powerful Minister for Economic Development, Tom Mboya, a Luo, was assassinated. Kenya felt then just as it did during this crisis. The glue that had been holding the country together was no longer working. One feared that the country would descend into chaos. The difference in 2008 was cell phones and the Internet. In 1969 we had to rely solely on rumor. In 2008 we could contact people we knew in other parts of the country by calling or texting with our cell phones to ask what was happening. Then we could make reports to the outside world, as I did, of the events as we saw them.

The campaign period leading up to December 27 was also very violent with at least twenty-five people were killed. Lastly, almost every few days I read in the newspaper of people killed by mob justice. The attitude that makes this acceptable is the same attitude that allows a person to attack a neighbor because they happen to be from a different ethnic group.

7. Centralized government: The nature of colonial rule is that everything is controlled by the colonial power from the center. Consequently, when the British gave Kenya independence it also gave them a very strong central government. When Jomo Kenyatta was president, this centralization was increased as he was an icon that could not be challenged. As far as the election was concerned, President Kibaki appointed all twenty-two members of the Electoral Commission of Kenya — the same commission that announced that he had won the December 27 election. Therefore it was a partisan body.

A result of this highly centralized government is that winning the election becomes crucial as the candidates either win "everything" or nothing. It also dictates that the control of wealth and power goes to the group that controls the presidency. As a referendum on centralized power, Raila Odinga's Orange Democratic Movement won six of the eight provinces, ninety-nine members of parliament, and control of almost all the cities outside of Central and Eastern Provinces which were won by Kibaki. So the violence was a demand for "devolution" of power, as it was called.

8. International Community: We must not let the international community off the hook. I will give three examples of how actions of the international community have adversely affected the situation in Kenya.

The first is birth control. In 1980 when there was a big debate about abortion in the United States, the Reagan administration cut off funds for family planning accusing them of promoting abortion. In Kenya, this came to mean opposition to birth control. When I was in Machakos District, Kenya in 1970, the family planning clinic had two people for a population of almost one million. At that time Kenya had one of the highest birth rates in the world. It was the large number of children born during this time who grew up to become the disenfranchised youth who participated in the violence after the election.

The second is the structural adjustment program placed on Kenya in the 1980's by the International Monetary Fund. This meant that the Kenyan government could not increase the number of public servants, including teachers. As the population of school aged children was increasing rapidly, the number of teachers was not. Moreover, in 2003, the Kibaki declared free primary school education and about one million additional children showed up for school. The result is classes of up to one hundred students with few resources for their education. The large group of children born in the 70's and 80's did not receive adequate education.

Lastly there is the issue of corruption. The centralized form of government in Kenya also allowed for gigantic corruption at the center. This will be covered in more detail in Chapter 14.

9. Spiritual/religious: The zeitgeist of modern Kenyan society is Hobbesian economics — if everyone does things in their own (and family, clan, and tribal) interest, society will function for the best. This has long ago been determined to mean that the fortunate few exploit the many. Among the middle and upper classes in Kenya, personal and family greed is more important than societal prosperity. This is true from the rulers at the top to those at the

236

bottom who believe that stepping on others is a legitimate method of getting ahead. Rather than praising Kikuyu for their hard work and emulating their success, the violence after the election was an attempt to bring down to the level of everyone else those who were perceived to have succeeded. The Biblical injunctions to love one's neighbor, to do unto others as you would have them do unto you have been ignored.

You may select those interpretations that seem most logical to you. I would say that a solution to the violence will require much more than a political settlement by the two sides. Rather it will necessitate a major restructuring of Kenyan society that addresses the underlying causes mentioned above. Kenyans are well aware of these issues and the need for corrective action. Unfortunately in the past whenever there has been a crisis in Kenya, the tendency has been to ignore the underlying causes as the country returned to "normal." But "normal" in Kenya has meant allowing pressure to build up beneath the surface. Pressure which will eventually explode into violence again unless these issues are addressed. It is still too early to determine if fundamental changes will be made this time or if all will soon be "back to normal," if there will be significant improvements for all, or another round of violence, perhaps during the next election in 2012.

Section 4

Understanding the Role of the West

In July 2008, I took this picture of this UN peacekeeping tank, guarding an intersection in Goma, North Kivu, Democratic Republic of the Congo. It illustrates for me one thing that is wrong with UN peacekeeping missions.

A few months after I took this picture, the Tutsi rebel warlord, Lauren Nkunda, attacked the outskirts of Goma and threatened to take over the city. The Congolese army which was defending the town went on a looting, killing, and raping rampage of their own citizens in Goma. The UN peacekeeping force, MONUC, did nothing. Why? Because they could not. How do you stop a rape with a tank? Do you blow everyone to smithereens? As in the wars in Iraq and Afghanistan, the military thinks that more firepower, bigger and more lethal weapons will bring "victory." What is needed is not the militarization of the conflict with heavy weapons, but police work with the UN officers actively in the field providing security, in this case not only from the many rebel groups, but from the Congolese army itself.

Chapter 12
Media Projections of Africa

The Context

Africa is 11.7 million square miles or more than three times the area of the United States. Over two thousand languages are spoken in fifty-five countries. The genetic diversity among Africans is greater than among all the people of the rest of the world. This was obvious to me one day when I was sitting by the roadside in Bukavu, a city in eastern Congo. As I watched the people go by, there were extremely tall, thin people, tall broad shouldered people, very short people, both thin and broad shouldered. The color of their skin ranged from almost pitch black, to tan, to a very reddish hue. Almost every person had a unique combination of physical characteristics.

Africa is a huge, diverse continent. For some, the whole of Africa is seen as one country. Each country and even parts within a country have their complexities. I have had many requests from people asking for help as they parachute into Rwanda for a few days to interview some Rwandan genocide survivors in order to understand the genocide. This is impossible. It takes a long time to grasp what is happening in just one country.

When Africa is discussed in the Western media, the issues are usually broken down into thirty second sound bites and Africa makes up a very small percentage of the news. When was the last time you saw a piece on Burundi in the US nightly news?

The Need to Create Division in Rwanda and Burundi

As I mentioned earlier, the conflict between Tutsi, Hutu, and Twa began during the colonial period between 1895 and 1961, based on media stereotypes to provide a method for the Germans and the Belgians to rule in Rwanda and Burundi. The consequences were the Rwanda genocide in 1994 and the Burundian Civil War from 1993 to 2005. European racism has had dire consequences.

With the demise of Adolph Hitler, blatant racism has gone out of fashion. Yet the world is left with remnants of this racism, often undetected without investigation into its roots. A prime example is the division of the Tutsi, Hutu, and Twa in Rwanda and Burundi which was implemented at the grassroots level by local government officials at the behest of the colonial power. During the colonial period, Rwanda and Burundi were lumped together as Ruanda-Urundi since both countries had similar cultures, but as always with significant differences that are glossed over by expatriates.

As the European explorers traversed the African continent in the late nineteenth century, they made not only observations, but theories to explain these observations. When Europeans entered the area of Rwanda and Burundi, they found Tutsi people who, to their biased observations, looked more like Europeans than other Africans they met. They then concluded that these people must have come from Ethiopia.

Why was this important? Nineteenth and early twentieth century race theory did not just have three or four races. It put all people into a hierarchy of races so that Germans, for example, were much superior to Slavs. Italians and Greeks were lower on this hierarchical scale because they were darker skinned than northern Europeans. The bottom rung of the white race was the Ethiopians. Therefore, if some people — called the Tutsi — came originally from Ethiopia that means they were of the white race, even if it was the lowest rung. According to this theory, they would then be destined to rule over the African races of Hutu and Twa.

This bogus theory had consequences. During the 1994 genocide in Rwanda, the hate radio station instructed people to kill the Tutsi, throw their bodies into the river, so that they could go back to Ethiopia. The idea was that the bodies would float down the Kagera River into Lake Victoria, down the White Nile to Khartoum, then up the Blue Nile back to Ethiopia. Preposterous? Yes. But the Tanzanians pulled twenty thousand Tutsi bodies out of the Kagera River where it empties into Lake Victoria. Quite rightly they were afraid that the dead bodies would pollute the whole lake.

Originally Rwanda and Burundi were part of German East Africa. When Germany lost World War I, Tanganyika was given to the British. The Belgians had to have their reward and were given Ruanda-Urundi as their prize. The Belgians had a problem in Rwanda and Burundi. There was no way to divide and rule because everyone spoke the same language, intermingled, and intermarried.

They developed the following theory which is still referred to in many media reports about Rwanda and Burundi. The Twa, who are less than one percent of the population, were the original "pygmy" inhabitants. They were considered "primitive" hunters and gatherers. They were, and still are, despised in Rwanda and Burundi.

Then, according to the mythology, sometime at the beginning of the Christian era, the Bantu speaking, agricultural Hutu arrived, mostly displacing the Twa. In race theory, being a farmer is clearly superior to being a hunter/gatherer. In Europe, being a tiller of the soil — a peasant, a serf — was considered low class. It's still this way in much of Europe. Yet these peasant classes had to be the majority of the population because the ruling class has to be relatively small.

So the Tutsi, as low rung "whites," were assigned to the role of rulers. They were cattle keepers which is superior to being a hunter/gatherer or a farmer. Remember that the ruling classes in Europe are descended from the horse riding knights — since there were no horses in the region, cattle had to be the substitution. In the 1930's in Rwanda, the Belgians classified everyone as a Tutsi, Hutu, or Twa. They counted the number of cows a person had, measured the size of their nose, noted the color of their skin, and then gave them a classification — ruler, peasant, outcast. It is not remarkable that they found that 14% or so of the people were Tutsi, about the upper limit needed for a ruling class.

The Belgians then issued everyone identity cards with the person's racial classification. If people were allowed to be classified as mixed due to intermarriage, this system would not have worked. Therefore, they adopted the common rule in Africa that a person has the identity of their father.

Adrien Niyongabo, the Burundi HROC coordinator, has an interesting story about this. In Burundi, the Belgians did not put the racial identity on the identity card. Like "race" in the United States a child had to figure out his or her classification since no one tells him or her. Adrien was born in Bujumbura and when he was seven, his father returned up-country leaving his mother behind. He did not know his ethnicity until one day, while he was cultivating with his mother, a Tutsi, he asked her what group he belonged to. She told him that he was a Hutu because his father was a Hutu. Since that time, Adrien accepted that identity. Yet this led to later problems as Adrien describes:

> In October 1993, the death of the first Hutu elected president gave rise to a new round of massacres between

Test you ethnic discernment. There is one *mzungu,* two Hutu, and five Tutsi in this picture. I am sure you can pick out the *mzungu* on the left, me. One of the stereotypes of a Tutsi is that they are tall. You can pick the man, third from the right, as a Tutsi. This is Adrien Niyongabo who is a Hutu. This illustrates the problem with ethnic stereotyping.

Hutu and Tutsi. The night of the 23rd, the government military [Tutsi], attacked my suburb. The Hutu were forced to leave the area or to hide themselves. As many others did, I followed the queue toward the hills surrounding Bujumbura. Unfortunately, after just one mile, I was stopped by two men with guns; stopped and forbidden to follow the others. Before I could even ask why, they added that I was a Tutsi who followed the Hutu so that I could investigate how things were settled and maybe go back to tell the government army. "So, we are going to kill you," they said. I kept quiet waiting, expecting to see God in few seconds.

In a short time, a man came up to where we were and asked them what I was doing there. They answered him the same way they had told me before. And the man said, "Please, I know who is his Father, who is his Mum. He is a Hutu as we are. Let him join the others." One of the two men asked him: "Do you know him really?" The man responded by saying, "Yes, yes!!!" Turning to me, the two men with guns said, "You are saved, guy. You can keep on following others!" Could I believe it? Like a new morning, the dark night looked to me. My life was given back to me again. Praise the Lord! This entire incident came from the stereotypes, which we use in Burundi to say that this person is a Hutu or Tutsi. In some cases, one can be totally wrong mostly with our patriarchal system, where one relies on his father's ethnic group independently from the mother's ethnic group. This event encouraged me to have an inwards look. Many other innocent Burundians, men, women, girls, boys, like me I thought, would have been murdered in similar circumstances. I felt great bitterness and wished that I would get an opportunity to participate in reconciling the two groups.

During the colonial period this mythical racial theory was taught in Ruanda-Urundi schools as historically true. It gave intellectual justification for the divisions of the society into hostile groups. Many Tutsi imbibed their superiority and many Hutu believed that their humble background made them inferior. Ironically more recent DNA analysis of Tutsi, Hutu, and Twa indicate that all three groups are closely related and this theory of separate origins is without basis in fact.

As the Belgians implemented this racist policy, they gave all benefits — education, jobs, government employment, etc. — to the Tutsi at the expense of the Hutu and Twa. On each hill of mountainous Rwanda and Burundi, Tutsi were appointed as local government leaders and required to fulfill the dictates of the *Mwami* (king) who was told what to do by the few Belgian colonists.

When I was a boy, my Polish peasant grandfather, Frank Zarembka, told me that around the turn of the twentieth century, when he was sixteen, he was sent off from his home in Russian controlled Poland to Dazing (now Gdansk) which at that time was controlled by the Germans. At the docks he unloaded cement boats and sand barges, twelve hours per day, six days per week, with the only holiday being Christmas. As part of a long file of men, he would pick up a fifty kilogram (one hundred and ten pound) bag of cement in the boat, put it on his shoulder, and walk out onto the dock and into a warehouse where the cement was piled in huge stacks. When the sand barges came, six of the men would be given shovels and a certain amount of time to fill a big bucket that a crane lifted to the shore. In all these activities, there were German supervisors with whips who did not hesitate to beat any of the "Slavs" whom they thought were not working hard enough. This was the reality in Europe at the turn of the century. Do you think it would be better in Africa?

The Germans and then the Belgians believed in forced labor in their colonies. Rwanda and Burundi are filled with very steep hills. Road making was back-breaking work done with only a pick and shovel. The Tutsi appointed by the colonialists were required to marshal a gang of Hutu and force them to work. The liberal use of the whip was prevalent. Any Tutsi who did not perform as expected was beaten and dismissed by his superiors.

At the end of World War I, each of the victorious powers were given parts of the former German colonial empire as League of Nations trust territories. Britain was given German East Africa which was renamed Tanganyika. But that corner of German East Africa, Ruanda-Urundi, close to the Belgium Congo was given to Belgium as their spoils of war. For reasons that I have not been able to determine, a small part of Rwanda, next to Uganda, called Kisoro was given to Britain. It still is a district now in Uganda. The people there speak Kiyarwandan, the language of Rwanda. Unlike their Belgium counterparts, the British colonial government in Uganda did not stress the Tutsi/Hutu/Twa divide. As a consequence until this day, ethnic division is not an issue in that district. This is a prime illustration of how these divisions were a product of the colonial rulers and their need to divide in order to rule.

"Ancient Tribal Hatreds"

Reporting on Africa is frequently based on the sole assumption that conflict is due to "ancient tribal hatreds." The basic underlying assumption is Africans are "tribal" and thereby cannot really be understood because they have this mystical "tribal" component that enlightened Westerners can never understand. Other normal, understandable explanations are ignored.

On April 24, 1994, only eighteen days after the beginning of the genocide in Rwanda, I wrote the following letter to the editor of *The Washington Post*. It was not published.

Jennifer Parmelee's ("Fade to Blood," April 24) analysis of the slaughter in Rwanda must be music to the ears of those responsible. Human Rights Watch-Africa has publicly identified Colonel Augustin Bizimungu, Captain Pasqual Simbikangwa, and Colonel Theoneste Bagasora as those at the top responsible for the killings. These were the leaders of a well-orchestrated coup by the ultra right-wing Hutu military, which has systematically targeted their opponents, whether Hutu or Tutsi, and have completely eliminated them. Considering the killings to be "tribal hatred" that "defies comprehension" excuses those responsible for the slaughter. This excusing allows a similar slaughter to occur in Burundi or another country in Africa or elsewhere as politically motivated killings are cloaked in "an eternal hell of ethnic violence." Rather we need to analyze the situation in places like Rwanda and put blame on those who are responsible, convening international tribunals such as Nuremberg to hold responsible those who murder their fellow countrymen.

If this is our analysis, then World War I and II can be explained by the "ancient tribal hatreds" between the British, French, and Russians and then the Americans on one side and the Germans and Italians and then the Japanese on the other. We would still need to explain how the "ancient tribal hatreds" between the British and French, which lasted for centuries, turned them suddenly into allies.

African leaders and rebels are acutely aware of this Western interpretation of African events. When it is to their advantage, they skillfully play into this simplistic explanation which covers more than it explains. For instance, during the Rwandan genocide the Hutu *genocidaires* told the international community that the killings were just due to old animosities between the Tutsi and Hutu and that, while they were trying to stop the violence, the bitterness was so great that they were unable. Unfortunately, many foreigners accepted this erroneous explanation.

There are two intertwining stereotyped images of Africa. One is that the African is perceived to be a simple, happy, over-sexed, singing/dancing person who, as I was once told in the United States, "can not think in the abstract." He is the "noble savage" who has not been corrupted by the wantonness of Western civilization such as Coca-Cola. One of the recurrent themes in reporting about

Africa now is the AIDS epidemic. This is seen as an example of the "over-sexed" African, with little discussion that the AIDS virus in Africa is more virulent than the one found in the United States, that poor nutrition and medical services are a contributing factor, that preventive measures like the use of condoms are opposed by conservative Christian and Muslim groups, and the AIDS epidemic was out of control before significant measurers were taken to combat it.

As I mentioned above, the other stereotype is that the African is viewed as a superstitious, violent savage full of ancient tribal hatreds. The reporting on the 2008 post-election violence in Kenya is a good example of this outlook. Almost all media reported the violence as due to the conflict between the Kikuyu and Luo. Starting on page 232, I indicated why this interpretation was invalid and have given other possible interpretations for the violence.

As a result of these two stereotypes, Africa's problems are seen as intractable. Since they are based on flawed human characteristics, they are immune to improvement. Hopelessness for the development of Africa results, reinforcing rather than solving the problems that do exist. As you notice these stereotypes in the reporting on Africa, be aware of their implications. Of course, people these days are too nice and they do not write so crassly as they once did. The fact that it is done subtly, frequently by unwritten assumptions, makes it even harder to detect unless one is extremely critical of what one hears and reads.

International Reporting on Kenyan Post Election Violence

During the post election violence in January and February 2008, there was, for an African issue, an extraordinary amount of international media coverage. Since I was witness to the events, I analyzed carefully what was being written both in Kenya and internationally. Here are some of my observations.

On Monday, January 7, Elizabeth A. Kennedy of Associated Press filed a report, "Kenyan Rivals Make Concessions." It included the following paragraph:

An official in neighboring Uganda said over the weekend, 30 fleeing Kenyans were thrown into the border river by Kenyan attackers, and were presumed drowned. Two Ugandan truck drivers carrying the group said they were stopped Saturday at a roadblock mounted by vigilantes who identified the refugees as Kikuyu and threw them into the deep, swift-flowing Kipkaren River, said Himbaza Hashaka, a Ugandan border official. The drivers said none survived, Hashaka said.

The Kipkarren River is about three miles from my home in Kenya and where the post office has my mail box. The day after I read this I walked over this bridge. As I expected, the river was a rather placid, slow moving pool of water since there had not been any significant rain for over two months. If someone had thrown me off the bridge into the water, I would have just stood up and walked up the bank. Moreover the "border river" is about seventy-five miles from the Uganda border and closer to Eldoret than Uganda. When I asked Florence Machayo, a neighboring Quaker peace activist, about this story, she curtly replied, "It is a lie."

If it had been true, it would have been one of the largest massacres in the 2008 post-election violence in Kenya. If the Kenyan papers had reported this story —.and they did not — it would have incited further violence in the country. Nonetheless, *Time* and CNN reported the story. The fact that this was shoddy reporting — an unverified report told by someone who was not a witness to the event — is not the point here. The point is that it was believed and promoted because it fit into the stereotyping of Africa. I emailed both *Time* and CNN asking that they retract this untrue story, but never received a response from either.

Here is a January 7 story from Agence France Presse, titled "Police cheer as Kenya's witch-wary looters return war spoils."

Dozens of looters who profited from Kenya's post-election unrest began returning or dumping their ill-gotten gains around the port city of Mombasa Monday, frightened of cursed goods, police said.

The Kenyan papers had other explanations for the return of the goods. First, the government in Mombasa, a majority Muslim area, had declared an amnesty period of two days during which anyone who returned looted goods would not be prosecuted. This was reinforced by the Imams who preached in their mosques that people should return stolen goods. Christian preachers also advised the return of stolen goods. The Kenyan reports had no mention of the alleged witchcraft. The peacemaking effort by the Muslims was not reported because it contradicts the jihadist stereotype that Muslims are violent. Would this article have been published in the Western media if its title had been "Muslim Imams preach peace — ask looters to return stolen goods?"?

As a third example, on January 27, Reuters wire service distributed a picture of a woman lying dead on the floor in a pool of blood with her baby boy crying on a chair behind her.

This picture would not have appeared in papers or TV in the United States. There is a voluntary censorship of not showing dead bodies in the US media. Until recently, the US government censored the filming or photographing of caskets of American soldiers killed in Iraq or Afghanistan. This sanitizes Americans perceptions. Pictures showing body parts of people in Iraq or Afghanistan blown apart by American missiles are never show to the American public. If they were, would not American public resistance to the wars occur much sooner than it now does? Exactly — that is why the media and US government keep this out of the media.

Contrary to the caption, this woman was not a victim of ethnic hostility. She was a Luo married to a Kikuyu — the two antagonistic ethnic groups — but she was shot and killed by the police. Police killings were the major story in the Kenyan press as over 40% of the people who were killed were shot by the police. Contrary to international law, the police were using live bullets on demonstrators and looters. A stray bullet had hit this woman now lying in a pool of her own blood.

In these cases, Western readers were fed the African stereotype of savagery and witchcraft. The events on the ground were reported using biased assumptions about Africa, regardless of the actual facts. There is a synergetic aspect to this misreporting. Readers more easily absorb information that conforms to their mindset which the reporters must pander to in order to be published.

The reporting on this one two-month long conflict is only glimpse at how Africa is portrayed in the media. As long as the stereotypes continue and this simplistic explanation is what the media thinks people in the United States wants to hear, they will continue to serve us this pap. As a result, Americans will continue to be uninformed.

How These Stereotypes Play Out in the Bigger Picture

Estimated Deaths Due to War		
Middle Africa—Total (from 1980 to 2010)		11,201,300
Darfur, Sudan	100,000	
Southern Sudan	2,500,000	
Uganda	300,000	
Kenya	1,300	
Rwanda	500,000	
Burundi	300,000	
Democratic Republic of the Congo	5,000,000	
Angola	2,500,000	
US Civil War		1,100,000
World War I		8,500,000

As I said above, the media give a snapshot — on TV it is only a few minutes and in the papers it is two thousand words or less. Consequently the historical context of the events are either overlooked or made into a sound-bite. Let us look at the larger picture. as indicated in the table above, that shows the deaths that have occurred in the middle of Africa in the last forty years, compare it to some other major conflicts.

Before continuing, I want to offer a caveat: Naturally, talking the large numbers of deaths in the table are only ballpark estimates as no one knows the real number. Once when I was in Burundi there was a massacre just south of Bujumbura. Some reports said that one hundred twenty-five people were killed, while the government reported fifteen. What was the truth? Who really knows but the accepted total in the media was one hundred twenty-five. So when we are talking about hundreds of thousands, the actual number of men, women, and children who have died is really unknown. But overall the numbers are staggering, surpassing the deaths in World War I.

Note that my figure for Darfur, one hundred thousand, is much lower than the four hundred to five hundred through reported by the Save Darfur Coalition (SDC). This illustrates another problem — various actors in these conflicts inflate or deflate the figures. The SDC needed large numbers to sustain its viewpoint in pushing for the US government to intercede in the conflict.

Notice also, as I explained in Chapter 2, that I put the Rwanda genocide at five hundred thousand and not the eight hundred and fifty thousand to one million usually given.

Another issue is that these numbers are not obtained by counting bodies. As a kid I once got a roll of adding machine paper and decided I would write all the numbers up to one million. I quit shortly after I passed the one thousand mark and I learned that counting to one million was a gigantic undertaking. Most of these African numbers are estimates based on mortality rates — that is, how many people are missing as compared to a peaceful society.

One of the main reasons that the media usually does not cover these conflicts is that most of the deaths — 90% in the case of the Congo — are due to exposure, lack of medical attention, and starvation when people flee their homes during violent attacks. I met a young man in Rwanda who had lived for more than six months in the forest. I think he survived by coming out of the forest at night and robbing people's fields for food. He was young and strong. The weak, the sick, children, and the elderly would not have this strength and these are the ones who succumb to the rigors of flight. Each time there is a report about a fight in the region and that people are fleeing, remember that some of those who are fleeing will not survive. Since the days of the cavemen, it is clear why people live in houses and not under the open sky where rain, mosquitoes, animals, and whatever can bring sickness and death. When most of the deaths are private affairs in the obscurity of the forest, how is the media going to record this? Where are the flashy pictures of fire and brimstone? Yet if a person is dead, he or she is dead regardless of whether that person had been shot or died of exposure.

One of my great-grandfathers had two brothers killed in the Civil War. All three of the brothers of another of my great-grandfathers served in the Civil War. All were wounded, all became alcoholics, only one married (for a brief time), and all died young. My two great-grandfathers "survived" (lucky for me) because they were too young to fight. The one million one hundred thousand deaths in the US Civil War were approximately 3% of the total population of the United States at that time. Soldiers fought great battles where the two sides killed each other with utter abandon. Even in this case, most of those soldiers died from their wounds, poor sanitation, and inadequate food and medical attention.

Those Civil War reenactments which are so popular these days at the sites of the various Civil War battles completely overlook how brutal the Civil War was. By the end of the Civil War one quarter of the Union Troops was African-American. Whenever they were captured — contrary to the rules of war — they and their white officers were executed and frequently mutilated. In retaliation, Union soldiers executed Confederate soldiers in the same grisly manner. As soon as a battle was over, looters robbed the bodies of money, shoes, and anything else remotely useful. Soon the stink was overwhelming. Dogs and pigs gnawed on the remains. As General Sherman famously said, "War is hell!"

As the Union armies invaded the South, they continued to kill, loot, and destroy, frequently, living off the land. There may have been a good deal of raping going on also, but due to the Victorian sensibilities of that time, I suspect that this was omitted from the records. I also suspect that the figure given in the table for the deaths during the Civil War underestimates the number of civilians, including the just freed slaves, who died of exposure, hunger, and disease. We have forgotten this brutality. Since we have forgotten, we do not understand why the South is still so bitter one hundred and forty plus years later and why they have taken their bitterness out on the freed slaves and their descendants.

I bring all this up to remind the reader that atrocious violence has occurred in the United States. Additionally little healing was done after the Civil War and the trauma of the war continues down through the generations and is still an important dynamic of current American events. For example, the recent controversy over the issue of flying the Confederate flag at the Georgia state house indicates the continuing level of race bitterness. Some white southerners see the Civil War as due to state's rights and that slavery was a side, minor issue. African-Africans and many northerners consider slavery, and therefore race, to be the defining characteristic of the Civil War. There is no common history that combines both of these interpretations so the bitterness continues.

As we look at the African conflicts in the table above, each conflict has its specific causes, history, and details, but all are also intertwined. For example, those *genocidaires* responsible for the genocide in Rwanda were later found fighting in Angola, at least one thousand miles away and in the Central African Republic in a totally different direction. The Lord's Resistance Army, the rebel group in Northern Uganda, can also be found creating havoc in southern Sudan, northeast Congo, and the Central African Republic. Weapons, such as an AK-47, which can be bought for the equivalent of a cow, know no boundaries. Many of the guns came from the disintegration of Somalia in 1993 when President Barre was overthrown and the arms supplied by the Russians and Americans during the Cold War, were spread throughout the region. Other weapons were imported cheaply after the collapse of the Soviet Union. But "traditional weapons" — machetes, clubs, bows and arrows, and spears — can also be used when hundreds of youth attack as a group.

In the table, the post-election violence in Kenya resulted in thirteen hundred deaths. With such a small number, the deaths could be counted. Yet this conflict had a tremendous amount of media coverage, rivaled only by the Rwandan genocide and the situation in Darfur (see below). Why? Some of the reasons include:

- much of the media for the region is based in Nairobi;
- although simplistic and wrong, the conflict could be reduced to sound-bites citing ancient tribal hatreds;
- much of the violence reported was in Nairobi, Kisumu, Mombasa, and Nakuru/Naivasha, the major cities and towns in Kenya;
- the looting and burning made for graphic pictures;
- Kenya had been considered by some to be stable country;
- the close connection with Britain/America because English is widely spoken and used in Kenya;
- the extensive involvement of the international community including Archbishop Desmond Tutu and former UN General Secretary, Kofi Annan, as soon as the violence broke out;
- the lack of any other graphic conflict in Africa at the time.

Clearly the amount of media coverage is not indicative of the severity of the conflict.

Using the Stereotypes to Sanction Military Interventions

Another use of these stereotypes and biases can be found in the issue of Darfur. There have been numerous calls for the United Nations or the US military to put large numbers of troops in Darfur in order to stop the "genocide" there. I think these calls are misguided. When officials and pundits cannot think up a better solution, they propose military intervention. Let us begin by reviewing some recent history of Western interventions in Africa. The unspoken, underlying assumption of these interventions is that Africans are brutal savages who can only be subdued by the brute force of enlightened Westerners.

In 1993, with the use of a new doctrine — Humanitarian Military Intervention — the US military invaded Somalia, landing on the beaches in the bright lights of TV network cameras. As the US tried to impose its solution on the problems in Somalia, those opposed resisted, Black Hawk down, seventeen American soldiers killed, and the US "cut and ran." Since "Humanitarian Military Intervention" could have been an excuse for all kinds of military adventures, it is fortunate that this was the death of the concept.

Later in Rwanda, there was a small United Nations peacekeeping force in place when the genocide began. Ten Belgian peacekeepers were intentionally disarmed and killed because the Hutu Power *genocidaires* predicted that the Belgians would then "cut and run" — which they did. The UN had not given their peacekeepers the mandate that could have stopped or curtailed the genocide. With extremely few resources and little political backing, the small force did the best it could

It is naïve to think that the UN can do effective peacemaking under the current arrangements. It is the major governments of the world who dictate the policies of and pay for UN peacekeeping missions. Each of the major powers has its own interests, not the interest of the area in conflict, as its central concern. The Clinton administration excused inaction during the Rwandan genocide as "The United States has no strategic interests in Rwanda."

Let us remember the important distinction between the military and the police. Ideally, police protect a community internally, keeping order and tranquility. The military protects a country from outside forces and invades other countries with the policy of preemptive strike, a favorite of the second Bush administration. The difference between the military and the police is being blurred more and more as police increasingly act like the military and the military take over police functions. The military invasion of New Orleans after Hurricane Katrina and the US military involvement after the Haitian earthquake illustrate accurately the problems with using the military for police and humanitarian functions.

When people advocate military UN peacekeepers for Darfur, they are not taking into account this distinction. An assortment of military contingents, a non-cohesive force, is brought to Darfur and expected to do the work of policing — a task for which they have not been trained. In Burundi and eastern Democratic Republic of Congo, I noted UN peacekeepers with amazingly heavy equipment and armor against groups armed with machetes and small arms. They enforced a peace of intimidation, if you will that does not solve the problems of the country. Military training and good police training are significantly different. The proposal is to bring the wrong experts into Darfur for the job that needs to be done. I understand that the United Nations peacekeeping department knows well their limitations and is seeking alternatives. We should be working to help them make a transition from military intervention to skilled policing.

At best, military solutions bring about an enforced "peace." It does not address the underlying problems that made violent military action seem necessary. This type of enforced peace can go on for a long time, for instance, in Tito's Yugoslavia. In the end, the military solution fails because the underlying problems resurface. In many instances, military solutions — after destroying much property and killing many innocent people — make the problems worse; for example, World War I, the Vietnam War, the US invasion of Iraq, and Israel's assaults on Lebanon. Why are the failures of so many military solutions rarely acknowledged, even by pacifists?

The Save Darfur Coalition (SDC) was a highly successful lobbying campaign in the US, equal to the 1980's anti-apartheid movement. As I mentioned above they had to inflate the numbers of dead to four hundred thousand in order to make the issue "significant" and for it to be considered genocide. I have given the number of one hundred thousand in the table above. SDC also had to simplify the conflict into one between Africans and Arabs, although these two groups, both Africans by any definition, intermarry and, when dressed, alike would be indistinguishable. This was done to make it look much more like the anti-apartheid movement. While the movement raised millions of dollars, these funds went into advertising to collect more funds for advertising, while little went to actual relief of Darfurians in Chad or Darfur.

My biggest skepticism is that the Save Darfur movement mirrored the foreign policy objectives of the Bush Administration and diverted the idealism, energy, and concern of American youth from the real American problems of the wars in Iraq and Afghanistan. More people were dying by violence from US military operations in

Iraq and Afghanistan than in Darfur — where again, the greatest percentage of death was due to exposure rather than violence. It should also be noted that deaths from disease and hunger are not added to the figures given for the deaths in Iraq and Afghanistan. Moreover, during the 1990 to 2003 international sanctions against Iraq, between 175,000 and 1,500,000 children died because they did not have access to clean water and proper medical care. I think that this deflection of media interest from Iraq and Afghanistan to Darfur was the real agenda. Students and others should have been protesting the atrocities of their own government rather than those of a perceived enemy of their own government. This is an example of projection of our "sins" onto the "sins" of others?

Why Do Some African Conflicts Get Media Attention and Others Do Not

Why is there such an interest in Darfur compared, for example, to the situation in northern Uganda where the number of displaced persons and deaths are roughly similar? The conflict in northern Uganda has been going on for over twenty five years. Given that President Clinton mistakenly bombed a factory in Sudan after the US Embassies in Kenya and Tanzania were destroyed in 1998 and given that President Bush declared Sudan to be in the second string "axis of evil," the US government has little leverage with the government in Sudan. On the other hand, Uganda was one of only four countries out of the then fifty-four in Africa which joined the "coalition of the willing" in support of the attack on Iraq in 2003. Here the US government has lots of leverage and the Ugandan government could be pressured to negotiate the end of this conflict. Why have we left the Ugandans to die with little protest, while protesting loudly for the people of Darfur?

For the last twenty plus years the Ugandan government, much like the US government, has pursued a military solution to this conflict. The Ugandan government frequently destroyed peace making opportunities which the communities in northern Uganda strongly supported. It is necessary to stress the use of negotiation to end conflicts and not heed the many "excuses" of various governments and rebel forces for the need of a military solution through continued fighting. In the case of Uganda, the Museveni government did not wish to resolve the conflict for two major reasons: First, the greatest opposition to Museveni's rule was in northern Uganda so it was politically useful for him to keep that region in turmoil. Second, it gave him an excuse to continue maintaining his bloated army that had brought him to power in 1986.

Consider the Democratic Republic of Congo (DRC) where there has been fighting since 1996, particularly in the eastern provinces of South Kivu, North Kivu, and Ituri. An estimated five million people have died — mostly from disease and exposure as the various militias, many supported by American allies, Rwanda and Uganda, and the weak government forces vie for the loot that is being stolen from this area. There has been very little media exposure and therefore little protest in more than a decade and a half and the fighting continues even with the presence of a UN peacekeeping force. Why the silence?

One explanation for these differences is that being anti-Sudanese and pro-Darfur is right in sync with the US foreign policy objectives, while involvement in the DRC and northern Uganda would upset American allies. Are we inadvertently using our political protest power where it will be ineffective while remaining silent about conflicts where we might actually have a chance of making a difference?

We should be promoting the development of an international peacemaking center with the expertise and experience to negotiate successful peace accords. Such an effort should be independent of governments including the United Nations which too often are interested parties to the conflicts.

In southern Sudan, the issue was framed as Arabs against Christians and traditional religions. The Darfur "crisis" is discussed as Arab versus African. It is as if a problem is somehow understandable if it can be classified as ethnic, racial, or tribal. All over the world populations are racially, ethnically and religiously mixed and most of the time this does not lead to conflict until some demagogues use these divisions for their own purposes of dividing and conquering in order to seize power. When the media buys into these stereotypes, it perpetuates the conflict as it diverts attention from the real underlying issues that need to be solved.

At one our early workshops in Rwanda, a person took the Rwandan quote, "God sleeps in Rwanda" and changed it to "God fell asleep in Rwanda" during the genocide. It is not surprising that Rwandan felt that God had forsaken them in their time of trials.

But if there is that of God in everyone, then the flight of all expatriates and the reluctance of anyone to visit during the genocide indicates that, as God's hands in this world, members of the international community failed in their response to the genocide.

At the height of the 2006 bombing of Lebanon, one of my friends, Kathy Kelly of Voices for Creative Non-Violence, traveled to Beirut in order to join an international, inter-religious group that was going to walk unarmed to southern Lebanon in order to bring relief supplies. I understand that during the previous conflict between Israel and Lebanon in 1983, ten thousand non-violent resisters participated in non-violent actions in Lebanon.

Let us use our imaginations. What if there had been one hundred and fifty thousand Tom Fox's in Iraq? Tom Fox, a Quaker member of Christian Peacemaker Teams, was kidnapped and executed while trying to bring non-violent solutions to the problems in Iraq. What if there had been a nonviolent peacemaker in place of every soldier the US had in Iraq? Would this have brought about better solutions to the problems there? I am certain we would be discussing the peaceful resolution of the conflict.

Let us imagine that in the last decades the international community had supplied everyone in Darfur (as well as northern Uganda, Burundi, Rwanda, North and South Kivu, and Ituri provinces in the DRC) with clean water and sanitation, basic medical care, universal primary education, decent housing, and those other things that are needed for a wholesome life — the basic human rights all people have. I believe that this could be accomplished for less cost than what is presently spent on the military costs in these conflicts. If the world had done this, would there be conflicts in Darfur, eastern Congo, and other places today? This type of "prevention" should be at the top of our peace agenda.

As in all conflicts, the situation in Darfur is complicated, belying attempts to boil it down to one or two simple explanations. Since 1970 the Sahara desert has expanded south about a hundred miles and still seems to be continuing its southward trek. This has squeezed the pastoral camel-keepers south putting pressure on the environment there which also has become drier during this time. This used to be called "desertification," but now it is being called global warming. People and animals are competing for increasingly scarcer resources. In the first decade of this century, this part of Africa has experienced three, five, or seven years of drought. In my time in Africa, along with other signs of climatic change, I have seen the snows of Kilimanjaro melt, mosquitoes — and therefore malaria — come to areas which were formerly too cold for them, and the rainy season change so much that farmers no longer can predict when to plant. If Americans wanted to really deal with one of the root causes of the conflict in Darfur and elsewhere in Africa, they could focus on the environmental roots of the conflict. But it is simpler just to send some troops to Darfur.

Americans should not view Africans with the stereotypes depicted by their media, but rather as human beings who need the basics of human existence. When those stereotypes lead to a fatalistic acceptance of the untenable status quo in Africa, they need to be challenged. If those resources used for war, preparation for war, and proxy battles between the US and the Soviet Union and now the war on terror, had been spent toward these goals, the African population would be more prosperous and wealthy. As a result the knee-jerk military reactions proposed as the solution for conflicts in the region must be considered suspect. In their place, there must be human enhancing creative solutions which begin long before the outbreak of violence.

Chapter 13
The Reputation of International NGOs

Why Africans Are Suspicious of International NGOs

While international non-governmental organizations (NGOs) often have stellar reputations in the US and Europe, many of them are not well-regarded in Africa. Many Africans have concluded that the billions of dollars donated for their benefit are, instead, eaten up by the NGOs themselves through overhead and greed. What else, they argue, can account for the fact that fifty years of intensive work by international NGOs, foreign aid, the World Bank and International Monetary Fund, and UN agencies has not improved the well being of the average African?

In the United States, NGOs include the large well-known ones — the Red Cross, Catholic Relief Services, Care, World Vision, Lutheran World Service, International Rescue Committee, Doctors without Borders, Oxfam — and thousands upon thousands of smaller ones. All of these organizations raise funds through donations from Americans. They have perfected excellent public relations and fundraising campaigns. One technique that some organization use is to put out wretched pictures of starving African children and then ask for contributions. They promote the AIDS epidemic in Africa since it fits nicely into the stereotype of a failing continent. In order to be successful in their fundraising efforts, they have to play into and enhance the negative stereotypes of Africa as described in the previous chapter. The quest for American dollars is intense so the NGOs have to hype up both the needs and the success of their response. In the end, those with the most heart-wrenching stories obtain the most funds.

One of the most outrageous examples of this involved a Rwandan Quaker we work with who was part of a documentary. In describing her, the film crew noted that she had two children and then showed a picture of starving children sitting dirtily on the ground. I had just taken a picture of this woman with her two healthy, well-dressed happy children. I made a copy of this picture and sent it to the movie producers and asked them to insert the

Children on Christmas Day

 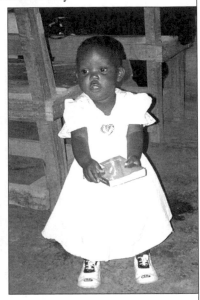

| Joshua. Age 1 | Dorothy, age 1 |

As an antidote to all those pictures of starving, emaciated African children, I took these pictures at Lumakanda Friends Church on Christmas Day, 2010. These pictures are millions and millions times closer to the reality of African children than the ones you normally see in those advertisements to donate money. It is the custom here that on Christmas Day children are given a new set of clothes. They then all come to church in their new clothes. I took a representative sample of various ages. The people attending Lumakanda Church are not wealthy. Gladys and I are the only ones with a vehicle, although one man has a motorcycle and a number have bicycles. On the other hand, members of Lumakanda Church are not poor either. Rather they are much like most Kenyans and other Africans in the region. These are truer pictures of real African children.

picture of her real children in place of the derogatory one. I am uncertain if this happened.

To me, it is much more inspiring to tell stories of healing and hope because it shows the resilience and strength of Africans and their societies. The African Great Lakes Initiative tries not to play into these stereotypes. We never show pictures of emaciated children, cars burning in the streets, or sick and dying people. While we have to be realistic in our descriptions of the violence in these

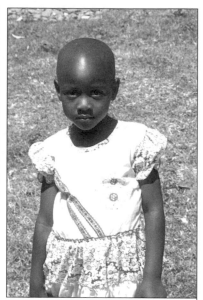

Dianah, age 15 and Ian, age 3   Connie, about 5 years old

countries, we focus more on how people respond to their tragedies — how they recover and reconcile. We do not wish to raise funds by exploiting the sufferings of Africans.

There is criticism of international NGOs in Africa, but somehow these criticisms do not reach the American media and, therefore, the average American. To do so would mean confronting the negative African stereotypes and questioning the seemingly altruistic nature of American giving. At best, Africans feel that these organizations' priorities have little to do with the needs and concerns of Africa, but rather the needs and concerns of the donating organizations themselves. At worst, these organizations are considered the newest form of neo-colonialism and exploitation of Africa. Here are a few examples:

1. Burundi and Kosovo: In 1999, Burundi was in the midst of a civil war and under international sanctions with hundreds of thousands of internally displaced people (IDPs). These IDPs were helped by various NGOs and food was being supplied at the equivalent of twenty cents per day per person. When the Kosovo war broke out and world attention focused there, some of these NGOs withdrew their funds from Burundi and sent them to Kosovo where IDPs were fed at the rate of $1.20 per day. As Africans

261

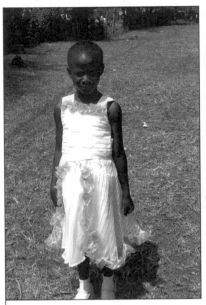 

| Our niece, Gloria, age 7 | Alvin, age 9 |

read about the food given to their fellow Africans versus the enhanced nutrition given to those in Kosovo, they made the obvious conclusion that white Europeans were worth six times more than black Africans. This shift did not take into consideration the still real needs of the Africans but focused on the needs of the NGOs.

Yet the NGOs, in order to keep their funds flowing, had to follow what was capturing American interest at that time. If they did not, they would have lost funding and if that happened consistently, they would have gone out of business.

2. Red Cross in Kenya: On March 22, 2008, the Kenyan Red Cross placed a four page advertisement in the *Daily Nation* reporting on the work they did during the post election crisis in Kenya. One sentence read, "This has enabled humanitarian aid to reach each person in the IDP camps countrywide." This is public relations only. Through the Friends Church Peace Team, Gladys and I distributed food to those who did not receive help from the Kenyan Red Cross during and after the violence. We heard comments many times from internally displaced people that the Red Cross trucks just passed them by. Since the Red Cross mostly supplied Kikuyus and mostly passed by non-Kikuyu, the Red Cross contributed to the unrest and unhappiness of the conflict.

| Colin age 11 | Our niece, Lorene, age 17 |

Moreover, we found in our own distributions to the IDPs at Lumakanda Primary School and the Turbo police station that the Red Cross only gave beans and corn. The corn came from storage at the National Cereal Board and was full of insecticide so that children got diarrhea when they ate it. We had to supply rice for the children, sick, and old people to eat. We also had to supply cooking oil, salt, sugar, soap, tea leaves, Vaseline, and other essential items.

The advertisement had a nice picture of IDPs in tents supplied by the Red Cross, but at Turbo IDP camp, the IDPs had to build "houses" out of poles and plastic tarps.

The Red Cross advertisement illustrated another point. Americans, regardless of their self-serving reputation as being generous, in this case they can be called nothing but stingy. The ad included a long list of everyone who had contributed to the relief work:

American Red Cross	$50,000
Netherlands Red Cross	$2,261,538
Canadian Red Cross	$105,788
Under governments, they report:	
USAID	$192,978
British (DFID)	$2,076,923

As you will note above, the Canadian Red Cross gave more than twice as much as the American and the Netherlands gave forty–five times as much. The British government gave eleven times more than USAID.

I would therefore not accept American claims to generosity. Frequently large sums of help are announced by the US government and various NGOs, but the amounts pledged are not forthcoming. Were the funds pledged actually delivered? If so, were they put to good use?

3. Mozambique Floods: When Mozambique experienced extensive flooding in 2000, it was reported extensively with pictures in the US media. An American NGO which had a small program in Mozambique suddenly received almost half a million dollars in donations for flood relief. The organization was not equipped for this kind of service and by the time funds had been received and action plans developed, the floods were long over. The organization, instead, decided to use the funds for redevelopment work in an area hard-hit by the flooding. This illustrates the fact that collection of donations does not necessarily mesh with the needs and/or possibilities on the ground.

Another point I noticed is that after the civil war in Mozambique was over and the country was recovering from the conflict, 90% of the health expenditures for the country were being spent by the various NGOs in the country. There was no central planning and no rational geographic sharing of the limited resources. The health priorities of the Mozambique people were secondary to the priorities of the NGOs.

4. HIV/AIDS, malaria, and family planning: Besides wars, conflicts, and famine, the major Western media interest in Africa is HIV/AIDS. This is partly because it fits in so nicely with the stereotypes of Africans, particularly as a modern day update of their supposed sexual prowess. The result of this inordinate coverage of the AIDS epidemic is that a tremendous amount of aid has been channeled to AIDS research, community outreach about AIDS prevention, anti-retro viral drugs (ARVs), and other medical needs of HIV+ people, and innumerable programs to support the estimated fifteen million AIDS orphans. ARVs only recently became commonly available in Africa when the pharmaceutical companies were forced to sell the medicines in large quantities and at a discounted price, allowing them to be manufactured under license in other third-world countries, particularly India. Even with the lower prices ARVs are still not reaching many who need them because there are not enough funds to pay for all the medicines needed and the proper medical services to deliver the drugs.

Malaria with an estimated almost one million deaths per year, mostly of children under the age of five, is one of the major diseases in Africa. While inordinate amounts of funding were going to the AIDS epidemic, malaria funding was miniscule. Since it is mostly poor people who get malaria, the big drug companies were unwilling to put any significant funding into malaria drug research and development. At the same time the old malaria drugs were losing their effectiveness. It is only recently, with the Global Fund for AIDS, Tuberculosis, and Malaria, that significant attention has been given to malaria. Since most of those who die from malaria are children, this seemingly ought to pull the heart-strings of donors.

In one year, Kenya with the help of the Global Fund for AIDS, Tuberculosis, and Malaria, the World Bank, and others was able to cut the number of child deaths from malaria by 40%. They did this by spraying vulnerable houses — our house in Lumakanda has been sprayed for the last three years — and by handing out free mosquito nets to all expectant mothers and those with children under age five. Although there were many stories of people using the mosquito nets for fishing nets or bridal veils, there was a strong push by the donors and health officials of the Kenyan government for mothers to actually use them. I myself am surprised at how fast the culture changed. Kenyans rarely used mosquito nets, but as soon as this campaign was launched, it became quite the norm to use mosquito nets, even in houses and rooms where they are not all that easy to install. Where were the various NGOs and government aid organizations in the decades before this sudden improvement. In other words, many of those children who have died of malaria since the time of independence in the early 1960's should not have died. With an easily doable plan, organization, and funding, half of them could have been saved.

Ironically, as the children died from malaria and emphasis was placed on HIV/AIDS, resources for family planning decreased. As more children were dying, more children were being born. It seems weird that extra children should be born to take the place of those children who should not have died. In all the counties of the region, the demand for family planning services is not being met by the resources allocated to them. Kenya has the lowest birthrate in the region with an average of 4.6 children per woman at the end of childbearing years. This is still an extremely high level of population increase. Uganda and Burundi are closer to seven children per female, two of the fastest growing populations in the world.

5. Eastern Congo after the genocide: One place where academics and NGOs have made an assessment of their shortcomings was their support of the Rwandan refugee camps in North and South Kivu, Democratic Republic of the Congo, from 1994 to 1996 after the Rwandan genocide. This assessment happened because their collaboration with the perpetrators of the genocide challenged their creditability as organizations charged with the task to relieve suffering. This then became a threat to their base of their supporters who might turn to other organizations to give their donations.

At the end of the genocide in July 1994, the *genocidaires* forced the Hutu population of western Rwanda to flee as refugees to North and South Kivu in the eastern part of what was then Zaire and is now called the Democratic Republic of the Congo (DRC). Around two million Hutu fled, partly in fear of the *genocidaires* and partly in fear of the conquering Tutsi Rwandan Patriot Front. As they fled into gigantic camps, those, who had organized and implemented the genocide and its five hundred thousand deaths, controlled the camps under the brutal methods that they had used in committing the genocide in Rwanda. The international community, which had been essentially paralyzed during the genocide, all of a sudden had an opportunity to do something they knew how to do very well — feed, house, and give medical support to refugees. The international community responded with large sums of funds which the NGOs used to launch a massive humanitarian response. Even this massive response was inadequate to deal with the two millions souls needing everything.

Unfortunately, due to the magnitude of the crisis, a large number of refugees died of cholera and other diseases that are normally easily treatable. It is estimated that fifty thousand people died during the first month only.

The NGOs had to work through the camp structure which was militantly controlled by the *genocidaires*, who allocated the distribution of food, giving more to their soldiers, *interahamwe*, and other supporters. Less was given to the general population and anyone who accused or opposed them even slightly was cut off. They inflated the number of people in each camp so that they got additional rations which they sold in the local markets. With the cash thus generated, the *genocidaires* planned to return to Rwanda and "finish the work," meaning to continue the genocide until they had killed all the Tutsi. The international NGOs trapped themselves into supporting those who had just killed half a million people. They rationalized that this was not a political problem but a humanitarian problem because almost two million people were in need of food, shelter, and medical care. If they withdrew, those people would be vulnerable. Since the *genocidaires* were in control of the camps, the NGOs had to work through them. But in doing so they became accomplices to the crimes committed.

One Hutu woman told me how she fled with all the others from North Kivu with her husband and little baby. She was pregnant with her second child and had gotten sick. The only way for her to get medical attention was to pay for services at Congolese hospitals and clinics which were forbidden to treat the refugees. She and her husband paid until they ran out of money. They then decided to return to Rwanda, an action that the *genocidaires* forbad with the sanction of death for those caught returning. The couple did not tell anyone of their plan, not even the husband's brothers as they were afraid that they might turn them in to the *genocidaires* for certain death. The wife tied her young child on her back and the husband took whatever documents they had. Each went off in a different direction as if they were going about their daily activities. They had agreed on a place near to the border to meet and then, after meeting at the rendezvous, quickly slipped into Rwanda safely. The couple and their children then did fine.

Ironically, while the international community was pouring millions of dollars into the relief of the Rwanda refugees in North and South Kivu, almost no support was going into Rwanda itself so that it could recover from the devastating effects of the genocide. Those who committed genocide were given support which allowed them to envision attacking Rwanda while those who had suffered the genocide or had remained in Rwanda after the genocide were given minimal support.

A few of the NGOs realized the implication of their support for the *genocidaires* and withdrew from North and South Kivu. But most continued with the excuse that they were politically neutral and that they had to continue supporting the status quo or people would die of starvation and disease. For a detailed description of this, see Samantha Power's book, *A Problem from Hell: American and the Age of Genocide.*

6. Post genocide Rwanda: After the end of the genocide in July 1994 and the details and extent of the Rwandan genocide filled the media in the Western world, it became clear that raising funds for Rwandan survivors of the genocide was "good business" for NGOs. Soon there were well over a thousand NGOs in Rwanda. Some of these were clearly frauds, such as one American NGO a Rwandan told me about, that collected over a million dollars but spent only ten thousand dollars on relief in Rwanda. Due to cases like this the Rwanda government required every NGO to justify what they were doing in Rwanda and then expelled over seven hundred NGOs that were not adequately contributing to the redevelopment of Rwanda. This is an amazing indictment of the NGO community. Unfortunately, by the time these NGOs were forced out of Rwanda, they were already turning their attention to the next lucrative international crisis that would bring sympathetic contributions to fill their coffers.

Foundation Priorities

My son, Tommy, went into the Foundation Center in Washington, DC and pulled up all foundation grants given to Burundi from 2005 to 2007 and sent the list to me. Since Burundi is one of the poorest nations in the world and had just finished a twelve year civil war in 2005, one would think that support for Burundi would be a priority. Alas, this is not the case.

In those three years, American foundations gave only twenty-three grants that included Burundi. Moreover, only eight of these grants were solely for Burundi with the other fifteen including many other countries in the region. In addition, twelve of these grants, totaling $3,565,000, were for wildlife conservation — a high priority for the developed world which long ago killed most of its wild animals, but this is not a high priority for the Burundians trying to recover from a civil war.

Of the eight grants for Burundi, by far the largest grant was a four year grant given in 2007 to Catholic Relief Services by the Bill and Melinda Gates Foundation in the amount of $21,876,316. Its purpose was "to increase small farmer cassava productivity." This was a useful grant. Burundi at that time was experiencing disease in its cassava plants. Cassava is, frankly, a not nice food to eat since it is mostly starch. But Burundi experiences recurrent drought and cassava is not only drought resistant, but once planted it takes only about six months before it can be harvested and can be harvested any time after that for the next two or three years. It is mostly used by people as a famine reserve as they typically harvest it when other foods are not available. Therefore, the disease that was killing the plants could have had dire consequences. Part of this project was to "access disease resistant planting material" and the disease is now under control.

The grants then decline in value tremendously.

If we leave aside the large Gates Foundation grant to Catholic Relief Services, the remaining seven grants totaled $53,000 for the year 2006. To put this in perspective, in 2006 AGLI spent $86,798 in Burundi. In 2005 and 2007, when there were no foundation grants to Burundi alone, AGLI spent $61,398 and $65,989, respectively Isn't this sad? Well, actually, outrageous that, with the exception of one large grant, a small organization like AGLI can spend in Burundi more than all the US foundations put together.

Non-governmental Organizations and Wages

Another large criticism of international NGOs concerns wages, benefits, and perks.

First it is necessary to understand how low wages are in the region. Here is an example. When I recently returned from the US, I was in a *matatu* in Eldoret on my way home and I heard an advertisement on the radio for three waitresses/waiters. The restaurant was offering $33.33 per month plus room and board. There is no tipping in local Kenyan restaurants. As I mentioned, the wage for day labor here in rural western Kenya is $1.33 plus lunch. And Kenya is by far the highest wage country in the region.

Large international NGOs pay their expatriate staff salaries equivalent to those of the expatriates' peers/co-workers employed in the United States. This can be in the realm of $50,000 to $150,000 per year. These employees also receive the usual fringe benefits of health insurance, pension, national holidays, sick leave, and vacation.

Additionally, expatriates often get some or many of the following additional benefits:

- **Hardship pay:** This goes by many names but it is based on the assumption that living and working in Africa is a hardship. This extra pay can be 25% or more of the base salary.
- **House:** Large NGOs will provide a house or housing allowance for their expatriate staff. This can also include guards, gardener, house servant, and/or cook.
- **Vehicle:** A vehicle may be given for the use of the expatriate, frequently with driver included.
- **Education allowance:** If the expatriate has children, funds may be used to support them going to an appropriate (and expensive) private school including, if necessary, boarding schools.
- **Home leave:** It is common for the expatriate and family to be given a one month's leave per year to travel home.
- **Extra holidays:** The expatriate is not only given the host country holidays, but additional US national holidays. No wonder the impression in Africa is that expatriates do not work hard.

If you add up these wages and benefits, you can see that the cost will be from $100,000 to $250,000 for each expatriate.

I have known a number of Westerners who make a living by taking temporary assignments under these conditions, saving most of their salary, and then spending the next three to twelve months on extended leave, usually having "adventures" on the African or other continents.

With this great salary and benefit package, one would think that Americans would be flocking to these positions. Except for the case of Nairobi, which is a cosmopolitan city, it is difficult to find Americans to fill these positions. I know one American NGO in Burundi that had a different director each year — I would meet the current director on one of my visits and the next year there would be a new person. Rather than hire a local person, these big NGOs have found it necessary to hire nationals of other foreign countries for these positions — an Ethiopian is in South Africa, a Cameroonian is in Burundi, or a Kenyan in Rwanda.

How do these NGOs pay their local African staff? I once saw an American contract where the one expatriate employee alone was receiving in salary more than the eight local Africans employees together.

Nonetheless, the NGOs pay many times more than the national governments pay local Africans. In Burundi, I was told that while someone might receive $60 per month working for the government, he or she could get $600 per month doing the same thing for the an international NGO. Consequently, working for an international NGO is a much sought after position and competition is intense. One of the major complaints from Africans is that this disparity between what the governments and NGOs offer means that the best and most qualified people are working for the NGOs and the governments are left with the NGO rejects.

How does AGLI deal with this issue? If I were paid according to the international NGO standards listed above, much of AGLI's income would be going to my salary, benefits, and perks. Our strategy has been, on the one hand, to pay the local Africans more than the dismal wages they would otherwise get but not near the amounts that other NGOs pay. On the other hand, foreigners working for AGLI in Africa are paid more or less the same amount as AGLI pays the local Africans — this means that they have to be called "volunteers." I find it remarkable that AGLI has more success in finding Americans willing to work in Rwanda and Burundi at our "volunteer" wages than some of the big NGOs have with their excessive salaries. One former AGLI volunteer, who latter worked for one of the large NGOs in North Kivu with all the salary and perks, told me he appreciated working for AGLI at its minimum standards because it showed him how things could be done.

I want to qualify the "more or less" tactic described above to indicate how difficult it is to be fair. If we pay a local African and an American volunteer the same amount, which we try to do, this is not "fair" because the African has a family, many relatives, local church, family obligations, and other responsibilities, while the "volunteer" only supports himself or herself. In at least one case that I know about, a three month AGLI experience in Africa was sufficient to give the former "volunteer" a decided advantage in being hired at a normal NGO salary by an American NGO in the United States.

But nothing is going to change much until the donors in the United States and elsewhere realize that their funds are being solicited under false pretenses — claiming that the funds will be used in Africa when most is used in the US or to support an elaborate lifestyle in Africa — and that little actually is received by that starving, dirty child in the advertisement.

Sitting Allowances

Many international NGOs pay "sitting allowances" for people to attend meetings, seminars, workshops, and other activities promoted by the NGOs. This might surprise you — people are paid to be involved in learning opportunities for their own benefit. Sometimes this pay is significant. I have heard of $35 per day payments for attendance to participants when the daily wage was $1 per day. I was told that in Burundi an important person is given $200 to attend a seminar. No wonder people want to attend and give glowing reports of how good the workshops were that day. I do not know of any NGO in the region except some Quaker ones that do not pay sitting allowances. This includes the United Nations organizations, for example, which pay peace committee members in Kenya $10 per day to attend one of their meetings.

This "sitting allowance" payment is called by many names; "transport or travel" (even though people are only walking from nearby), per diem, stipend, "*chai*" (which means "tea" in Swahili and is a euphemism for "a bribe"), or "*kitu kidogo*" (something little).

It is AGLI's policy not to pay any "sitting allowances." Because of this, we are at total odds with the prevailing custom of the other NGOs and the expectations of the people in the region. People come to the workshops expecting to be paid. I remember when we first implemented this "no sitting allowance" policy in Burundi in 2001. The trauma healing workshop was for teachers from Kibimba Primary School and Kibimba Secondary School. The teachers from the secondary school refused to come since they were not being given a sitting allowance so the workshop was only half full. My own feeling was that the teachers were coming for the pay and not for the learning. AGLI's AVP and HROC workshops are voluntary and that is critical to their success. If people were paid, it would be an inducement that renders them no longer "voluntary." Do those other NGOs who pay sitting allowances think that their activities are so unproductive that no one will come unless they are paid?

We have learned to tell people beforehand that they will not be paid. Sometimes people show up and expect to be paid and then leave when they realize that they will receive nothing but a good meal. In IDP camps in North Kivu, for instance, the fact that a good meal will be served is an inducement in itself. But eating together is part of the reconciliation process because in the cultures here only friends eat together.

We have had many testimonies from people, who came expecting to be paid, yet decided to stay and by the end realized that what they got was more valuable than being paid. Here is one such testimony from Jérome who attended a HROC workshop in Burundi.

> One time when I was coming from the workshop, going home, they said, "Where are you coming from?"
> I said, "I'm coming from the workshop."
> They said, "You must have received a big stipend for three days?"
> I said, "Big stipend?"
> One said, "Yes, of course if you are there for three days."
> I told him, "Yes, I got a lot out of the workshop." I gave him this example, "You know *ugali* [corn mush]?"
> "Yes, of course, I am Burundian, I know *ugali.*"
> "Imagine that you have a lot of *ugali* in front of you, but your heart is bleeding, will the *ugali* take away the hurt and bitterness from the wound in your heart?"
> He said, "No."
> "That's why it's a lot of money because I come home with peace. If they had given those big stipends, there would be no meaning for me because my heart was still bleeding, but now I have my heart. So peace is more meaningful than money."

Here are the reasons for not paying sitting allowances:

1. As mentioned above, the workshop would no longer be voluntary, but would have an inducement. In a poor country this inducement can be more important than the content of the workshop.

2. If sitting allowances were given, we could not trust the positive evaluations we receive and the motivations for requests for more workshops

3. When compensation is given, people compete to get in. The recruiters who can be pastors, government officials or other HROC participants try to fill the workshop with their relatives and friends.

4. In some cases, when participants are selected and a sitting allowance is given, the recruiters demand some or all of the allowance for themselves.

5. Giving out small amounts of money is a real hassle and destroys the end of the workshop as people jostle to be paid quickly so they can leave.

6. Less people would be able to attend the workshops. Since AGLI has a set amount of funds, when the funds are finished, there is no more. I calculate that if AGLI gave the usual sitting allowance we would be able to offer five workshops while we would be able to do six workshops without the allowance. One hundred participants would be paid using funds that could, instead, have provided the workshop for another twenty participants. Those twenty would-be participants are the ones who would be paying.

7. When participants are paid, it implies that they are in a victim role and AGLI's facilitators are the rescuers. The purpose of the workshops is to change people's attitudes and not being paid to attend is the first attitude that needs to be changed. This becomes the first step out of the victim role.

8. In the end, the paying of the allowance retards community responsibility. The NGO custom of paying sitting allowances has destroyed civil responsibility since the culture now says that a person does not need to do anything for the community unless he or she is paid. People now wait until there are substantial funds available, usually from foreign NGOs or the government, before they will participate in an activity.

9. If the sitting allowance is for attendance at a board meeting of a local non-profit organization, then the board members, since they are being paid by the management for attending, are no longer disinterested members, but beholden to the administration. As a result they will be subservient to the administration and approve whatever is brought before them.

I have to admit that our refusal to pay sitting allowances gives us a lot of problems. NGOs have spoiled the environment and we are trying to change that environment.

Obliviousness of NGOs

NGOs seem to be oblivious to the implications of their practices and policies. In the discussion on sitting allowances above, they do not seem to understand the implications that their paying people to attend NGO functions destroys voluntary civic responsibility, a necessary ingredient for any society to improve itself.

In May 2001, I was in Burundi. At this time the civil war was fierce and I could hear the booms of large guns from the hills surrounding Bujumbura every night. The Tutsi government was still firmly in control of Bujumbura. David Niyonzima, the general secretary of Burundi Yearly Meeting, took me to visit some of the NGOs in Burundi at that time. His reason was that, as a Burundian, he would never have access to these NGOs unless he used me as an "excuse" to meet with appropriate NGO bureaucrats. At one NGO, it barely succeeded because, even though we had an appointment, David had to talk his way past the secretary to get into the office.

Then we visited Africare. The conversation with the Africare Director at that time became surprisingly heated. David had asked him to justify the fact that all the senior positions in the organization were filled by Tutsis. David commented that while Hutu could clean the floors and be drivers, they were given no positions of responsibility. Africare's Director responded forcefully saying that they did not discriminate but chose only the best qualified candidates. David pushed him on why there were no qualified Hutu candidates. It was clear that David, a Hutu, would not be able to be employed by Africare. What is ironic about this situation is that Africare is a US African-American organization and the defense that the Director gave echoed exactly what predominantly white organizations say when asked about their lack of diversity.

In Burundi, as far as I can tell, all senior positions in NGOs are held by Tutsi. If there are exceptions, I do not know about them. How can this happen? Once an international NGO I know was hiring for the director of the organization in Burundi. A Hutu, who might conceivably have applied for the position, was called by one of the senior Tutsi in the organization and told that no Hutu should apply for the position. As I indicated in the NGO wages discussion above, NGO positions are some of the best paid opportunities in a country such as Burundi. If the Tutsi have a monopoly on the positions, I predict they are not going to let any Hutu destroy their stranglehold on those lucrative positions.

This exasperates the conflict between Tutsi and Hutu in the country. Do the NGOs realize what they are part of the conflict!? They should make sure their senior staff is ethnically balanced.

With the 2005 elections in Burundi, the government became Hutu dominated, but with certain percentages everywhere allocated to Tutsi and Hutu. The NGOs remained firmly Tutsi dominated. Consequently the NGOs have all taken extremely anti-government stances, while the government on its side is extremely suspicious of the NGOs. This is not a healthy situation. The Peacebuilding Commission at the United Nations in New York was so concerned about this conflict along the ethnic divide that it was brought to the attention of the Quaker United Nations Office in New York. They contacted me and other members of Burundi Yearly Meeting to see if there was any means for us to mediate this dispute. Unfortunately our leverage on this was too small to have any effect.

This is the style of house rented by NGOs in the region for the expatriate staff and offices. This is picture of a house in Goma in North Kivu, Democratic Republic of the Congo. As the number of houses like this were overbuilt, this particular house was turned into a hotel where Gladys and I stayed. It cost us $50 per night, the cheapest that could be found in Goma. Right across the border in Gisenyi, Rwanda, the cost of a night in a hotel would be about $20. This is the difference between a country at war with high levels of corruption and an organized one with little petty corruption. These mansions for expatriates are common in Rwanda, Burundi, and the eastern Congo.

In Kigali (capital of Rwanda), Bujumbura (capital of Burundi), and Goma (capital of North Kivu), there are tremendous mansions being built. These mansions are built to rent out to the international NGOs at a tremendous price of around $3000 or $4000 per month, clearly out of the range of any African except the elite. I know one

Less then ten miles away from the mansions rented by NGOs, Congolese internally displaced people were living in housing like this plastic tarp. It's height is less than four feet so it is just a place to crawl in at night.

large NGO in Goma that has rented one large mansion where its expatriate staff lived and a second for its offices. The ostentiousness of these mansions in areas of conflict and poverty is debilitating. Do not the NGOs realize that every African can see how they are living, divorced as much as possible from the local population as if they were living in the Green Zone in Iraq?

Whenever a crisis develops and NGOs move in, they quickly secure the best housing, not only for their "mansions" mentioned above, but also for their much better paid African employees. The result is a housing shortage and a significant increase in the cost of land, rental properties, and building costs. In other words, for the average person in the capital city, the most immediate effect of the arrival of NGOs is a considerable rise in the cost of living for the middle and upper classes. While the NGOs do not control the cost of housing, they do need to be aware of how their sudden arrival is going to upset the market.

International NGOs have short-term contracts that do not lead to sustainability. They come and go willy-nilly. Is the AIDS epidemic going to be solved in a year or two? Is peace coming immediately to a country that has been at war for more than a decade? I think that ten years is the minimum timeline that NGOs should use for planning. Things are going to change and evolve over a decade, but the response to this should be flexibility to meet new conditions as the situation changes.

For example, after the flare-up of violence in North Kivu in 2008 and early 2009, the situation calmed down when the governments of Rwanda and the Democratic Republic of the Congo agreed to work together to disarm the many rebel groups in the province. Soon the two presidents met together in the no-man's land between Goma in the DRC and Gisenyi in Rwanda and declared that peace had returned. The Congolese government then closed all the IDP camps with hundreds of thousand of people in them and sent them back to their homes — with no planning, inadequate assistance, and great bitterness between those who fled and those who remained. The NGOs closed up shop and left. If a new outbreak of violence occurs, a likely event, and people again flee to the IDP camps, few NGOs will be available to service the needs of the IDPs.

The African Great Lakes Initiatives' philosophy is to stay with the people on a long term basis — we have been in the region and have no plans to move elsewhere. People ask AGLI to go to Darfur, Zimbabwe, or even Sierra Leone, but the response is that AGLI has its hands full where it is and does not wish to expand to other regions. We are more than happy to advise others on what we recommend, but others have to do the work.

NGOs support a lavish style. Just recently I was speaking to an African Quaker peace activist from North Kivu and he was complaining how he was being sent to conferences in swank hotels in Bujumbura and Nairobi, while he was seeking modest funds for his programs in North Kivu. He calculated that over $1,500 was spent for him to attend one conference in Nairobi. At the same time, he was desperate for funds to run workshops in North Kivu. At $500 per workshop for three days for twenty people, the cost of his attendance at the conference could have instead have been used for sixty participants for a three day workshop. This particular partner has decided to boycott any more of these conferences and to lobby his co-workers in the region to also boycott them.

My last comment on the obliviousness of the NGOs is their frequent complicity with corruption. During the 2008 crisis in North Kivu, the large NGOs, including the World Food Program, reported that they were sending sufficient food from Mombasa to Goma to feed the over five hundred thousand people in the IDP camps. But when I visited those camps, people reported that they received only a one fourth to one third of what was claimed. The rest was stolen and readily available for purchase in the shops in Goma. Most merchants did not even worry about putting the flour or other goods into another bag. I live right off the main road that goes from Mombasa to Goma and I would see the food trucks go by. They were open trucks with bags of goods. The driver could stop anywhere and sell a few. The truck could be easily looted. Merchants, who cannot afford to lose valuable merchandise, no longer do this and, today, everything is shipped in a sealed, locked container. If the relief food were done like this, it is much more likely to arrive intact at its destination. The NGOs seem to consider the theft of a significant amount of their aid as part of doing business in Africa. Their complacency condones continued theft.

Reform NGO's

Non-government organizations are part of the problem. They need drastic reform. NGOs need to calculate, not just how much is spent on fundraising and administration, but how much actually gets to the people intended for the services. Gladys once was watching an infomercial on TV for an orphans' program in Tanzania. They were asking $320 — less than a dollar a day as they continually said over and over — to support an orphan. As I watched the program and started thinking of how much it cost to produce the infomercial and then put it on TV, I had to question how much did that orphan receive in actual services for that $320 donation. AGLI has an orphan program in Bududa, Uganda named Children of Peace and we ask sponsors for $100 per year and 100% of it goes towards the children as AGLI itself covers the administrative costs.

One important step is to stop considering the Great Lakes region of Africa as a hardship posting. I surely do not experience any hardships and I am not given any of those perks and benefits that are routinely bestowed on expatriates. It is absurd to give foreigners the local holidays plus the home country holidays. Salaries need to be pegged, not to the level of America and European countries, but to that of the host country that the expatriate is living in. All those perks — house, gardener, cook, house servant(s), guards, driver, vehicle, and so on — need to be abolished as a leftover from the long gone colonial era. All workers in NGOs, regardless of where they come from, should be expected to live modestly rather than extravagantly as is now routine.

One counter argument is that if this were the case, then Americans would not be willing to work in Africa. This has not been AGLI's experience. We send expatriates as volunteers for one month to over three years and we give them $400 per month to live on with no extra perks. We find people, both young and old, willing to do this. I feel that too many of the highly paid expatriates are there, not to do the work that NGOs hired them to do, but to enjoy an easy, well paid life that they could never lead in the United States — only the super-rich could have the number of household servants that are customary in Africa. Another response to this criticism is that, if there are no Americans willing to work under these modest circumstances, then there are more than enough well-qualified Africans willing to do so — if only the NGOs were willing to hire them.

For their African staff, the NGOs need to pay the equivalent of government wages so that they do not "steal" the best people from the government. I just noticed in an article on the Internet that a USAID grant in Uganda for HIV/AIDS work will pay their nursing staff the same rate as the government nurses. This should become standard practice among all NGOs.

Sitting allowances, regardless of what they are called and how they are sometimes hidden in budgets, should be abolished.

I have found that NGOs with a small, narrow focus do much better than the larger "let's do everything" NGOs. I think that this is because the focused NGO has clear objectives, knowledge and skills on its small area of expertise, and being smaller, adapt much more quickly to changing circumstances.

I find that many large, bureaucratic NGOs with multi-million dollar budgets frequently fritter away their funds on extensive strategic planning, expensive evaluations by highly paid professionals, conferences in plush hotels, and other wastes of funds. When I see the funds being misspent while I realize the many needs around, I become angry and discouraged. When I consider the people from far away who are making donations, and I see how the funds are wasted in the region, I feel that the donors have been hoodwinked by slick advertising.

NGOs must start with a much longer time frame than one to three years, the timeline of most grants. Significant change does not happen quickly. NGOs need to pick a community they wish to work with and stick with it — through thick and thin — for many years and decades. Partners in Health has this philosophy, which should be adopted by of all NGOs.

NGOs need to stop reacting to disasters only and then withdraw. It takes at least a decade after the end of a conflict to return to "normal" as defined before the beginning of the conflict. When NGOs leave too quickly, the seeds of the next conflict are being sowed.

As the donors to these NGOs, I ask you can to demand reforms. Demand the kind of changes I have outlined in this section. Find NGOs that fulfill these criteria and donate to them. Then be vigilant. Watch how they perform in the field. Remember that it is better to do something small, well, rather than something big, poorly.

Chapter 14
Corruption

Basic Assumptions of Corruption

Corruption is endemic throughout the world. For instance, in the United States, Bernie Madoff embezzled somewhere between $18 billion and $65 billion in a gigantic ponzi scheme. As in many cases of grand corruption, it is difficult to access the exact amounts that Madoff stole. How Madoff was able to continue this scam for twenty-eight years without being caught is a mystery.

Then on the U.S. government side, we have billions of dollars of no-bid contracts to Blackwater for work in Iraq, with Vice-President Dick Cheney smoothing the way. In addition to all the other criticisms of the wars in Iraq and Afghanistan, the fact that the US Treasury is being looted by unscrupulous contractors that seem to get away with the largest thefts imaginable should be another grave concern about the US war making machine. War has become a façade for corruption on a grand scale.

Kenya is noted for being one of the more corrupt countries in the world. Yet its total gross domestic product is only $30 billion, about the middle that Bernie Madoff is estimated to have stolen. We therefore can not assume that Africans are more corrupt than others.

The second major assumption that needs to be questioned is that the Africans are doing this corruption on their own. The kleptomaniac President of former Zaire, now Democratic Republic of the Congo, Sese Seko Mobutu, is supposed to have said, "I know I am corrupt, but who is corrupting me?" Almost all of the cases of grand corruption in Africa include foreign companies or international organizations. This includes corporations, the United Nations, foreign governments, and non-governmental organizations. The fact is that when funds come from overseas, local citizens have little knowledge or resources to track how these funds are spent. The foreign donors are extremely lax as they consider siphoning off of funds as normal. It is only when the missing funds become outrageous that any action is taken.

The third assumption is that because corruption is so common, it must be tolerated. Corruption is based on the basic greed in human nature. This is the way the world works and it is fruitless to try to change things. These are excuses that need to be rejected.

That embezzlement and corruption usually results in impunity is amazing. The fact that Bernie Madoff got one hundred and fifty years in prison for his theft occurred only because his case was so gigantic. If a person in the United States is caught with a little crack cocaine, he can spend years in jail, while a white collar embezzler, if caught, frequently does not have to spend time in jail. This is true all over the world. In other words, embezzlers usually succeed even when they get caught. Most, of course, do not get caught.

International Bribery

To become really rich, do not become a Wall Street stock broker, become the president or minister of an African country. Two of the sons of former Kenyan President Daniel Arap Moi — both of whom were members of parliament at various times — are reported to have wealth of over $500 million. The Mars Group, an anti-corruption organization, estimates that Philip Moi's net worth is $770 million. None of this wealth would have been inherited since former President Moi is still alive. Superstar Michael Jackson's wealth at the time of his death was considerably less than this amount. International bribery is the reason that warlords and rebels try to overthrow governments in Africa, looting, killing, and raping in the process. To them, these are only small costs in comparison to the potentially huge rewards.

In late 2008, Siemens Corporation of Germany was fined $1.6 billion in a "bribery corruption scandal." I am not certain there was much of a "scandal" as this is normal operating procedure for multi-national corporations. It was labeled a "scandal" only because Siemens was caught.

Siemens, a German conglomerate employing four hundred thousand people worldwide, is involved in many enterprises, from nuclear power plants to light bulbs. Siemens bribed everybody in the world — not only the often suspected Chinese and Nigerians, but the supposedly honest Norwegians. Siemens' contracts included bribes of 5% to 40% of the value of each of their contracts. Until 1999, this bribery was legal in Germany and companies could deduct bribes as an expense to be deducted from the bottom line. But when bribery was made illegal, Siemens went underground with their bribery.

Why does a company need to bribe? The company will be submitting a contract for some goods or scope of work. Other companies from throughout the world will also submit bids. It would be nice to assume that all the bids are competitive and the best will win the contract. Alas, this is naïve. If one company bribes the people deciding on the contact, they are going to win the contract. Others have to participant in bribing if they wish to win. Once bribing becomes part of the process in awarding contracts, the details of the bids become relatively unimportant. The largest briber or the company that places it bribes in the right place wins the contract.

The company does not lose anything on their bribing since they add the bribes to the cost of the contract. If there is a contact for $1,000,000 and to win the contract the company has to pay $250,000 in bribes, then they put in a bid of $1,250,000 to cover their cost of bribing. Of course, those who are being bribed understand this perfectly and are willing to agree to an inflated price because they are receiving part of the "loot."

Behind these bribes is a developed under-the-table cartel of people who manage the bribing system. These are the fixers. A company will not send in one of their employees who, if caught will bring problems to the company, but more importantly will not have developed the "proper channels" for not only bribing those who are awarding the contract, but then hiding the bribing so that those being bribed can not get caught. As time goes on and people get entrenched, informal bribery networks develop and become quite efficient at looting the treasury of their country.

As this develops, those accepting the bribes become embolden. They develop or find bogus companies, usually outside the country, and then aware them contracts. In these cases, 100% of the bid is a bribe and the looters run away with the total amount of the funds. The Anglo-Leasing schemes developed in Kenya beginning in 1997 were fictitious companies which looted the Kenyan treasury of hundreds of millions of dollars. Wikipedia states: *The new revelations indicate that Anglo Leasing Finance was just one of a plethora of phantom entities, including some UK companies, used to perpetrate fraud on the Kenyan taxpayer through non-delivery of goods and services and massive overpricing.*

As the 2008 trial in Germany revealed, at one time Siemens paid a $5 million dollar bribe to the son of the prime minister of Bangladesh and another time $12.7 million dollars to senior government officials in Nigeria. As I indicated above, these amounts are much better than being a Wall Street stock broker. Siemens used everything, suitcases full of cash, offshore banks, secret Swiss bank accounts, and shell companies, to hide their activities. As the court case against Siemens revealed, Siemens had a cadre of two thousand seven hundred agents throughout the world — usually nationals of the country in which they were making the bribes — who actually handled the transactions for them. Reinhard Siekaczek, a Siemens executive put in charge of the bribery program, was considered to be an "honest" man because he never stole any of the bribe funds for himself. He claims that he never handled a bribe. He just organized everyone one else to do it. His rationale was that since everyone was paying bribes if Siemens did not, they would lose the contracts and their employees would have to be laid off.

Siemens settled out of court. For their cooperation, the names of people all over the world that accepted their bribes were kept secret. Their bribery agents are also unknown. This destroys the success of the case. The crooks have been let go scot-free with their "earnings" intact. I cannot emphasize enough that this out of court settlement that protected all those bribers and those who received bribes is the main reason why bribery will continue — no one gets caught. Moreover, none of the $1.6 billion fine will go to those who overpaid up to 40% for their Siemens light bulbs. Moreover the informal bribery network remains intact and I am certain it is used by many other companies in addition to Siemens.

Government contracts in Africa include bribery, probably closer to the 40% than the 5% of the value of the contract. So the African citizen is being robbed by an alliance of big international businesses and local government officials.

This explains why a person is willing to take up arms and flee to the bush in the hopes of overthrowing his government — or at least making such a nuance of himself that he is given a "peace deal" to become a minister and begin his rapid climb to becoming one of the wealthiest in his country and in that small group of world multi-multi-millionaires. Many leaders in the region from Robert Mugabe of Zimbabwe to Yoweni Museveni of Uganda, whose wealth is estimated by a Ugandan newspaper at $1.6 billion, have followed this path to riches.

How Grand Corruption Works

In the *Daily Nation* of December 3, 2010 ("Sh270bn of budget 'to be lost in graft'"), the Permanent Secretary for the Kenyan Treasury Department, Joseph Kinyua, reported that $3.375 billion of Kenya's government budget of $12.5 billion would be lost through corruption. This is 27% of government funds. Other sources estimate that the loss is between 33% and 50%. Kinyua claimed that he had been trying to close the loopholes that were allowing this to happen, but the process was "slow and painful."

An example of how corruption works concerns a recent Production Sharing Agreement (PSA) between the government of Uganda and Tullow Oil and Heritage, two large oil exploration companies. Up to two billion barrels of oil have been discovered in the Lake Albert basin of western Uganda. This may be just the first of future finds since major exploration in the basin continues. At $80 per barrel, this field is worth $160 billion. This compares with a gross domestic product for Uganda of under $16 billion for the whole country of thirty-three million people.

A secret Production Sharing Agreement was negotiated between the Energy Ministry of the Ugandan Government and Tullow Oil and Heritage, the oil exploration companies. Fortunately for the anti-corruption community, the agreement was leaked and put on the Internet. There is no doubt why it, like almost all of these kind of agreements, are kept secret. The agreement was remarkable disadvantageous to the country of Uganda.

The biggest issue was that it was signed when the price of oil was $30 to $40 per barrel. The Production Sharing Agreement has no provision if the price of oil climbs above this price. These types of contracts normally have a windfall tax to cover this eventuality. The Ugandan agreement did not. Since a windfall profit tax is routine in these kinds of contracts, there is no possibility that those who negotiated the agreement could not have been aware of this possibility. If oil is at $80 per barrel and if the concession would reach one hundred thousand barrels per day, as is quite possible, then the oil exploration companies would reap the amount due to the increase in the price of oil. This would equal almost $1.5 billion per year. If oil goes higher than $80 per barrel, then Uganda will lose even more.

Moreover the contract includes the provision that Uganda can set up a national oil company which would own 20% of the venture without putting in any capital. This was an unknown provision before the agreement was made public. When the contract was made public over two years after it was signed, no one in the Uganda Government had begun to set up such a national oil company. I do not know what would happen if the national oil company is not formed, but I would presume its shares would remain in the hands of the two international exploration oil companies.

How was this lopsided Production Sharing Agreement made? How could the Ugandan negotiators give away so much to the oil exploration companies? The agreement included a signing bonus of about $1 million dollars. Where has this $1 million dollars gone? No one knows. It definitely did not go into the accounts of the Uganda government. These are bribes paid to the Ugandan negotiators for giving away potentially billions of dollars due to price increases. Since $1 million is insignificant regarding the billions of dollars involved in the contract, it was of unimportant to the bottom line of the oil exploration companies. It is amazing how little money was needed to bride the Ugandans to negotiate this terrible agreement.

When production begins, there is another $5 million bonus. Will this again go unaccounted for? The loss of the first $1 million suggests that Uganda will go the way of most oil producing countries in Africa; Nigeria and Angola are only two prime examples of this. Most of the funds will be embezzled and little will benefit local Ugandans.

The reaction of the Uganda government to the leaking of this official Ugandan government document was to denounce those who leaked the documents: "Stealing government documents is espionage and criminal...These documents contain commercial confidentiality details that the concerned companies have invested in." What an excuse for the corruption involved in a very detrimental agreement with Uganda.

Here is an example from Kenya. Safaricom is the most profitable company in East Africa with fifteen million cell phone subscribers. At one time it was wholly owned by the Kenyan government. A few years ago, they sold 30% of the shares to Vodafone, a large British telecommunications company. Later it was revealed that the government had only 65% of the shares left because another 5% had been given to a mysterious company called Mobitelea Ventures. The public does not know who the officers or shareholders of this company are. It is therefore assumed that this was the "bribe" that Vodafone paid Kenyan officials and politicians for buying the Safaricom shares.

Clearly the medicine for this disease is transparency. No government contracts or agreements, including those in the United States, should be secret. All must be made public before any agreement is signed by a government. Surely, though, this would be a brave, new world.

Agricultural Imperialism

The farm is blessed with perfect climate, plenty of surface water, fertile soils, the equatorial sun and a large, enthusiastic labor pool.
Dominion Farms webpage

One of the biggest issues in Africa today is the "re-colonialization" of Africa by wealthier countries which are leasing large areas of Africa for highly intensive, mechanized agriculture. These include China, Qatar, Saudi Arabia, and American corporations. The biggest of these schemes is a million acres (an area forty miles by forty miles).

I read an article in Business Week written by Jessica Silver-Greenberg, a reporter who visited a project called Dominion Farms, near Bondo, Kenya where we have an active AVP group. The Dominion Group, based in Guthrie, Oklahoma, is owned by Calvin Burgess and a few other private investors who have made money in real estate, manufacturing and aviation. It has no agricultural investment except Dominion Farms in Kenya. This seventeen thousand acre farm (an area more than five miles by five miles) is situated on the swampy land where the Yala River empties into Lake Victoria. It is being developed as a rice farm where the husks are being fed to tilapia in a large fish farming operation.

Calvin Burgess explains in an article he wrote for a Kenyan newspaper, "Desperation, hunger, and corruption reign and life was helpless; this simply must change...Food shortages, hunger, and corruption reined over a land full of superstitions and traditions; this simply must change." In his blog written at the same time, he reports that he visited Barack Obama's grandmother who lives nearby indicating that life is not nearly as bleak as Burgess thinks since her grandson has become president of the United States.

A Peace of Africa

Burgess claims that he never pays brides, regardless of the consequences. Nevertheless in order to rent this land for a twenty-five year lease renewable for another twenty years, he "made a series of agreements in confidential documents signed by members of the local councils and tribal chiefs" and these were approved by the Ministry of Lands. Note that the Luo people of this area do not have traditional "tribal chiefs" but that these are low level government functionaries appointed by the Kenyan government. He paid the Siaya County Council $100,000 and the funds vanished. He paid another $120,000 to the local Lake Basin Development Authority and it also disappeared. Burgess is aware of this. Is he so naïve that he does not realize that these are bribes?

He pays an annual rent of $140,000 — it is not clear to whom he pays the rent and what that "rent" is used for. This is $8.23 per acre. Gladys, my wife, is renting a small plot to grow corn and beans and it is costing her $53.33 per acre.

Dominion Farms claims it is hiring hundreds of local workers, but most of these, according to Silver-Greenberg, are women paid $2.66 per day to pull weeds and scare away birds, hardly the uplifting of the surrounding population that Burgess claims. Of course, those people, who are not longer able to graze their cows, goats, and sheep and harvest papyrus and other naturally growing crops, are unhappy on how they have been pushed aside. Dominion Farms has also built a dam on the Yala River which displaced an estimated three hundred families. According to Dominion Farms, those moved received compensation for their houses — $60 on average, according to Silver-Greenberg.

The farm has a rice mill, two rice combines, and an airplane for spraying fertilizer and herbicides on the rice. Burgess claims that he does not spray pesticides, but a former manager disputes this claim. Dieldrin, a chemical in some pesticides and long banned in the US, has been found in the local water supply. The local inhabitants also complain that their drinking water now has a metallic taste from the fertilizers Dominion Farms puts on its crops.

Dominion Farms has two thousands acres in rice cultivation. What is it doing with the other fifteen thousand acres?

In his blog, Burgess admits that the enterprise is struggling financially. While this does not surprise me, as rich countries such as Qatar and Saudi Arabia can put in as much capital as they need to grow food that can not be grown in their own countries, will the economic aspects of these enterprises be of any significance. This may be true even of Dominion Farms — Burgess explains that he is doing this as a religious calling to help the Africans.

Since the end of World War II, Africa has been noted for the failure of numerous capital intensive, mechanized agricultural schemes. In my Peace Corps days in the 1960's, I was involved in one such scheme to grow cotton in the region east of Lake Victoria. It was a total disaster because the altitude was too high for good cotton yields. The funds invested were mostly wasted. It is not clear that Dominion Farms will not suffer the same fate. Burgess recently blogged about that his rice crop was destroyed by hailstorms, a common occurrence in this region.

If Africa is going to develop agriculturally, is this the model that we want to see? In the 1960's, after independence in Burundi, the Chinese developed a rice scheme on the plains north of Bujumbura. This was not a large scale mechanized scheme but rather small holder plots. People can rent a plot for the growing season which pays for the water and irrigation. They can then grow the rice, sell it to the rice factory, and keep the proceeds. As I previously mentioned, a Quaker women's group has been renting one of these plots for over ten years and with the profits have been able to send all their children to school. This is a much better model for development than a large mechanized farm.

To think that no one was using this land before Dominion acquired it is contrary to facts. In almost all the schemes that alienate land to foreign concerns, any people living on the land are neglected, uninformed in secret deals, and, at best, given minimally compensated with nowhere to go.

Rice could easily be grown in this area. Rice is a capital intensive crop to develop and all the savings of all the people in the region would not be sufficient to develop even a modest, shareholding rice cooperative. The problem then is not "superstitious and traditional" people, as Burgess claims, but lack of adequate capital and financing. With proper inputs and developments, Africa can clearly feed itself and sell its surpluses to such agriculturally marginal places as the Middle East.

Not only has Dominion Farms paid bribes to secure it use of the seventeen thousand acres, but it dispossessed the surrounding people without their knowledge, agreement, or compensation. This is corruption as much as paying off officials with bribes.

Petty Corruption

With so much corruption at the top, it is not all surprising that petty corruption occurs at the grassroots level. In Kenya this is often called *chai* (tea), soda, *kitu kidogo* (a little something), and other euphemisms. These names are the same ones used in the "sitting allowance" that NGOs pay. The rationale is this: local bureaucrats are paid so little that they can not survive on their salary so that they need to "earn" extra money to support themselves. That this is a completely false rationale is illustrated by the fact that, when this excuse was used to dramatically increase police salaries in Kenya a few years ago, no noticeable drop in police corruption occurred.

People do not always pay the bribe themselves. Others do it for them. The best example is the *matatu* conductor. In Kenya, there are numerous police roadblocks. At each roadblock, the conductor pays a bribe. Coins are too obvious and heavy so the bribe has to be paper money. The amount cannot be less than sixty-seven cents, the value of the smallest paper note of fifty shillings. A *matatu* conductor can easily pay twenty of these bribes per day and the amounts therefore add up. This is paid even if there is no obvious illegality occurring. If so, for instance, when the *matatu* is overloaded, the bribe can be bigger. Naturally, the bribes are recouped by increased fare prices, meaning that the conductor is paying the bribes on behalf of all the passengers.

Foreigners have told me that they never saw a *matatu* conductor give a bribe. One needs to be very sharp to notice it. The conductor puts his hand out the window with the bribe in it. The police looks in the *matatu*, perhaps seeing if passengers have their seatbelts on and like a magician that works by slight of hand, receives the bribe from the conductor. The best place to notice this is the seat right behind where the conductor sits.

I think many people assume that the police at the roadblock are the ones receiving the loot from the bribes. Actually this is just the first step in grand corruption. Those police officers have to give their "proceeds" from the day to their superiors who, according to some formula, give most to their superiors and so on until some reaches the head office in Nairobi. We need an inside whistleblower to understand exactly how the system works from the police officer on the road to the head office in Nairobi.

A more obvious example is when we recently got our vehicle inspected. We gave our garage man $13.33 for his service in getting the inspection at the official government inspection station. It took most of the day. In the end, our garage man said that he had to pay $6.67 as a bribe or the official would never have given him the inspection certificate. I then realized that this was common procedure and that half of what I was giving our garage man was for him to bribe the government official.

As I have said above, the one who receives the bribe must have support from the one giving the bribe. I am amazed at how easily Kenyans give a bribe. Once I went to a hotel and after paying the night's charges, I asked for a receipt. The clerk at the counter replied, "How much do you want it for?" Naturally I replied the amount of the charge. The clerk at the counter was surprised. I had previously received a receipt from that hotel from a person who wanted reimbursement for the night which was twice what I paid

As I mentioned before, in Kenya one of the euphemisms for corruption is *kitu kidogo*, "something small." The problem with this is that there are many layers asking for "something small" so that by the end it is no longer a small thing but rather, something very big. Too many people assume that a certain level of bribery is just the way things are and therefore is acceptable. I am aware of an institution where the administration was taking an extra $10 to $15 every day or two for excess gas for the institution's vehicle. I calculated that after five months about $1333 had been embezzled. This was leading the institution into bankruptcy.

The concept in Kenya is that if someone is caught embezzling money, he or she immediately reimburses the shortage and all is well and forgotten. Once at an institution, I noticed $133.33 missing from a deposit. When I sent an email inquiring about this missing amount, the funds were in the account within two hours and no follow-up, no investigation was made of this attempted embezzlement. In another example, I found that someone had twice embezzled funds. Her superior responded, "We agreed to have a *harambee* [a fundraising event] to help her pay the funds she owes." The thief would keep the funds she embezzled while others would cover her theft. As far as I know the stolen funds were never reimbursed to the organization. No wonder petty theft is rampant in Kenya.

I have seen Kenyans pay bribes when the person could easily have just said, "No" and there would have been no repercussions. Ironically, it is common knowledge that *wazungu* are not asked for bribes because the bribers know that they will not pay them or perhaps complain to higher ups if they do.

Once I got caught in a speed trap near the neighboring town of Turbo. About ten people were stopped while I was there, but only three of us were given a speeding ticket. The others just paid a bribe to be let go, but this had to be in the $13.33 to $26.67 range. As an *mzungu* I was given a ticket and had to deposit the fine of $26.67. This was on a Saturday and I was told to report to court in Eldoret on Tuesday. Tuesday morning I showed up in court. But the police from Turbo, about twenty miles away, had not brought in the paperwork. I was told to come back at 2:00 PM after lunch. This I did and there was still no paperwork. So the staff stamped my ticket and told me to go back to the police station in Turbo and speak with the officer in charge. I did so and he was very nice and polite and, to my amazement, gave me back my $26.67 deposit on the fine. It is clear that Kenyans who are given tickets never show up in court and therefore forfeit their fine deposit. Consequently, the police do not even bother to file the paperwork with the court.

In the years I have lived in Africa, I have found that there are bedrock values that should not change. One of these is the condoning of bribing and embezzlement of funds. I have opposed this whenever I have seen it. On at least two occasions, people who I was accusing of embezzlement threatened to kill me. I have received numerous nasty emails. I have been called names — bully, CIA agent, "big brother" are some of them. Yet those Africans who oppose those embezzling funds have always been supportive of my stance and this has led to a strong following. One of the things I am accused of when I speak out is that I think all Africans are thieves but Americans are not. However, I have also uncovered a fair share of the misuse of funds by Americans, such as wanting to use funds donated for the work in Africa to go on a family safari. One should not think I am any less strict on these Americans.

American Complicity with Petty Corruption

As I mentioned in Chapter 5 on visiting Africa, Americans visiting Africa frequently are enablers for this petty corruption. They give cash to Africans or send funds to Africans through Western Union or other cash transfer agencies that are designated for organizations or institutions. When a donor does this, there is no accountability, no way of finding out if the funds were spent as directed, and therefore no transparency. Americans would never do this in the United States — they would write a check to the organization they wish to support. Frequently the person receiving the funds is very nice, polite, and convincing — the attributes of con men all over the world, including Bernie Madoff.

There is another aspect to these cash donations. If an African is given funds, people in his community will think that he has turned over only half or a quarter of the funds he or she had received. Since they will be suspicious, the person receiving the funds will have no method of verifying the value of what he or she has received. In other words, giving cash donation to an individual leaves that person open to accusations — whether true or false — of fraud. Therefore, when funds are routed though the proper channels, the receiver is also protected from false accusations.

Here are some guidelines that should be followed when giving funds to programs in Africa or anywhere else in the world including the Unites States.

1. Funds should only be given to a registered organization with a valid bank account. If the organization does not have a bank account, then it is a "briefcase organization" which is a scam. Even in the case of a scholarship, funds should be sent directly to the educational institution or routed through a dependable organization.

2. In order to qualify for funding, the donor should receive a proposal from a legally recognized organization which has approved the proposal at a board meeting of the responsible people. This proposal should include a detailed budget. A neutral person, knowledgeable about the country and type of proposal, should review it with an onsite visit.

3. Over-budgeting, currency transactions, over-pricing, salary hiking, and vague or unclear line items should be thoroughly questioned. The proposal including purpose, timeline, budget, and delivery of funds must be public information.

4. After funds are sent, monthly or quarterly program and financial reports should be regularly received. Frequently these should include pictures which can easily be done by email anywhere in the region. No further funding should be sent until such reports have been received and accepted as proper.

5. At the end of the proposal period, a final report and financial accounting must be submitted. There should then be another onsite visit by a neutral observer who should verify the accounting by

looking at the bookkeeping and supporting receipts. This protects not only the donor but also protects the implementer from any charges of mismanagement of the funds.

6. This implies that small donations are difficult to monitor and verify. Consequently, it is advisable that those who are unable to make the appropriate site visits channel their funds through organizations that have this capability, allocating a proper amount for this administrative task.

7. When theft, misuse, wastage, or unacceptable accounting is encountered, the donor must pursue these problems with the same diligence they would use for a similar case in their home country. Corruption cannot be excused under any rationale. If a donor is not willing and prepared to follow-up such misconduct, it should not accept proposals and disperse funds.

8. When theft, misuse, or unacceptable accounting is uncovered, the donor organization will discretely tell other donor organizations of such problems so that implementing organizations are not able to move from one donor to another with impunity.

In short, fiscal responsibility should be a top priority for anyone sending funds to programs in Africa.

"Legal" Corruption

Legal corruption occurs all over the world. In the US, when a lobbying organization gives funds to re-election campaigns and the senators and representatives then "respond" with a law that benefits those companies, this is legal corruption.

As I have noted in previous chapters, Kenya is not a "poor" country when compared with Rwanda, Burundi, Uganda, and the war-torn Kivu provinces in the Congo. Nonetheless, when it is to its benefit, it pretends it is a "poor," destitute country. During the drought in 2009, Kenya pleaded for outside aid to feed the estimated ten million Kenyans who were unable to feed themselves. Kenya received what it asked for. At the same time, Kenya had a bloated cabinet with almost half the members of parliament being ministers or assistant ministers receiving additional "perks" for their positions. During the public offering of Safaricom shares of the most profitable company in East Africa, almost $4 billion was tied up in the bidding when less than $900 million was required to fulfill the public offering of shares. This was only a fraction of what was needed to feed those hungry millions.

In the early 2000's, foreign donors who were subsidizing Kenyan and Tanzanian recurrent expenditures realized that less than 50% of the taxes were being collected as the rest was lost through tax evasion. They required the governments to improve their collection procedures so that from 2003 to 2007, Kenya tax collection increased almost three times in amount and to over 90% of the amounts due. Why had foreign governments and organizations like the World Bank and IMF been subsidizing this for decades?

In 2010 the program in Kenya that was supplying ARV (antiretroviral) drugs to HIV+ people in Kenya was not refunded due to the massive fraud in the previous rounds of funding. As a result large numbers of HIV+ people needing ARV's would not get them. The Kenyan government then floated a proposal to tax cell phone time and flights at the airport which would raise most of the funds that had been cut. What! Why is the international community supplying these drugs when Kenya has the ability to take care of its own needs? This, I think, is another example of "legal" corruption.

There is another kind of "legal" corruption — when the government or other institution pays more for services and goods than it should. I am not talking here about fraud where the purpose is to embezzle funds, but overpayment even when no fraud is intended.

In Kenya, misuse of funds has reached an art form. In a country where $3 per day is the official minimum wage, board members of the country's Truth and Reconciliation Commission are paid $120,000 per year. Ministers who go on foreign trips spend an unbelievable $100,000 per day on themselves and their entourage — I have difficulty even imagining how that much money could be spent in one day. Overcompensating people, misuse of "expense" accounts is just another method of corruption.

In my work with the African Great Lakes Initiative, I am always pruning budgets as people think, "It is not my money so I'll just put in a higher amount." This is misuse of funds. For instance, I just advised an organization to stop buying diesel from the closest gas station because it was higher in price than another gas station that they routinely went by. In this region the price of many things is still determined by bargaining as there are no set prices. Everyone needs to bargain to obtain the best and proper price.

I suspect that to many people, this may all seem rather trivial. Yet when unnecessary price increases across the board, funds do not stretch to where they should. I have had Americans complain about how much food is given at AGLI workshop lunches and how the Africans can not possibly consume the mounds of food that they are served. Over time, AGLI has cut the cost of the lunch by 40% by demanding that a decent, but not extravagant meal, be served. Since food is the largest expense in any one of our workshops, this is an important item in how many workshops we can do on a given amount of money. I calculate that this food savings in workshops allows us to do about 25% more workshops with the same amount of funds. Regardless of what people think, the amount of funds is always limited. Therefore they should be handled prudently.

Do Not Negotiate with Rebels

The biggest fallacy during the last half century is the custom of negotiating with rebel groups by giving them plush positions in government in order to placate them. Thus, the rebels become "strong" by destroying, looting, raping, and killing their own family, friends, neighbors, and countrymen so that the international community will negotiate with them. Destroying one's country is not proper training for running a government, and instead should be a ticket to trial at the International Criminal Court (ICC).

In 1996, the international community allowed rebel Charles Taylor to take over Liberia which he had been destroying for the previous seven years. He became president in an election overseen by the UN peacekeeping mission. He won 75% of the vote because people feared that, if he lost, he would go back to the bush and continue destroying the countryside. Taylor used his new authority to help destabilize the surrounding countries of Sierra Leone, Guinea, and Ivory Coast. In time, two other rebel groups challenged him and took over much of the country. He was given asylum in Nigeria, but, when the new president of Liberia asked for his extradition to face charges of war crimes, he was sent to the International Criminal Court where he is now on trial. If he had gone there directly, those four countries would have been spared years of war and fighting from which they have yet to recover.

It should become an absolute rule that any person who has used violence against his own country in order to obtain power —

which in the West is called "terrorism" — should be disbarred from all government positions. The current policy encourages any ne'er-do-well to take up arms and create chaos in order to seize the plum of state. As long as this policy is accepted in the region there will never be peaceful development.

During the Burundi civil war, there were seventeen sides, the Tutsi controlled government, the country's parliament plus fifteen rebel groups. They sat for seven years, but in plush hotels negotiating the end of the conflict. Every time negotiations resumed the country itself suffered since the rebel groups would attack to show that they were "strong" actors and needed appropriate "rewards" to stop their violence. Rebel groups split so that they had more bargaining power. In the end, all these rebel groups, together with the current government, were given positions in the government according to how "fearsome" they had been as rebels. The most militant Hutu rebel group, the NFL (Forces Nationales de Liberation), refused to sign the agreement and continued fighting, killing, and destroying. Even though beginning in 2005, the government was Hutu and the FNL was a Hutu group, all ethnic considerations were cast aside as they continued disrupting the country.

This was finally put to an end when the South African government, which had been instrumental in the negotiations that ended the civil war, told the FNL that they either agree to a ceasefire and negotiated settlement turning themselves into a political party or they would be attacked, captured, and sent to the ICC. The FNL given this ultimatum, accepted a peace agreement and turned themselves into a political party. The FNL were given a number of nice positions in the Burundi government. This part was a mistake. They should not get government rewards, but trial and jail.

❀ ❀ ❀
Sanction Other Countries that Support Rebels

The "habit" of supporting the foes of your foes is a remnant of the Cold War where pro-US governments were supported by the United States against countries that were pro-Soviet or pro-Chinese. These alignments have sometimes continued long after the end of the Cold War. We need to be reminded that it was immoral to export the "Cold War" to proxy countries where destruction and death ended up occurring. This habit has not died so that countries keep playing their favorites against those that are out of favor.

Almost every rebel group is supported by least one governments. This is how they get arms, ammunition, training, funds, and recognition. In the case of the eastern Congo, Rwanda and Uganda supported various rebel groups which were their proxies in the flow of mineral resources to the West. The Congolese government supported the former *genocidaires* from Rwanda. The most ironic clash was when two rebel groups in eastern Congo, both supported by Uganda, fought against each other. The United States was also involved since both Rwanda and Uganda are staunch allies of the US. I once was at a Great Lakes Policy Forum meeting in Washington, DC where a spokesperson from the US military said that the US military was not giving any support to the Rwanda and Uganda governments to support the rebel groups in the eastern Congo. This was followed by a UN peacekeeping spokesman who claimed that American bodies of hired American mercenaries were being carried out in body bags.

One salient aspect of the Rwandan genocide was that the French continued supporting their client Rwandan *genocidaire* government before and during the genocide because they wished to keep their influence in the region. When the genocide failed, Rwanda moved from the Francophone sphere of influence to the Anglophone sphere of influence. France and England, in their foreign policy in Africa, are still playing out their rivalries that began during the late nineteenth century scramble for Africa.

The Rwandan Patriotic Front that invaded from Uganda and defeated the *genocidaires* spoke English rather than French because most of them had grown up in English-speaking Uganda and attended schools there. In 2004 when I visited the Ministry of Local Government, I found that everyone spoke English. At that time French, Kiyarwandan, and English were official languages. In late 2008, the Rwandan government decreed that everything would change from French to English. The language of instruction in schools changed overnight. Teachers, who had been teaching in French for years, had to scramble to learn English in order to retain their teaching positions.

One of the underlying changes occurring in Central Africa is the move from French to English; from Francophone to Anglophone. This is occurring not only in Rwanda, but also Burundi and the eastern Congo. When I visited the region in 1999, almost no one could speak to me in English. Frequently I had to converse in Swahili, but then found that most up-country people did not know

Swahili either. Now, many people who could not speak English with me in 1999 speak to me quite fluently. Many Rwandans and Burundians are sending their children to schools in Uganda so that they can learn better English. Those former French speaking teachers who are now trying their best in limited English do not give a quality education.

This move from English to French might seem beside the point. But the rivalry between the French and English is an important factor that needs to be remembered in the politics of Africa.

International pressure does work. Recently, it worked very effectively in North Kivu in the eastern Democratic Republic of the Congo. In Chapter 7, I described how Laurent Nkunda controlled the resources of this very rich Masisi region.

Laurent Nkunda became the Tutsi rebel leader who headed a group called CNDP (French initials for "National Congress for the Defense of the People"). He was strongly supported by the Rwandan government. Nkunda's stated purpose was to defend Tutsi who lived in North Kivu against the former *genocidaires* who still roamed the forests and had formed another rebel group that exploited North Kivu's resources. Reports, including from the United Nations, claim he was actually a surrogate force for Rwandans to loot and exploit various minerals and other resources in North Kivu. People from Goma told me that they saw truckloads of demobilized Rwandan soldiers traveling at night through town on their way from Rwanda to the Masisi area he controlled.

In late 2008 and early 2009, Nkunda's forces attacked and almost captured the city of Goma. My sense is that the only reason that he did not take Goma was that he did not have sufficient troops to control a city of six hundred thousand people. The international community began to put pressure on Rwanda to stop supporting Nkunda and his rebel forces in the Kivus. They had done this in the past and Rwanda had claimed that they were not supporting Nkunda and could not control him and his forces. Nonetheless, the Netherlands and Sweden cut off economic assistance to Rwanda until they stopped their support of Nkunda. This was real pressure. Rwanda, before the genocide, was the highest recipient of foreign aid per capita of any country in Africa. After the genocide, Rwanda again became the highest recipient of foreign aid per capita of any country in Africa. At that point in time, 50% of Rwanda's recurrent budget was supplied by the international community and the Rwandan miracle of economic revival would have stopped dead in its tracks if aid had been cut off. Rwanda quickly changed its policy.

As a consequence, in January 2009 Rwanda arrested Lauent Nkunda when he was in Rwanda and Nkunda's rebel group was re-integrated with the Congolese Army. Rwanda, after more than a decade of hostility with the Congolese government, signed a peace agreement where the Congolese and Rwandan armies would jointly attack the remaining *genocidaire* rebels in North Kivu. By September 2009, détente had progressed to such an extent that the two president of Rwanda and the DRC were able to meet in the no-man's land between Gisenyi, Rwanda, and Goma, DRC, to seal a peace agreement between the two countries. President Kabila of the DRC declared that the war was over. The internally displaced people's camps were closed and the IDPs returned to their homes. My contacts in North Kivu tell me that exactly the same people control Masisi as before — except now they are part of the Congolese Army rather than the CNDP. I do not know if this is the beginning of the end of war in North and South Kivu or just another lull before fighting breaks out again.

The point of this story is that countries can be forced, perhaps against their own desires and interests, to stop supporting rebel groups that are creating havoc in other countries. This should become standard operating procedure for the region. Any country that supports the rebel group in another country should be hit with sanctions by donor governments, by the United Nations, and by the World Bank, the International Monetary Fund, and all other international organizations.

Can the world community do this?

Tackle Corruption

There is a worldwide organization called Transparency International (TI) which "leads the fight against corruption, brings people together in a powerful worldwide coalition to end the devastating impact of corruption on men, women and children around the world. TI's mission is to create change towards a world free of corruption." Part of the solution is to support the campaign initiated by Transparency International to expose corruption. It is necessary to strengthen the laws that exist against bribery and corruption, but even more important to implement and enforce the laws that do exist. Siemens was caught, in part, due to international cooperation of the investigative arms of a number of governments including the US. Secret Swiss bank accounts must be opened for inspection and all those off-shore secret banks need to be shut down. Moreover when companies, governments, or individuals are caught, their names must be made public, they must make restitutions for their ill-gotten gains, and those responsible should, like Bernie Madoff, be given jail sentences. All of this should be without regard to nationality.

If the world put more resources investigating corruption, there would be a lot less "terror" in the world and certainly less bribery. The poor countries would then have up to 40% more funds to invest in their development. Most importantly, rebels and warlords would lose one of their major incentives for looting, burning, raping, and killing. This would help bring peace to Africa.

Impunity for large scale corruption must be faced squarely. As long as people know they can become exceedingly rich by seizing some part of a government, there will be people who will destroy, rape, and kill to do so. One of the most remarkable aspects of President Julius Nyerere of Tanzania was that when he voluntarily left office, he and his family were not wealthy like the Kenyatta family in Kenya when Jomo Kenyatta died in office. This is partly the reason that Tanzania has not had the civil conflicts that have occurred in neighboring countries.

How can corruption be tackled? I consider the out-of-court settlement of the Siemens case — where there was a large fine but the bribers and those bribed were kept secret — to be criminal. The prosecutors and judges allowed those two thousand seven hundred bribery agents, plus the tens of thousands people who were bribed, to stay with their ill gotten loot. The first way to tackle corruption is to disallow plea bargaining that hides the bribers and those that they bribed. This should all be public knowledge and those who have given or taken bribes should face the consequences in their home countries. Imagine if all those Siemens' bribers and those bribed had been exposed to justice and had to return their loot with time in jail to think about what they did. This would have been revolutionary. Other cases will soon be coming up. Will there be transparency to the whole world or will a plea bargain hide those responsible? Moreover I am not so naïve to think that the Siemens' worldwide corrupt system has collapsed. By keeping it secret, it allows that bribery network to continue to function. I doubt that this elaborate system functioned only for Siemens, but the network, informally, was responsible for many cases of bribing.

Another important step is to close those secret bank accounts in Switzerland and all offshore banks. When Siemens bribed the Nigerian government officials with $12,700,000, did they carry 127,000 hundred dollar bills in suitcases? These funds had to be deposited somewhere in secret bank accounts. If there were no secret bank accounts, grand bribery would be much more difficult. For good reason, the US government does not issue $1,000 or $10,000 notes. Switzerland prides itself as the home of the Red Cross, but it should rather be vilified as the enabler of world corruption. I suggest that, as was done to help bring down apartheid in South Africa, there should be a boycott of Switzerland and all its products, athletic events, etc. until the Swiss banks become as open to inspection as any other banks in the world. Those offshore banks in mini-nations could easily be forced to close if the international community decided to do this. So let's decide to close them.

If the international community put the same effort into challenging international corruption as they have been putting into money laundering and tracking funds to terrorist organizations, the pay off to the world would be substantial. As happened in the Siemens case, many nations need to work together to catch those very clever bribery thieves. Then the court cases must be pursued vigorously to destroy the roots of the problem. I do not understand why egregious bribers should not be hauled in front of the International Criminal Court since they destroy their home country as much as, perhaps even more than, any gun-toting rebel.

As part of this effort, the international community, meaning national governments, the United Nations and its many agencies, the World Bank and IMF, the large NGO's like the Red Cross, Catholic Relief Services, World Relief, and the many much smaller NGO's, must all challenge the corruption they find in their programs. They should not be afraid to lay down extremely tough conditions for transparency — they must all become much more transparent themselves — and not hesitate to withdraw funding when corruption is revealed.

Moreover, when corruption is uncovered, restitution must be demanded and received before funding is restored. The current custom is to cut off funds, demand reforms, and then re-engage. In the meantime, whoever did the looting is waltzing to the bank. This practice, too, must end.

The petty bribing must also be curtailed. Westerners must stop giving cash, sending funds through Western Union and other agencies, to private individuals. If they wish to be charitable and donate funds, they must also be willing to demand accountability and results.

If we wish to rectify the problems in the Great Lakes region of Africa, this attack on corruption is essential. Does the world have the moral and political will to do it? I do not know. To date, I have not seen much evidence of it. In the past, Quakers attacked slavery when it was accepted everywhere in the world. There is always hope that a better world, a Peaceful Kingdom as the Quakers call it, can be built here on earth.

Chapter 15
Elections

The Problems with African Elections

As has been indicated in this book, after violent overthrow of the government, elections are the method used to seize or retain power. Controlling the government not only gives the victor a nice salary with many perks, but opens the way to immense illegal wealth through corruption. Unlike the United States, where a defeated politician can usually make much more money after he or she retires from a government position, African politicians who lose will have nothing more than whatever they collected during their time in office.

Mo Ibrahim, a wealthy Sudanese businessman, has launched the Ibrahim Prize, given to an African leader who has peacefully led the development of his or her country and who has voluntarily left office at the end of his or her term. According to its webpage, "The prize consists of $5 million over ten years and $200,000 annually for life thereafter. It is the largest annually awarded prize in the world. The Foundation will consider granting a further $200,000 per year, for ten years, towards public interest activities and good causes espoused by the winner." Out of fifty-four countries in Africa, in 2009 and in 2010, the committee for the Mo Ibrahim Foundation could find no worthy recipient.

In these systems, the winner does take "all." The temptations to use every possible method to win are exceedingly strong. Consequently, every method of increasing one's vote while decreasing the opponents votes are used. For instance, in the 2010 Burundi election, the Quaker Peace Network election observers found these cases of fraud just in the registration process for the election:

- people registering more than once,
- underage children being enrolled as voters,
- buying of voter identification papers,
- the spreading of rumors to keep people from registering,
- hard to find election enrollment offices in opposition strongholds which would benefit the ruling party,
- a ruling political party official taking the enrollment books home at night and adding unauthorized names to the polling list.

To capture the presidency the fraud has to be large. Yoweni Museveni in Uganda is supposed to have had one million ghost voters in his last three elections in 1996, 2001, and 2006. There were mythical polling stations which voted 100% for him. He probably did not need these ghost voters in 1996 and 2001, but in 2006 the ghost votes kept Museveni from a runoff which he may well have lost.

It is unclear how many ballot boxes were stuffed in the 2007 Kenyan election. In some cases, there were more votes than registered voters. Any constituency where this happened was supposed to be discounted, but that did not happen. As I related in Chapter 11, the actual polling at my polling station, as was true throughout Kenya, went well. It was when the results were taken to Nairobi and counted by the electoral commission, solely appointed by President Kibaki, that the fraud occurred. In the case of Kenya, the losing voters felt cheated and resorted to violence. The government responded with violence of its own.

There are so many fraudulent methods of stealing elections. President Daniel Arap Moi, the twenty-four year "elected" dictator of Kenya, had one interesting method. In 1992 and then 1997, he was forced to have multiparty elections. One of his techniques was to register numerous parties, some with names very similar to opposition parties, that were secretly allied to him, but were manipulated to confuse the voting public.

Here is a list of some possible ways that the ruling party will rig the election in its favor:

- The electoral commission is stacked with government supporters appointed solely by the current president.
- Fraudulent enrollment of voters.
- Entire ghost polling stations can be counted on to give 100% of the votes to the ruling party.
- The government in power can hassle their opponents, putting them in jail before the election, accusing them of disturbing the peace of the country, or not allowing their opponents the freedom to campaign.
- The ruling party, and opposition parties, form youth militias to intimidate, beat up, and sometime kill opponents.
- Bribing of voters can be done on a massive scale.
- Miscounting of votes to favor the ruling party can occur.

I visited Burundi in February 2010 shortly before their five elections for different levels of government between May 21 and

September 7. I met with diplomats from the Belgian, French, South African, and the European Union. I also attended a meeting with IFES, International Foundation for Electoral Systems, the consortium of NGOs concerned with the elections, and a meeting of NGOs with a delegation from Germany. On the grassroots side, I met with more than twenty election observers from the Quaker Peace Network and attended the first of five days of training for "citizen reporters" that we were training to cover the election at the local level. Naturally, I talked with all kinds of people in between and asked how the registration of voters went the week before.

Everyone was in agreement about one thing, namely that the election was not about ethnicity, that is, the division between Hutu and Tutsi which has defined Burundian politics since independence in the early 1960's. All parties were multi-ethnic and the divisions were between regions of the country and political personalities. This was seen by all as a substantial improvement. But there was little political difference between the more than forty parties as none seem to have any kind of political platform that they are running on. Only one of the major seven political parties even had an up-to-date webpage. In other words, the election was not at all about issues. If that is the case, then what is the election about? Power, wealth, and influence for the winners.

There was a major split between the international community and grassroots activists as to how the situation was developing. The international consensus was expressed by one of the diplomats from South Africa, "The election, which cannot be expected to be perfect, is progressing satisfactorily." The following problems were considered "normal" and not something that should invalidate the electoral process:

• two politicians had been assassinated,
• youth groups from two of the major political parties in one province fought each other in a battle,
• there are substantial indications that various political parties were organizing and training youth groups who do the election intimidation and violence in places such as Burundi,
• one of the opposition party's office near where I was staying was raided at eleven o'clock at night by men with guns and rocks and the police did not show up until the following morning,
• there were reports of fraud in the enrollment of voters

The Quaker Peace Network-Burundi (QPN-Burundi) is comprised of nine Quaker and Quaker affiliated organizations in Burundi including the AGLI supported programs of HROC-Burundi and the Friends Women's Association. In the past, QPN have realized that observers concentrate on poll watching on the day of the election, but neglect all the activities during the enrollment of voters, the election campaigning period and then the post election period of potential violence. So QPN-Burundi had decided to observe throughout the whole election process. QPN-Burundi had thirty-five observers during the two weeks of voter enrollment

Quaker Peace Network election observers, Josephine Nizigama and Desire Nduwimana, on right in white hats, are observing the Burundian communal election on May 21, 2010.

When I met with over twenty of these observers, they were not nearly as confident that the election was going smoothly. They observed many of the incidences of fraud indicated above. In a number of cases, they reported the misdeeds to the Burundi Electoral Commission and the Commission did respond by investigating and correcting the fraudulent practices. But how many of these were not caught by election observers? Since in order to win, every political party needs to seek whatever unfair advantages that it can get because otherwise its opponents will win, will these numerous frauds cancel each other out? Or can there be a "free and fair" election when there is a substantial grassroots fraud? The answer is "no" because the ruling party, through its control of the organs of government, has much more power to instigate fraud than any of the other political parties. I was told that one of the "tricks" of the out-of-power political parties was to accuse the ruling party of fraud at every instance to build up the case that the ruling party was "stealing" the election. But is this a "trick" or true? The conventional wisdom was that the ruling party, if it lost, would not be willing to go back into the bush to start another civil war because they have become too used to the good life brought by governing the country. But this same statement can be used to indicate that the ruling party will do everything possible to win re-election.

What is important to note here is that the international community as represented by the embassy officials I met with had a low bar for a free and fair election. If there was not massive, obvious fraud and if there was no significant post-election violence, the international community was going to announce that the voting was free and fair. Therefore the winner, regardless of what they had done to get elected, will be considered legitimate. Burundians in their local communities are very likely to decide otherwise.

Then, if elections, such as those in 2010 in Sudan and Ethiopia are not considered free and fair, nothing of consequence happens and the ruling party continues in power. If, by chance, the voting is close as in Kenya in 2007 and Zimbabwe in 2008, then the Presidents, Kibaki and Mugabe in these cases, just announce that they have won and refuse to give up power. Both of these cases resulted in wide-spread violence and a compromise through a grand coalition of the "winning" and "losing" parties. As can be expected this leads to great difficulty in governance of the country.

This discussion implies two things. First, if in order to win a candidate has to use numerous devious means including large scale bribing, the candidate will want to recoup his expenses. This is frequently given as one of the reasons for the massive embezzlement of funds in Kenya where winning (that is, "buying") the election costs enormous sums. Voters who have been bribed feel that the winner has bought his position and therefore is no longer answerable to the constituency. The politician feels likewise. He had to chance so much to win that once he wins, his main focus is to recoup his expenses and then much more. It is ironic that in Kenya, very unlike the United States where it is almost impossible to upseat an incumbent, most incumbents lose. This means, though, that the MPs wish to get all they can during their five year term because there may not be another one.

The second important point is that, when the election is so fraudulent, no one believes in "democracy," that those who won did so in a legitimate matter. As the ruling party and "elected" dictator become more unpopular, there is no chance of up-seating him, unrest and violence become the only means of "voting." This is one of the major causes of violence in Africa today.

The Exception: An Election Where the Ruling Party Lost

After the 2010 clearly rigged elections in Sudan and Ethiopia were over, I read a comment in the *Daily Nation* in Kenya, that elections in the greater eastern and central African region, the ruling party always wins. Therefore there is no need to hold elections which are expensive, lead to violence and counter-violence, and make the population unsettled. Since in most countries, there are no term limits, or if there are term limits, they are abolished when the incumbent has reached his limit, this statement is true.

But there is one major exception in the region, the overthrow of the Kenya African National Union (KANU) in the 2002 election in Kenya. It is instructive to learn how this was done. In the 1992 and 1997 elections the president, Daniel arap Moi, had won re-election through various legal and illegal methods. By 2003 he had been in power for twenty-four years of a brutal dictatorship. The country was clearly tired of him and wanted a change. Moi, by this time, was too old and unpopular to run again, so he anointed Uhuru Kenyatta, the son of the first Kenyan president, Jomo Kenyatta, to run as president on the KANU ticket. If he won, it would have been business as usual. Much to the surprise of many, including myself, Uhuru Kenyatta, lost and the new president became Mwai Kibaki. How did this happen?

I considered this as an important development as the election of Nelson Mandela in South Africa, since the ruling party was removed from office through a fair election. I assumed, wrongly, that the methods used to overthrow the KANU regime, would be used in subsequent elections in Kenya and elsewhere in Africa.

All the religious groups in Kenya which included not only the Christians and the Muslims, but also the Hindus and other smaller religions, banned together under the Ufungamano Initiative to ensure a fair election. First, they had to challenge the methods of voting and counting the votes. They lobbied for a system where all the votes in a polling station had to be counted at the polling station itself with all the election observers present. Then the tally had to be posted at the polling booth. The Ufungamano Initiative made sure that they had an observer at every polling station. These agents called in the result to the Initiative's vote counting center which announced the votes as they came it. The result was that the Ufungamano Initiative's results came out faster than the official count. Their results showed that KANU and its candidate, Kenyatta, were losing badly with less than 33% of the vote. Because of this, it was impossible for KANU henchmen to stuff the ballot boxes. Nor could Moi and Kenyatta stage a coup as it was clear to the whole world that they were soundly defeated. I was in Kenya shortly after this happened and I could not believe the euphoria at that time of having finally gotten rid of President Moi and his henchmen. Note that this civic monitoring of the election needed extensive organization and funds to carry out its task of ensuring a fair counting of the votes.

For reasons that I can not quite explain, the Ufungamano Initiative disbanded as an election observing organization. If they had continued doing what they did in the 2002 election during the 2007 election, the stalemate and post election violence probably would have not occurred. The religious leaders, rather than working together, became very partisan, supporting one candidate or the other on ethnic lines. They had become part of the problem. Later the religious leaders publicly apologized for their biased leadership during the election and post election violence.

Election Reforms

The world has decided that those who control governments are elected by the population. This is an excellent theory. The problem is the practice. In the United States, elections now mean inordinate expenditures on advertising, much of it on TV. Therefore, wealthy candidates and those to whom lobbyists are willing to contribute — in return for future favors — fill the election rosters. Elections are determined by such dirty tricks as the Swift Boat attacks on John

Kerry or the attempts to discredit Barack Obama by the "birthers" who say he was not born in the United States. Every African that I have spoken with believes that Jeb Bush, as governor of Florida, handed his brother the presidency in 2000 because this happens all the time in Africa.

Elections are a non-violent method of bringing desired change in leadership to a country. This is one reason that the Quaker Peace Network-Africa is so involved with election observing. What is the result when the election is clearly a fraud? Those in power manipulate the system in such a fashion that they win time after time. In any election, the incumbents have a decided advantage to start with and, if they want to use the powers of the state to help them conduct fraudulent elections, their advantage increases to the extent that no opposition has a chance.

As I reported above, in 2002 Kenya was able to overthrow the Moi dictatorship by observing the election from beginning to end. Some of the basic election process changes that made this possible included having votes counted at the polling station at the end of the voting day in front of all party and neutral observers and the results posted at the voting station. Results could then be called in to a neutral tally station. With current computer technology, the results from every polling station can be placed on a webpage immediately for everyone to see and verify. The use of Excel spreadsheets could have given an accurate addition of the totals for every candidate. It is possible to run an accurate tally of the votes even in such poor countries as Burundi. Unsurprisingly, the ruling parties in these countries oppose such methods of transparency.

Fraudulent elections are a cause of violence. Methods must be worked out, and consistently applied, that make elections as fair and transparent as possible. Otherwise post election violence will become more and more common and will destroy the political and economic well being of their countries.

Another related issue has to do with term limits. Presidents, such as Museveni in Uganda, should not be allowed to change their constitutions so that they can remain in power term after term. There should be a maximum of two five-year terms after which the President must move on. The current reality of "president-for-life" means that a president does not plan for a successor because, if qualified and astute, that successor could overthrow the president. When the president-for-life finally dies, or is overthrown, there is no obvious successor and unrest, even civil war, breaks out.

What needs to happen is that any country that tries to change its constitution to allow for perpetual presidents must feel the wrath of the international community by a total ban on economic and political assistance. Countries that do not have term limits in their constitution already must be required to amend them. In case after case, the longer the ruling president and his party stay in power the worse the corruption becomes because they have learned how to play the system better and better. Over time, extended rulership means the government must become more repressive to put down dissent and the country deteriorates until it creates a situation like the way-too-long dictatorship of Robert Mugabe in Zimbabwe. Rulers are more than willing to destroy their country in order to stay in power.

If there are fair, transparent elections, and if rulers can only stay in power for a maximum of ten years, countries in the Great Lakes region would have periodic changes of elected officials. Each newly elected government would start afresh and clean the stables, so to speak. If elected officials do not perform well, they can be dismissed at the next election. Proper pressure from the international community could make all of this possible. Again, is there the moral and political will to do it?

Do Not Agree to Low Standards

Recently there was an election in Sudan. The Carter Center and the European Union observer teams declared that the election was not up to international standards. The African Union — filled with leaders who know how to manipulate and steal elections — declared that the elections were fair and did not need to meet international standards because this was Sudan's first election in twenty-four years. This is nonsense. It was still a stolen election.

As I have observed in the Burundi elections, the international community has extremely low standards for what is a fair election. If election day itself is relatively peaceful with people lining up for hours at the polling stations, the election is considered free and fair. Voting on election day is only one small aspect of the process and free and fair must include much more than this criteria which naïve election observers consider the hallmark of a fair election, thereby giving credence to a process that is fundamentally flawed.

There is a theory that people perform to the level of the expectations others have of them. I once read of a study at an inner-city school, where the researchers artificially increased the IQ of a number of students at the bottom of the class. The teachers responded by expecting more from these students and the amazing thing was that after a year of this, the students did have higher IQ scores close to the fake ones they have been given at the beginning of the year. They became more intelligent because their teachers expected them to be intelligent. When there are very low expectations of African countries, they will fulfill those expectations. If there are high expectations — high standards for them to strive for — they will fulfill these and progress will occur.

As I explained in Chapter 13, the international media has a very biased standard of news from Africa as it must include conflict, fighting, war, and AIDS to be newsworthy. The positive is neglected because it does not fit in with the stereotype that the writers and readers have of Africa. I have heard numerous Africans, and read even more, who have decried this bias of the international media; another example of low expectations.

Likewise if people assume that corruption is natural and normal in Africa, they are not going to challenge that corruption. This, again, is a low expectation. African governments and organizations must be held to the same high standards as other countries. Americans should expect their donations to be handled as honestly as they expect donations in the United States to be handled.

In the Alternatives to Violence Project that we implement in the region, one of the guidelines for successful conflict resolution is "expect the best." With Africa, there is way too much of "expect the worst." Expecting the best is a sign of hope and encouragement. Expecting the worst is a sign of disillusionment and resignation. We need to "expect the best" with Africa.

Conclusion

When I visited Burundi during the civil war and went up country, I noticed that all houses were exactly the same. None was bigger than another with an extra room. There were no decorations to distinguish one house from another. At first, I thought Burundians did not have any aesthetic taste, but then I realized that if someone had a bigger or nicer house, both the rebels and the government troops would target them. All housing was at the lowest, common level. Yet at the same time, everyone was making bricks, both adobe and fired bricks. I realized that this extensive brick making was a hope for a better future. In time when peace finally did come in 2005, people quickly improved their houses and built new ones or additions.

Regardless of the advice that I should not shake hands with Africans as I reported in the introduction, I have made it a policy to shake hands with kids. Since I go to out of the way places where children seldom see *wazungu*, many are excited to see an *mzungu*. To be polite and friendly, I offer to shake their hand, if they are not too afraid of me. This for me is a symbol of the warmth and friendliness that I have always received while I am in Africa.

Such is the case in the region at this time. Since the beginning of the first decade of this century, the economy in the region has begun to improve. In most cases, this is clear at the local level with better houses, more bicycles, brighter clothes on the women and children, more activity on the road from Mombasa to Goma, and other signs of increased prosperity. Nonetheless, there is a long way to go, decades of slow, constant improvement, I would estimate, before the basics of food, housing, medical care, and education will include everyone in the region.

Yet there are still great dangers. Any one of these countries could explode into violence, particularly during elections. If this happens, that country and even the whole region could be set back and, depending upon the severity of the violence, could negate all those improvements of the first decade of this century.

Thank you for having reached this far in this book. Perhaps some readers will think that I have been too critical and harsh on American culture and society. Others perhaps will think that I have been too harsh on African culture and society. I have long ago learned that if I wish to comprehend an issue or problem in depth, I need to be straightforward and honest. Sometimes this offends others who are accustomed to a more complacent approach. My criticisms are mostly directly at how American or African society is organized on the macro-level. In both places, I find people themselves to be warm, friendly, interesting, concerned, and helpful. However, tackling a major reform in society, say deeply imbedded corruption in Kenya or the for profit health care system in the United States, is an overwhelming task. Yet as a good Quaker, I think one of our purposes for living in the world is to work to rectify such problems.

Gladys and I plan to continue to live in our home in Lumakanda and continue to work on peacemaking in the region. I have an email list serve where I send out reports whenever I have something of significance to say. If you would like to keep updated, you can sign up for this by going to the AGLI webpage, www.aglifpt.org. You can stay in touch with me by going to my website, www.davidzarembka.com

Acknowledgement

With such a long, interesting, and eventful life, it is impossible to list or even remember all those people who have given me insight, helped me grow, worked alongside me, and even confronted me. For me this is particularly difficult because I see my role not as an implementer, but rather as the organizer and cooperator bringing people, ideas, and resources together to implement programs. As a result, I am dependent upon others to perform the actual work. I will list those who have been most important for my African experiences with the hope that I do not miss someone important.

My first note of gratitude is for my late mother, Helen Jane Zarembka, not only for blessing my original trip to Tanzania in 1964, but also for the unfailing support she gave me over the years during my eclectic career.

This book would not have existed if my children, Joy Mutanu Zarembka and Tommy Mutinda Zarembka, did not push me to start the project and, more importantly, to help with the editing throughout the one and a half years of writing. I feel amply rewarded for all those Dr. Suess books I read to them when they were children. I need to thank my wife, Gladys Kamonya, for enduring the many hours I spent wedded to the computer screen as I wrote the book. She also unfailing in answering my many questions about Luhya and Kenyan culture and mores. She is the "deep throat" behind this book. (For those too young to know, "deep throat" was Bob Woodward's secret source of information in the Nixon White House during his crash from power.) Thanks to Douglas Kebengwa, my adopted Kenyan son, for keeping my computers working.

I need to express deep sense of gratitude to the late Alison des Forges and Karen Worth for encouraging me to join the Harvard program, Project Tanganyika, in 1964, the late John Gerhart and Gail Gerhart for finding me that first position in the Rwandan refugee camp, and Randy Kehler for partnering with me during that year. These have also all been my lifelong friends. I would also like to thank all my students at Muyenzi Primary School where I taught that year.

In Africa, I will mention people by country. Clearly without their help, support, and fantastic work under trying conditions of-

317

ten with little finances AGLI's programs would not have had the impact that they have had.

In Kenya, I have so many people to thank. I need to acknowledge my involvement with Gladys' family — her father, David Okwemba; her late mother, Selina Imali; her aunt, Katherine Mwandihi; her sisters, Florence Kageha, Janet Makungo, Mary M'mbone, Josephine Muhonja, and Eunice Mugasia; and her children, Douglas Mmbala Shukuunzi and Beverly Kang'azi. Since there are many other aunts and uncles, in-laws, nieces and nephews, and now grandnieces and grandnephews, rather than name them, I will just acknowledge them all as a group.

I also need to thank my former wife, Rodah Wayua Zarembka, and her father, Wilson Malinda. Thanks also to Kivuto Ndeti and the late Motheke Ndeti for inviting me to start the Mua Hills Harambee Secondary School. I need to also thank my driver in those years, Joshua Mwangi.

Lastly, my life and work in Kenya would not have been possible without the help of the following in Kenya: Getry Agizah, Eden Grace, Janet Ifedha, Elizabeth Kabankaya, Malesi Kinaro, Alfred Machayo, Florence Machayo, Jacinta Makokha, Joseph Mamai, Hezron Masitsa, Dorcas Nyambura, Bernard Onjala, Mary Kay Rehard, Ann Riggs, Peter Serete, Joseph Shamala, Donald Thomas, and Ruth Thomas

In Burundi, I need to acknowledge Charles Berahino, Bridget Butt, Marceline Girukwishaka, Elie Nahimana, the late Odette Nahayo, Alexia Nibona, Adrien Niyongabo, David Niyonzima, Florence Ntakarutimana, and Desire Nzeyimana.

In Rwanda, Theoneste Bizimana, David Bucura, Solange Maniraguha, Sizeli Marcellin, Josephine Mukangoga, Etienne Nsanzimana, Cecile Nyiramana, Innocent Rwabuhihi, and Augustin Simparaka.

In eastern Congo, Mkoko Boseka, Leon Mkangya Alenga, Levi Munyemana, Zawadi Nikuze, and Jeremy Nzabanita.

In Uganda, Helen Kabuni, Grace Kiconco, George Walumoli, and Teresa Walumoli..

Since 1998, the Friends Peace Teams has been supportive of my activities in Africa. Special thanks goes to Adrian Bishop, Ray Boucher, the late Elise Boulding, Andy Cross, Deborah Dakin, David Easter, Nadine Hoover, Val Liveoak, Mary Lord, Gail Newbold, the late Susan Rose, Chuc Smith, Kathy Wright, and Cece Yocum.

Without the support of these people involved in the African Great Lakes Initiative, I could not have accomplished much in these last twelve years: Laura Shipler Chico, Anna Crumley-Effinger, Rosalie Dance, Rachel Fretz, Rachel Mandenyika, Sue Nowelsky, Tom Paxson, Andrew Peterson, Dawn Rubbert, and Mumia Shimaka. Dawn Rubbert also was so good as to copy edit this book, correcting my many foolish inconsistencies in spelling, punctuation, grammar, and incomprehensible sentences. I need to acknowledge the encouragement and support of the members of Bethesda Meeting, St. Louis Meeting, and Baltimore Yearly Meeting, and also those around the country who have supported AGLI through the years.

I am also grateful for the many extended service volunteers and work campers who have been involved through these years: Brad Allen, Bob Barns, Alexandra Douglas, Ann Dusseau, Ginnie Floyd, Sandy Grotberg, Mary Kay Juu, Sheila Havard, the late Linda Heacock, Emily Higgs, David Kern, Carolyn Keys, the late John McKendy, Bethany Mahler, Gabe Morden-Snipper, Nancy Shippen, Karen Vaccaro, Barbara Wybar, and Peter Yeomans.

The photographs in this book were supplied courtesy of the following:

Roger Des Forges, page 25;

Adrien Niyongabo, pages 31, 33, 35, 47, 166, 168, 170, 172, 242, 308, and 315;

Patrick Angaya, page 151.

The remaining pictures were taken by the author.

Glossary

AGLI — (pronounced AG-lee) African Great Lakes Initiative of the Friends Peace Teams.

Bagaza, Jean-Baptiste — President of Burundi from 1976 to 1987.

Bantu — A group of similar, but distinct languages spoken in central, east, and southern Africa.

Bugusu — A sub-tribe of the Luhya living on or near Mt. Elgon.

Chang'aa — Cheap and potent liquor locally produced from molasses, Swahili.

DRC — Democratic Republic of the Congo, formerly Zaire.

Eldoret — The major town in the north Rift Valley, thirty miles east of Lumakanda.

FPCD — Friends in Peace and Community Development.

FRODEBU — The Front for Democracy in Burundi (French: Front pour la Démocratie au Burundi), the party of President Mechior Ndadaye who was assassinated in 1993.

Genocidaires — Those who participated in a genocide, French.

Harambee — self-help, "let us all pull together," Swahili.

Hutu — The majority group in Rwanda and Burundi, usually considered to be farmers.

IDP — Internally displaced people.

Interahamwe — "Those who work together." These were the youth militias that carried out much of the killing during the Rwandan genocide, language of Rwanda.

Isikuti band — A group of about six or so men who dance and sing traditional songs to a very lively beat, Luhya language

Jembe — A hoe, Swahili.

Jua Kali — "Hot sun," those who labor making things in the outdoors, Swahili.

Kakamega — The capitol and major city of Western Province.

Kalenjin — A group of related tribes in the Rift Valley of Kenya including the Nandi, Sabaot, and Kipsigis.

Kibaki, Mwai — President of Kenya from 2003 to the present, leader of the Party of National Unity (PNU).

Kikuyu — The largest tribe in Kenya based just north of Nairobi which has controlled the government and big business most of the time since independence.

Kinyarwandan — The language spoken in Rwanda.

Kisumu — The capitol city of Nyanza Province on the shores of Lake Victoria.

Lugari District — The northeastern most district in Western Province, formerly part of the White Highlands.

Luhya — A group of Bantu speaking sub-tribes in Western Province of Kenya including Bugusu, Marigoli, and Tiriki.

Lumakanda — The small town where we live, the seat of the government in Lugari District.

Marigoli — A sub-tribe of the Luhya to which Gladys belongs.

Mabati — Corrugated iron roofing sheets, Swahili.

Masai — A cattle keeping tribe in the Rift Valley of Kenya well know to tourists, speaking a language different from the Kalinjin and Luhya people.

Matatu — Minibus, Swahili.

Mgeni — Guest or stranger, Swahili.

Mt. Elgon — One of the highest mountains in Africa on the border between Kenya and Uganda which can be seen from our house in Lumankanda.

Museveni, Yoweri — President of Uganda from 1986 to the present.

Mwethia — Women's solidarity group, language of the Kamba.

Mzee — Old man or elder, a term of respect in Swahili.

Mzungu — A white person or foreigner, singular, Swahili.

Naivasha — A town in the central Rift Valley hard hit by the 2008 post election violence.

Nakuru — A city in the central Rift Valley hard hit by the 2008 post election violence.

Nandi — One of the Kalinjin tribes around Eldoret in the north Rift Valley.

NFL — Forces Nationales de Liberation, a rebel group in Burundi.

Odinga, Raila — Current Prime Minister of Kenya, leader of the ODM party, a Luo.

Orange Democratic Movement (ODM) — Raila Odinga's party which challenged the ruling party in the 2007 election.

Party of National Unity (PNU) — A coalition of parties formed in 2007 to support the bid of Mwai Kibaki for re-election as president.

Sabaot — A Kalinjin tribe living near and on Mt. Elgon.

Safaricom — Largest cell phone provider in Kenya and most profitable company in East Africa.

Shamba — A field or plot, Swahili.

Sugoi — A section of Turbo Division near to where we live.

Tanganyika — The mainland of Tanzania. In 1964 Zanzibar and Tanganyika joined together to form Tanzania.

Tiriki — A sub-tribe of the Luhya living near the original Quaker mission in Kaimosi.

Turbo Division — Part of Uasin Gishu District across the road from Lugari District.

Tutsi — Minority traditional ruling group in Rwanda and Burundi, usually considered to be cattle herders.

Twa — Very small, ostracized group in Rwanda and Burundi, considered to be potters, hunters of wild game, jesters, and buried the dead.

Ugali — A porridge made from milled cornmeal , often eaten daily, Swahili.

Ukambani — That part of Kenya inhabited by people from the Kamba ethnic group.

UPRONA — The Union for National Progress, in French Union pour le Progrès National, the mainly Tutsi party in Burundi.

Wazee — Elders, a term of respect, plural of *mzee,* Swahili.

Wazungu — White people or foreigners , plural of *mzungu,* Swahili.

White Highlands — Ten million acres of prime agricultural land in central Kenya, given out by the colonial government in large estates to British settlers.

Youth — In this region, a person under 35 years of age.